RESEARCH BIBLIOGRAPHIES A

NEW SERIES, 6

THE CYCLE OF GUILLAUME D'ORANGE

OR GARIN DE MONGLANE

RESEARCH BIBLIOGRAPHIES AND CHECKLISTS

NEW SERIES

ISSN 1476–9700

General Editors

Alan Deyermond

Abigail Lee Six

THE CYCLE OF GUILLAUME D'ORANGE

OR GARIN DE MONGLANE

A CRITICAL BIBLIOGRAPHY

Philip E. Bennett

TAMESIS

First published 2004 by Tamesis, Woodbridge

ISBN 1 85566 105 5

Tamesis is an imprint of Boydell & Brewer Ltd
PO Box 9, Woodbridge, Suffolk IP12 3DF, UK
and of Boydell & Brewer Inc.
668 Mt Hope Avenue, Rochester, NY 14620, USA
website: www.boydellandbrewer.co.uk

A catalogue record for this book is available
from the British Library

Library of Congress Cataloging-in-Publication Data
Bennett, Philip E.
    The Cycle of Guillaume d'Orange or Garin de Monglane : a critical
bibliography / Philip E. Bennett.
        p. cm. – (Research bibliographies and checklists. New series,
    ISSN 1476–9700 ; 6)
    Includes bibliographical references and indexes.
    ISBN 1–85566–105–5 (pbk. : alk. paper)
    1. Guillaume d'Orange (Chansons de geste) – Bibliography.   I. Title.
II. Series.
Z6521.G85B46 2004
[PQ1481]
016.841'1 – dc22   2004004788

This publication is printed on acid-free paper

Printed and bound in Great Britain by
Athenaeum Press Ltd., Gateshead, Tyne & Wear

CONTENTS

vi

INTRODUCTION

The group of poems which constitute the epic cycle most commonly known under the name of Guillaume d'Orange, who is the central hero around which the whole edifice revolves, is the most elaborately structured of the three cycles which Bertrand de Bar-sur-Aube, author of the poem *Girart de Vienne*, identifies as constituting the corpus of Old French epic poetry in his day. Bertrand refers to the 'geste [...] de Garin de Monglane' (548, ll. 46–47),[1] the suppositious ancestor of the whole clan, who are also known collectively as the 'Narbonnais' from the fief of the father of the most important generation of its epic heroes: Aimeri de Narbonne. For convenience the entire set of poems — including the sub-cycles of Vivien, Rainouart, and Aimeri — will be referred to in this volume as the Cycle of Guillaume d'Orange.

It is highly unlikely that our cycle was constituted in anything like its current form at the time Bertrand was writing, and, indeed, the other cycles, those of the king and of the rebellious barons, to which he refers, were never constructed into cohesive entities at all, although MS BNF f. fr. 860 does group a number of poems related to the *Chanson de Roland* and the Norse *Karlamagnús saga* constructs a neo-cyclic biography of Charlemagne from epic sources. It should also be noted that the three cycles referred to by Bertrand are far from constituting the totality of French epic production in the later twelfth century: he makes no reference to the Lorraine Cycle or the Crusade Cycle, for instance. Indeed it is most probable that Bertrand invented the 'three-cycle' notion to announce and account for his own programme of composition within *Girart de Vienne*, although he is unlikely to have invented the cyclic concept *ex nihilo*.

The exact manner in which poems dealing with the poetic biography of Guillaume, those associating him with Vivien and Rainouart in the great battle of *Aliscans* and the events which proceed from it, those which deal with Guillaume's more distant ancestors (including Garin de Monglane, the founder of the dynasty who also gives his name to the whole cycle) or with various nephews of the childless Guillaume, has been, and must remain, a matter for speculation. However, it is clear that what might be termed 'proto-cycles' were in existence by the *ca* 1200, perhaps sooner, although the first extant cyclic

---

[1] The first number in parentheses is that of the item in the continuous sequence of the bibliography; any numbers following a comma give the page or line numbers cited.

manuscripts survive only from the third quarter of the thirteenth century, while the only two witnesses to the completed cycle, B^1 and B^2, belong to the fourteenth. There is therefore a sense in which the process of cyclic construction belongs not to the period of epic creation, but to the period in which the classic texts of an established French literary canon were being collected by cultured bibliophiles.

Despite the intense interest in Guillaume, his family, and his legend which runs through the Middle Ages, producing three major redactions of the poems, and several minor ones, in the thirteenth and fourteenth centuries, the Guillaume Cycle impacted neither on national ideology, as did the legend of Charlemagne and Roland, nor on the popular imagination, as did individual poems like *Huon de Bordeaux* and *Les Quatre Fils Aymon*. Consequently, unlike these other products of medieval epic consciousness which continued to circulate either in official chronicle and history, or in the chapbook versions of La Bibliothèque Bleue, the poems relating to Guillaume and his clan excited very little interest from the sixteenth to the nineteenth century. It was the fortuitous, and gratuitous, identification of Guillaume d'Orange with the founder of the house of Orange-Nassau which led the Dutch scholar W. J. A. Jonckbloet to edit and translate the core poems relating the biography of the legendary ancestor of the kings of The Netherlands in the 1850s, an event which inaugurated a period of intense scholarly activity which has not diminished to this day.

The history of scholarship on the Guillaume Cycle falls into two important periods. The first runs from W. J. A. Jonckbloet's work to the discovery of the manuscript of *La Chanson de Guillaume* and its publication in 1903 (242). Although *Guillaume* is, strictly speaking, not a cyclic poem, its importance for defining relationships between other properly cyclic poems, and for the development of these poems in the Middle Ages, is incalculable. Theories which had been meticulously built up by irreproachable philological research were suddenly either confirmed or, more usually, overthrown at a stroke. It remains the most edited and the most studied of all the poems about Guillaume and his clan, rivalled only by *Aliscans* which is closely related to it. As a result it is natural that *Guillaume* has a central place in this bibliography. The second, post *Chanson de Guillaume*, period has been marked by a series of milestones which continue to inspire research, and are sometimes themselves the object of research. It was on the Guillaume Cycle that Joseph Bédier focused his attention in publishing the first volume of *Les Légendes épiques* in 1908 (56). The debate between traditionalists (later neo-traditionalists) and individualists (or *bédiéristes*) which this inaugurated shows no signs of abating. In 1956 and 1965 Jean Frappier published the two volumes of his monumental study of *Les Chansons de geste du cycle de Guillaume d'Orange* (79), which not only provided an incisive assessment of scholarship to date, but also inspired new work on the cycle and on the individual poems of which it was constituted.

What Frappier's book did for literary studies of the cycle Madeleine Tyssens did for manuscript studies with her thesis, published in 1967 as *La Geste de Guillaume d'Orange dans les manuscrits cycliques* (22). Like Frappier, Tyssens restricted her study to poems closely definable as belonging to the Guillaume Cycle, leaving out of account the poems dealing with the broader Narbonnais clan. However, like Frappier's work hers has provided a launch-pad for very important research on an aspect of medieval literature which late-twentieth-century scholarship with its fixation on literary theory is inclined to overlook: the manuscript versions of the poems and the relationships between them. The last of the milestones to inspire an important body of work on the Guillaume Cycle poems does, indeed, belong to the area of theoretical studies. It is the thesis of Joël-Henri Grisward, published in 1981 under the title *Archéologie de l'épopée médiévale* (635). Inspired by the three-volume study, *Mythe et épopée*, by Georges Dumézil (Paris: Gallimard, 1968–73), Grisward's work has in many ways proved as controversial as that of his mentor, whose work blends religion, mythology, social anthropology, and literature. It has, however, given a new vitality to epic studies, and a scientific focus to studies of the relationship of epic poetry to underlying mythographic systems which earlier excursions into myth and symbol criticism often lacked.

The present bibliography aims to cover all work published on the Guillaume Cycle, in its widest extension as the 'Cycle of Garin de Monglane' from Jonckbloet to the end of the year 2000. The very large number of comparative studies bringing together a number of poems from the cycle, and particularly those which concentrate on what has been described (106) as the core of the cycle — *Le Couronnement de Louis, Le Charroi de Nîmes, La Prise d'Orange, Le Moniage Guillaume* — shows the extent to which the Guillaume Cycle is viewed as an organic entity by scholars. It includes work published on the *Chanson de Guillaume*, because of the importance of that poem in the history of scholarship on the cycle, and regularly includes works comparing that poem above all, but also other poems from the cycle, with that immovable touchstone of Old French epic, *La Chanson de Roland*. It does not, however, systematically include work on foreign adaptations of poems from the cycle, or of the cycle as a whole, such as the *Karlamagnús saga*, Wolfram von Eschenbach's *Willehalm*, or Andrea da Barberino's *Le Storie Nerbonesi*. Comparative studies relating these works to poems from the cycle are included if the work concerned deals predominantly with the latter. Similarly works covering a whole range of Old French or other texts, and including a reference to a poem of the Guillaume Cycle, are not included, although some comparative studies concentrating on an item from the cycle and using other texts as minor comparators are included. Similarly excluded are the broad articles including material drawn from the cycle in early volumes of the *Histoire littéraire de la France*, and in the collective volumes of the *Grundriß der romanischen Literaturen des*

Mittelalters. There is an element of subjectivity in such judgements, which will include and exclude items to the irritation of some users of the bibliography, but I have tried to exercise that judgement consistently to produce a coherent account of scholarship devoted to Guillaume d'Orange and his *geste*. The bibliography also contains references to, and occasionally summaries of, reviews of monographs and editions, but not of articles or of collective volumes which contain one or more essays included in the bibliography; it also contains references to doctoral theses and dissertations, whether published or not, but does not include dissertations produced for masters degrees or Belgian *mémoires de licence*. Another category excluded is that of the simple reprint of a book, conference paper or article, despite the current fashion for re-issuing articles and conference papers in collected volumes of scholars' work. The only exception is for very early material, particularly editions of poems, which would otherwise be inaccessible to those intended to benefit from the present book.

While I have tried to read everything included in the bibliography some items have proved extremely elusive, and those I have not managed to see are marked by an asterisk (*).

The bibliography is numbered continuously from 1 to 815, but is broken into sections. The first deals with manuscript studies, the second with the very large number of editions and studies which have encompassed either the whole cycle or two or more poems from it; the third section presents studies and editions of individual poems listed alphabetically, not in the order of their appearance in cyclic manuscripts. Within each section editions and translations are listed in chronological order of first publication and studies in alphabetical order of author. Where an author has more than one entry in the same section publications are listed in chronological order. Reviews of books are also listed in chronological order to give an immediate overview of the reception of the work. To facilitate consultation there is an index of scholars and an index of titles, characters, and themes at the end of the volume.

This work could not have been undertaken, let alone completed, without help from many quarters. I am particularly grateful to the British Academy, to the Carnegie Trust for the Universities of Scotland, and to the Research Committee of the Faculty Group of Arts, Music and Divinity of the University of Edinburgh for financial support for research trips to libraries in the UK and in France. I am also grateful to the Faculty of Arts of the University of Edinburgh for allowing supplementary study leave and providing teaching relief to enable the work to progress materially.

Heartfelt thanks goes to the staff of many libraries, particularly at the universities of Edinburgh, Cambridge, and London, and in the National Library of Scotland, the British Library, and the Bibliothèque Nationale de France for their cheerful help with abstruse enquiries. I am also particularly grateful to all those colleagues who have helped me track down individual items, especially Dr

Anne Cobby of the Modern and Medieval Languages Library of Cambridge University and Dr Marianne Ailes of Wadham College, Oxford.

Although I have aimed at exhaustiveness, I am aware that items will have been missed. I shall be grateful to all who help to fill those gaps in the record.

ABBREVIATIONS

(i) THE MANUSCRIPTS AND THEIR *SIGLA*

A^1	Paris, Bibliothèque Nationale de France, f. fr. 774
A^2	BNF, f. fr. 1449
A^3	BNF, f. fr. 368
A^4	Milan, Biblioteca Trivulziana, 1025
Af	*BNF, n. a. fr. 934*
Ars	Paris, Bibliothèque de l'Arsenal, fr. 6562
B^1	British Library, Royal 20 D XI
B^2	BNF, f. fr. 24369–70
C	Boulogne-sur-Mer, Bibliothèque Municipale 192
D	BNF, f. fr. 1448
E	Berne, Bibliothèque de la Bourgeoisie 296
Harley	British Library, Harley 1321
M	Venice, Biblioteca San Marco, francese VIII
R	British Library, Royal 20 D XIX
S	Oxford, Bodleian Library, French e.32

(ii) POEMS OF THE GUILLAUME CYCLE AND RELATED TEXTS

Al	*Aliscans*
AN	*Aymeri de Narbonne*
BC	*Beuves de Commarchis*
BL	*La Bataille Loquifer*
ChG	*La Chanson de Guillaume / La Chançun de Willame* ($G1$ = ll. 1–1980; $G2$ = ll. 1981–3554)
ChV	*La Chevalerie Vivien (Le Covenant Vivien)*
CL	*Le Couronnement de Louis*
CN	*Le Charroi de Nîmes*
EnfG	*Les Enfances Guillaume*
EnfR	*Les Enfances Renier*
EnfV	*Les Enfances Vivien*
FC	*Foucon de Candie*
GA	*Guibert d'Andrenas*
GM	*Garin de Monglane*
GV	*Girart de Vienne*
MAN	*La Mort Aymeri de Narbonne*
MonG	*Le Moniage Guillaume*
MonR	*Le Moniage Rainouart*
PCS	*La Prise de Cordres et de Sebille*

PO	*La Prise d'Orange*
RomG	*Le Roman de Guillaume en prose*
SB	*Le Siège de Barbastre*
StNerb	*Le Storie Nerbonesi*

(iii) PERIODICAL AND SERIES TITLES

Archiv	*Archiv für das Studium der neueren Sprachen und Literaturen*
BBSR	*Bulletin Bibliographique de la Société Rencesvals*
BEC	*Bibliothèque de l'École des Chartes*
Boletín	*Boletín de la Real Academia de Buenas Letras de Barcelona*
CCM	*Cahiers de Civilisation Médiévale*
CFMA	Classiques Français du Moyen Âge
CN	*Cultura Neolatina*
DAI	*Dissertation Abstracts International*
FMLS	*Forum for Modern Language Studies*
FR	*French Review*
FS	*French Studies*
FSB	*French Studies Bulletin*
GRM	*Germanische-Romanische Monatschrift*
InfLitt	*L'Information Littéraire*
LR	*Les Lettres Romanes*
MA	*Le Moyen Âge*
MAe	*Medium Aevum*
MedRom	*Medioevo Romanzo*
MLJ	*Modern Language Journal*
MLR	*Modern Language Review*
MPh	*Modern Philology*
MR	*Marche Romane*
Neophil	*Neophilologus*
NM	*Neuphilologische Mitteilungen*
PMLA	*Publications of the Modern Language Association of America*
RBPH	*Revue Belge de Philologie et d'Histoire*
RF	*Romanische Forschungen*
RLi	*Revue de Littérature*
RLiR	*Revue de Linguistique Romane*
RLR	*Revue des Langues Romanes*
Rom	*Romania*
RoNo	*Romance Notes*
RPh	*Romance Philology*
RR	*Romanic Review*
SATF	Société des Anciens Textes Français

SF   *Studi Francesi*
SM   *Studi Medievali*
TLF   Textes Littéraires Français
TraLi   *Travaux de Littérature*
TraLiLi   *Travaux de Linguistique et de Littérature*
UNCSRLL University of North Carolina Studies in Romance Languages
            and Literatures
VoxRom   *Vox Romanica*
YFS   *Yale French Studies*
ZfSL   *Zeitschrift für französische Sprache und Literatur*
ZrPh   *Zeitschrift für romanische Philologie*

(iv) COLLABORATIVE VOLUMES

Burlesque et dérision
   Burlesque et dérision dans les épopées de l'Occident médiéval: actes du colloque international des Rencontres Européennes de Strasbourg et de la Société Rencesvals (Section Française), organisé à Strasbourg (16–18 septembre 1993), ed. Bernard Guidot, Annales Littéraires de l'Université de Besançon, 558, Série Littéraire, 3 (Paris: Les Belles Lettres, 1995) 381 pp.

Coloquios de Roncesvalles
   Coloquios de Roncesvalles, Agosto 1955, Publicaciones de la Facultad de Filosofía y Letras, Universidad de Zaragoza, cursos de verano en Pamplona (Zaragoza: Institución Príncipe de Viana, 1956).

Comprendre et aimer
   Comprendre et aimer la chanson de geste (à propos d'Aliscans), ed. Michèle Gally, Feuillets de l'ENS Fontenay-St Cloud (Fontenay-aux-Roses: École Normale Supérieure; Diffusion Ophrys, 1994) 107 pp.

Cyclification
   Cyclification: The Development of Narrative Cycles in the Chansons de Geste and the Arthurian Romances: Proceedings of the Colloquium, Amsterdam, 17–18 December, 1992, ed. Bert Besamusca, Willem P. Gerritsen, Corry Hogetoorn, and Orlanda S. H. Lie, Koninklijke Nederlandse Akademie van Wetenschappen Verhandelingen, Afd. Letterkunde, Nieuwe Reeks, 159 (Amsterdam: Koninklijke Nederlandse Akademie van Wetenschappen, 1994) 235 pp.

De l'étranger à l'étrange
   De l'étranger à l'étrange ou la 'conjointure' de la merveille (en hommage à Marguerite Rossi et Paul Bancourt), Senefiance, 25 (Aix-en-Provence: Publications du CUER MA, 1988) 493 pp.

Echoes of the Epic
   Echoes of the Epic: Studies in Honor of Gerard J. Brault, ed. David P. Schenck and Mary Jane Schenck (Birmingham, AL: Summa Publications, 1998) xxiii + 257 pp.

Études Lanly
   Études de langue et de littérature françaises offertes à André Lanly (Nancy: Université de Nancy II, 1980) xvi + 593 pp.

Farai chansoneta novele
   Farai chansoneta novele: hommages à Jean-Charles Payen: essais sur la liberté créatrice au Moyen Âge, ed. Huguette Legros (Caen: Université de Caen, 1989) 462 pp.

Festgabe Foerster
   Beiträge zur romanischen und englischen Philologie. Festgabe für Wendelin Foerster zum 26. Oktober 1901 (Halle: Max Niemeyer, 1902) 498 pp.

Festgabe Gröber
   Beiträge zur romanischen Philologie: Festgabe für Gustav Gröber (Halle: Max Niemeyer, 1899) 540 pp.

Guillaume d'Orange III
   Les Chansons de geste du cycle de Guillaume d'Orange III – Les Moniages, Guibourc: hommage à Jean Frappier, ed. Ph. Ménard and J.-Ch. Payen, Bibliothèque du Moyen Âge (Paris: SEDES, 1983) 359 pp.

Guillaume et Willehalm
   Guillaume et Willehalm: les épopées françaises et l'oeuvre de Wolfram von Eschenbach: actes du colloque des 12 et 13 janvier 1985, ed. Danielle Buschinger, Göppinger Arbeiten zur Germanistik, 421 (Göppingen: Kümmerle Verlag, 1985) 171 pp.

Hommage Delbouille
   Marche Romane, numéro spécial (1973: *Hommage au Professeur Maurice Delbouille*) 292 pp.

Il ciclo di Guglielmo d'Orange

> *Medioevo Romanzo*, 21.2–3 (1997: *La 'Chanson de geste' e il ciclo di Guglielmo d'Orange: Atti del convegno di Bologna 7–9 ottobre 1996*, ed. Andrea Fassò), 161–529.

Keller Studies

> *Studies in Honor of Hans-Erich Keller: Medieval French and Occitan Literature and Romance Linguistics*, ed. Rupert T. Pickens, Medieval Institute Publications (Kalamazoo, MI: Western Michigan University, 1993) xxviii + 540 pp.

Magie et illusion

> *Magie et illusion au Moyen Âge*, Senefiance, 42 (Aix-en-Provence: Publications du CUER MA, Université de Provence,1999) 634 pp.

McMillan Essays

> *Guillaume d'Orange and the Chanson de Geste: Essays Presented to Duncan McMillan in Celebration of his Seventieth Birthday by his Friends and Colleagues of the Société Rencesvals*, ed. Wolfgang G. van Emden and Philip E. Bennett (Reading: Société Rencesvals, British Branch, 1984) xi + 218 pp.

Medieval Alexander Legend

> *The Medieval Alexander Legend and Romance Epic: Essays in Honour of David J. A. Ross*, ed. Peter Noble, Lucie Polak, and Claire Isoz (Millwood, NY: Kraus International Publications, 1982) xviii + 288 pp.

Mélanges Delbouille II

> *Mélanges de linguistique romane et de philologie médiévale offerts à M. Maurice Delbouille, II: Philologie médiévale,* ed. Jean Renson (Gembloux: J. Duculot, 1964) 769 pp.

Mélanges Foulon II

> *Marche Romane*, 30.3–4 (1980: *Mélanges de langue et de littérature françaises du Moyen Âge et de la Renaissance offerts à Charles Foulon,* II) 307 pp.

Mélanges Fourquet

> *Littérature épique au Moyen Âge: hommage à Jean Fourquet pour son 100ème anniversaire*, ed. Daniel Buschinger, Wodan, 77 (Greifswald: Reineke-Verlag, 1999) 409 pp.

Mélanges Frappier

> *Mélanges de langue et de littérature du Moyen Âge et de la Renaissance offerts à Jean Frappier, professeur à la Sorbonne, par ses collègues, ses élèves et ses amis*, Publications Romanes et Françaises, 112 (Geneva: Droz, 1970) 2 vols, xx + 1176 pp.

Mélanges Horrent
   Études de philologie romane et d'histoire littéraire offertes à Jules Horrent à l'occasion de son soixantième anniversaire, ed. Jean Marie d'Heur and Nicoletta Cherubini (Liège: [s.n.], 1980) xxiii + 853 pp.

Mélanges Le Gentil
   Mélanges de langue et de littérature médiévales offerts à Pierre Le Gentil, professeur à la Sorbonne, par ses collègues, ses élèves et ses amis, ed. [Jean Dufournet and Daniel Poirion] (Paris: SEDES, 1973) xvi + 929 pp.

Mélanges Lejeune
   Mélanges offerts à Rita Lejeune, professeur à l'Université de Liège (Gembloux: J. Duculot, 1969) 2 vols, xxxii +1762 pp.

Mélanges Lods
   Mélanges de littérature du Moyen Âge au XXe siècle offerts à Mademoiselle Jeanne Lods (Paris: École Normale Supérieure de Jeunes Filles, 1978) 2 vols, xxi + 902 pp.

Mélanges Louis
   La Chanson de geste et le mythe carolingien : mélanges René Louis, publiés par ses collègues, ses amis et ses élèves à l'occasion de son 75e anniversaire (Saint-Père-sous-Vézelay: Musée Archéologique Régional, 1982) 2 vols, cliv + 1310 pp.

Mélanges Ménard
   Miscellanea mediaevalia, mélanges offerts à Philippe Ménard, ed. Jean-Claude Vallecalle, Alain Labbé, and Danielle Quéruelle, Nouvelle Bibliothèque du Moyen Âge, 46 (Paris: Champion, 1998) 2 vols, 1534 pp.

Mélanges Rychner
   Travaux de Linguistique et de Littérature, 16.1 (1978: Mélanges d'études romanes du Moyen Âge et de la Renaissance offerts à M. Jean Rychner, professeur à l'Université de Neuchâtel, par ses collègues, ses élèves et ses amis, ed. André Gendre, Charles-Théodore Gossen, and Georges Straka) 571 pp.

Mélanges Suard
   'Plaist vos oïr bone cançon vallant', mélanges de langue et de littérature médiévales offerts à François Suard, ed. Dominique Boutet, Marie-Madeleine Castellani, Françoise Ferrand, and Aimé Petit, UL3 Travaux et Recherches, 1–2 (Lille: Université Charles de Gaulle – Lille 3, 1999) 2 vols, 1040 pp.

Mélanges Subrenat
'Si a parlé par moult ruiste vertu': mélanges de littérature médiévale offerts à Jean Subrenat, ed. Jean Dufournet et al., Colloques, Congrès et Conférences sur le Moyen Âge, 1 (Paris: Champion, 2000) 584 pp.

Mélanges Wathelet-Willem
Marche Romane, numéro spécial (1978: *Mélanges de philologie et de littératures romanes offerts à Jeanne Wathelet-Willem*) xx + 757 pp.

Mittelalterstudien
Mittelalterstudien: Erich Köhler zum Gedenken, ed. Henning Krauss and Dietmar Rieger, Studia Romanica, 55 (Heidelberg: Carl Winter, 1984) 323 pp.

Mourir aux Aliscans
Mourir aux Aliscans: 'Aliscans' et la légende de Guillaume d'Orange, ed. Jean Dufournet, Unichamp, 39 (Paris: Champion, 1993) 244 pp.

Reading around the Epic
Reading around the Epic: A Festschrift in Honour of Professor Wolfgang van Emden, ed. Marianne Ailes, Philip E. Bennett, and Karen Pratt, King's College London Medieval Studies, 14 (London: King's College London Centre for Late Antique and Medieval Studies, 1998) xix + 340 pp.

Rencesvals 4
Société Rencesvals, *IVe congrès international, Heidelberg, 28 août – 2 septembre 1967, Actes et Mémoires*, Studia Romanica, 14 (Heidelberg: Carl Winter, 1969) 266 pp.

Rencesvals 5
Société Rencesvals: Proceedings of the Fifth Conference (Oxford, 1970) (Salford: University of Salford, 1977) 225 pp.

Rencesvals 6
Société Rencesvals pour l'étude des épopées romanes, *VIe congrès international (Aix-en-Provence, 29 août – 4 septembre 1973)*, Actes (Aix-en-Provence: Université de Provence, 1974) 763 pp.

Rencesvals 7
Charlemagne et l'épopée romane: Actes du VIIe congrès international de la Société Rencesvals (Liège, 28 août – 4 septembre 1976), Les Congrès et Colloques de l'Université de Liège, 76; Bibliothèque de la Faculté de Philosophie et Lettres de l'Université de Liège, 225 (Paris: Les Belles Lettres, 1978) 2 vols, 723 pp.

Rencesvals 8
VIII Congreso de la Société Rencesvals, Pamplona – Santiago de Compostela 15 a 25 de agosto de 1978 (Pamplona: Institución Príncipe de Viana, 1981) 582 pp.

Rencesvals 9
Essor et fortune de la chanson de geste dans l'Europe et l'Orient latin: Actes du IXe congrès international de la Société Rencesvals pour l'étude des épopées romanes, Padoue-Venise, 29 août – 4 septembre 1982 (Modena: Mucchi Editore, 1984) 2 vols, 1005 pp.

Rencesvals 10
Au carrefour des routes d'Europe, la chanson de geste: X^e congrès international de la Société Rencesvals pour l'étude des épopées romanes, Strasbourg 1985, Senefiance, 20–21 (Aix-en-Provence: Publications du CUER MA, Université de Provence, 1987) 2 vols, 1263 pp.

Rencesvals 11
Memorias de la Real Academia de Buenas Letras de Barcelona, 21– 22 (1990*: Actes du XIe congrès international de la Société Rencesvals – Barcelone, 22–27 août 1988*) 431 + 466 pp.

Rencesvals 12
Charlemagne in the North: Proceedings of the Twelfth International Conference of the Société Rencesvals, Edinburgh, 4th to 11th August, 1991, ed. Philip E. Bennett, Anne Elizabeth Cobby, and Graham A. Runnalls (Edinburgh: Société Rencesvals British Branch, 1993) iii + 545 pp.

Rencesvals 13
Aspects de l'épopée romane: mentalité, idéologies, intertextualités, ed. Hans van Dijk and Willem Noomen (Groningen: Egbert Forsten, 1995) ix + 526 pp.

Romance Epic
Romance Epic: Essays on a Medieval Literary Genre, ed. Hans-Erich Keller, Studies in Medieval Culture, 24 (Kalamazoo, MI: Medieval Institute Publications, Western Michigan University, 1987) xi + 241 pp.

Symposium Riquer
Symposium in honorem prof. M. de Riquer (Barcelona: Universitat de Barcelona and Quaderns Crema, 1984) 476 pp.

Technique littéraire

> *La Technique littéraire des chansons de geste: Actes du colloque de Liège (septembre 1957)*, Bibliothèque de la Faculté de Philosophie et Lettres de l'Université de Liège, 150 (Paris: Les Belles Lettres, 1959) 483 pp.

Troubadours and the Epic

> *The Troubadours and the Epic: Essays in Memory of W. Mary Hackett*, ed. L. M. Paterson and S. B. Gaunt (Coventry: The Department of French, University of Warwick, 1987) xi + 269 pp.

(v) GENERAL ABBREVIATIONS

Ars.	Bibliothèque de l'Arsenal, Paris
BL	British Library
BNF	Bibliothèque Nationale de France
CycG	The Cycle of Guillaume d'Orange
ed.	edited by / edition
f. fr.	fonds français
f.	folio
ff.	folios
l.	line
ll.	lines
MF	Middle French
MS(S)	manuscript(s)
n. a.	nouvelle acquisition
ns	new series (nouvelle série, neue Folge etc.)
OF	Old French
PUF	Presses Universitaires de France
ser.	series
trans.	translated by
UP	University Press
vol(s).	volume(s)

BIBLIOGRAPHY OF THE CYCLE OF GUILLAUME D'ORANGE

A. Manuscript Studies

1   Andrieux, Nelly, 'Un programme d'écriture et sa réalisation: les manuscrits B^1 et B^2 du Cycle de Guillaume', *Rom*, 104 (1983), 229–36.
Some preliminary reflections on the MSS as global writing projects, without any conclusions expressed. The article contains a useful table comparing the compositional structures of B^1 and B^2 with that of *D*.

2   Andrieux-Reix, Nelly, 'La dernière main: approche des fins cycliques', in *Mélanges Fourquet* (1999), pp. 109–20.
A meditation on the nature of closure and completion in the MSS of CycG, leading to the conclusion that the organizing principle of the MSS is less biographical than encyclopædic.

3   Delbouille, Maurice, 'Le système des "incidences": observations sur les manuscrits du cycle épique de Guillaume d'Orange', *RBPH*, 6 (1927), 617–41.
A close palaeographical study of MS B^2 indicates that the *incidences* are the work of a revisor, not of the main scribe responsible for the MS, and that there can have been no prior tradition of using *incidences* to produce chronologically coherent narratives in redaction B of CycG. Before the revision producing the current disposition of the Paris MS, B^2 and B^1 would have shown even more similarity in their transcriptions and compilations of the poems than they do now.

4   ——, 'Dans un atelier de copistes: en regardant de plus près les manuscrits B^1 et B^2 du cycle épique de Garin de Monglane', *CCM*, 3 (1960), 14–22.
Analyses the material processes by which the versions of CycG peculiar to the B family were generated in their scriptoria.

5   Dougherty, David M., 'La redécouverte du manuscrit de Cheltenham', *CCM*, 3 (1960), 27–31.
The article offers a brief description of the MS and a résumé of its contents.

6   Holtus, Günter, 'Les problèmes posés par l'édition de textes franco-italiens: à propos de quelques leçons problématiques de *V4*, *V8* et d'autres manuscrits', in *Rencesvals 10* (1987), pp. 675–96.

The article pleads for a complete and transparent representation of the linguistic difficulties posed by the artificial literary language 'Franco-Italian' in the edition of texts. Pages 683–87 deal specifically with problematic readings in the Marciana MS of *Al* (cf. 194).

7   Jodogne, Omer, 'Le manuscrit de Boulogne du *Charroi de Nîmes*', in *Coloquios de Roncesvalles* (1956), pp. 301–26.
A detailed comparison of *C* with redactions A (called by the author 'la version classique') and B produces the slightly odd conclusion that *C* is a careful 'critical edition' produced by combining readings of A^2, used as 'base manuscript', and an unidentified MS of the B family. This composite text was then further modified by the *C* redactor with inventions of his own.

8   McMillan, Duncan, 'Lectures sous les rayons ultraviolets, VI: Bibl. Nat. fr. 24369 (*Enfances Guillaume*)', *Rom*, 69 (1946), 93–95.
The exercise produced few results as the original text had been very carefully scraped, but enough survived to indicate that the erased text was *EnfG*.

9   ——, '*La Chevalerie Vivien* dans le manuscrit dit "de Savile": notes prolégoméniques', in *Etudes offertes à Félix Lecoy* (Paris: Champion, 1973), pp. 357–75.
A codicological study of MS *S* of *ChV*, and an assessment of its place in the MS tradition.

10   ——, 'Notes d'ecdotique: fantômes et mirages dans la *Chevalerie Vivien*', in *Mélanges Rychner* (1978), pp. 353–62.
The article, which takes as its starting point the difficulties of producing a satisfactory critical text of the poems of CycG because of the nature of the revisions and re-copyings to which they have been subject, uses the previously unknown MS *S* to suggest that certain readings of the other MSS contain camouflaged faults or 'corrections'.

11   ——, 'Propos sur un mini-problème de critique textuelle', in *Mélanges Louis* (1982), pp. 637–47.
Based on the concept of common omissions, the article demonstrates that there is no extra intermediary *(a')* separating the MSS $A^{1,2,4}$ and A^3 of CycG. It goes further in arguing against the habit then current of using undifferentiated variants as evidence in computer generated stemmata of medieval texts.

12   ——, 'Un manuscrit hors série: le cas du manuscrit *S* de la *Chevalerie Vivien-Aliscans* (Bodléienne, French e.32)', in *Symposium Riquer* (1984), pp. 161–207.

The detailed study of the differing *scriptæ* used in the MS and of the habits and linguistic differences of the half-dozen scribes involved in its preparation leads to the conclusion that the MS was never intended for circulation, but was produced by a copy-shop for internal use as a model for MSS for sale.

13   Rajna, Pio, 'Un nuovo codice di chansons de geste del ciclo di Guglielmo', *Rom*, 6 (1887), 257–61.
A brief description of the Trivulziana MS (A^4) and a list of its contents.

14   Régnier, Claude, 'Les stemmas du *Charroi de Nîmes* et de la *Prise d'Orange'*, in *McMillan Essays* (1984), pp. 103–16
Based on often minute readings of the MSS, the article is a polite but pointed criticism of McMillan's classification of the MSS of *CN* (365, pp. 19–26) and a defence of Régnier's own classification of the MSS of *PO* (646, pp. 16–28).

15   Rinoldi, Paolo, '"Dans un atelier de copistes": ancora sui manoscritti B^1 e B^2 del "grand cycle" di *Guillaume d'Orange'*, *MedRom*, 23 (1999), 359–87.
Building on the seminal studies of Maurice Delbouille (3 & 4) the study reveals that one scribe was responsible for rubrics, *incidences*, and linking passages in both MSS.

16   Schoesler, Lene, 'New Methods in Textual Criticism: The Case of the *Charroi de Nîmes'*, in *Medieval Dialectology*, ed. Jacek Fiziak, Trends in Linguistics, Studies and Monographs, 79 (Berlin: Mouton de Gruyter, 1995), pp. 225–76.
Using as a sample the lines appearing in the Paris fragment (BNF n. a. fr. 934), an attempt is made to establish a revised stemma for *CN* and to establish the dialect of the original composition by computerized analysis of readings. The methodology is not without flaws, and the application at times unsystematic. See McMillan's riposte (388).

17   Short, Ian, 'An Early French Epic Manuscript: Oxford Bodleian Library, French e.32', in *The Medieval Alexander Legend* (1982), pp. 173–91.
A very detailed codicological and palaeographical study of MS *S* of *ChV* and *Al*, concluding that the MS was copied in eastern France at the very end of the twelfth century. The intricate relationships of hand-changes between three scribes in the copy of *Al* support the author's view that the book was the product of an organized scriptorium; however, the fact that the whole of *ChV* was copied by one scribe, while *Al* is predominantly a collaboration between two scribes (one older [?]; one younger [?]), makes it harder to maintain his view that the book may have been a training exercise supervised by the older of the two scribes

responsible for copying *Al*. For an alternative explanation of the way the MS was produced see 12.

18 ——, 'L'avènement du texte vernaculaire: la mise en recueil', in *Théories et pratiques de l'écriture au Moyen Âge: Actes du colloque du Palais du Luxembourg-Sénat, 5 et 6 mars 1987*, ed. Emmanuèle Baumgartner and Christiane Marchello-Nizia, Littérales, 4 (Paris: Université de Paris X - Nanterre, 1988), pp. 11–24.
A general study including the important observation that *ChV* and *Al* in MS *S* although partly by the same scribe must have circulated independently in the Middle Ages.

19 Suchier, Hermann, 'Le manuscrit de *Guillaume d'Orange* anciennement conservé à Saint-Guilhem du Désert', *Rom*, 2 (1873), 335–36.
Identifies the MS described by G. Catel, which he found in the library at St-Guilhem-le-Désert in 1633, with A^1.

20 Tyssens, Madeleine, '*Le Charroi de Nîmes* et la *Prise d'Orange* dans le manuscrit B.N. fr. 1448', *CCM*, 3 (1960), 98–106.
The author shows that, despite its problems, MS *D* offers sound readings and is an independent witness to the archetype. Editions of CycG poems need to take more account of redactions *C* and *D*.

21 ——, '*Aliscans* dans le manuscrit français VIII de la Marciana', *CN*, 21 (1961), 148–54.
Attacks Paul Lorenz's view of the position of *M* in the MS tradition of *Al* (200), pointing out that much of his evidence is based on a poor appreciation of the readings of *M*. Identifies a family M-B^1-B^2-D- BNF f. fr. 2494, within which *M* is valuable as not containing the interpolation of Rainouart's combats against grotesque Saracens. Its treatment of Rainouart's marriage also helps redefine the relationships of *G2* and *Al*.

22 ——, *La Geste de Guillaume d'Orange dans les manuscrits cycliques*, Bibliothèque de la Faculté de Philosophie et Lettres de l'Université de Liège, 178 (Paris: Les Belles Lettres, 1967) 471 pp.
The definitive study of the poems and MSS of the narrowly defined cycle of Guillaume and that of Vivien and Rainouart, together with a minutely observed study of the development of the cyclic redactions. The work is divided into two parts: a study of the MSS as collections of poems, and a study of individual poems in the various MS redactions. This is the fundamental reference work for manuscript studies of CycG.

Rev.:   .1   Giuseppe di Stefano, *SF*, 36 (1968), 519–20.

.2   Ulrich Mölk, *RF*, 80 (1968), 572–74.

.3   Eugene Vance, *MLN*, 83 (1968), 941–43.

.4   W. M. Hackett, *FS*, 23 (1969), 395–97.

.5   Jean-Charles Payen, *MA*, 75 (1969), 529–39.

.6   Paul Zumthor, *ZrPh*, 85 (1969), 435–37.

.7   E. von Richthofen, *Speculum*, 45 (1970), 332–33.

.8   Peter Dembowski, *MPh*, 68 (1970-71), 71–75.

.9   Duncan McMillan, *CCM*, 15 (1972), 336–41.

23   ——, 'Vestiges lexicaux dans le manuscrit *D* de la *Prise d'Orange*', in *Mélanges Horrent* (1980), pp. 481–87.

A study of the rare eastern dialect forms *rende* and *soués* (= MS *soëf*), *D*, l. 19, leads to a conclusion that, although tentatively expressed, confirms Régnier's views (646, pp. 11 & 22) that *PO* was of eastern origin, and that a lost MS, O^2, links the families *AB* and *C*.

24   ——, 'Le style oral et les ateliers de copistes', in *Mélanges Delbouille II* (1964), pp. 659–75.

The study concentrates on material aspects of the production of the MSS of the different redactions of CycG, in particular on the articulations devised by the various heads of copyshops to produce a coherent text from inherited versions of the poems. Evidence drawn largely from the B family MSS demonstrates that these cyclic productions were intended for reading, albeit reading aloud by a professional to a listening audience, and to be preserved in libraries.

25   ——, 'Encore *Aliscans*: les enseignements du manuscrit Savile', in *Mélanges Louis* (1982), pp. 623–35.

Readings of MS *S* of *Al* not only allow us to confirm by another witness the particularly complex, shifting relationships between all the MSS of *Al*, but give clear proof in the division of hands, the layout, and the content of ff. 132–34 that within one scriptorium teams of scribes would work simultaneously on different parts of a text using models of differing provenance. This conclusion complements and completes Ian Short's tentative reference to a 'production-line technique' in commercial scriptoria (17).

26   ——, '"En *Aliscans* a merveilleus hustin"', in *Mélanges Subrenat* (2000), pp. 521–32.

The study reveals how the complexities of the transmission of MSS of *Al* were magnified by the concurrent circulation of competing redactions, leading to a high degree of contamination in all MS families. However, it also demonstrates that a comparison of *S, M, D* and the A family does permit a reasonable reconstruction of the archetype of all extant MSS.

*27   Walker, B. J., 'The Boulogne Manuscript of the *Charroi de Nîmes*' (PhD thesis, University of London (Westfield College), 1958).
See: *BBSR*, 1, p. 65.

B. EDITIONS AND STUDIES OF THE CYCLE AND OF GROUPS OF POEMS

(i) *Editions and Translations*

28   *Guillaume d'Orange: chansons de geste des XIe et XIIe siècles, publiées pour la première fois et dédiées à sa majesté Guillaume III, roi des Pays-Bas, Prince d'Orange etc*, ed. W. J. A. Jonckbloet, 2 vols (The Hague: Martinus Nyhoff, 1854) 427 + 318 pp.
Vol. 1 contains texts of *CL, CN, PO, ChV*, and *Al*, considered to be the ancient (eleventh-century) kernel of CycG. An ed. of *EnfG* and *MonG* was promised for a vol. 3, but never materialized. The ed. is essentially from A^1, with some readings and variants from A^3 and B^2; for *Al* variants are from *Ars*. Vol. 2 is a wide-ranging dissertation on the origins and development of the traditions behind CycG, relating the poems as far as possible to historical events, which explains the elaboration of the poems by the conflations and confusions inherent in oral tradition. While making soundly circumspect use of archival documents, with some pertinent comments on the relationship between oral tradition and official historiography, Jonckbloet consistently overestimates the age of the surviving poems by about a century. Few of the historical prototypes for characters and events he unearthed would now be accepted.

29   *Guillaume d'Orange: le marquis au court nez, chanson de geste du XIIe siècle mise en nouveau langage*, trans. by W. J. A. Jonckbloet (Amsterdam: P. N. van Kampen, 1867) xxiv + 385 pp.
A free translation into modern French of *EnfG, CL, CN, ChV, Al*, and *MonG*, reconstructing them as a continuous narrative in the manner of a modern novel. Dedicated to the King of the Netherlands, the Introduction, which still has some scholarly value, is historically oriented to explicating the character of the legendary founder of the House of Orange.

30   Meyer, Paul, 'Notice sur un recueil de fragments de manuscrits français (Bibl. Nat., nouv. acq. fr. 934)', *Bulletin de la Société des Anciens Textes Français*, 22 (1896), 59 – 75.
Brief notes on one fragment of *CN* (= *Af*) and four of *Al* with transcriptions of the texts (cf. 171).

*31 *Chansons de geste: Roland, Aimeri de Narbonne, Le Couronnement de Louis*, trans. by Léon Clédat, Bibliothèque du Moyen Âge: Traductions Archaïques et Rythmées (Paris: Garnier, 1899).

32 Tuffrau, Paul, *La Légende de Guillaume d'Orange* (Paris: Piazza, 1920) 272 pp.
A retelling of CycG linking *CL*, *PO*, *ChV*, *Al*, and *MonG* adapted to 'modern taste' (e.g. by modifying the end of *PO* and reducing Rainouart's burlesque features).

33 *La Geste de Guillaume Fièrebrace et de Rainoart au Tinel d'après les poèmes des XIIe et XIIIe siècles*, trans. by Alfred Jeanroy, Poèmes et Récits de la Vieille France, 6 (Paris: E. de Boccard, 1924) xiv + 156 pp.
An elegant prose translation for a general audience of extracts from *EnfG*, *CL*, *CN*, *PO*, *ChV*, *ChG*, *Al*, and *MonG* arranged to make a biography of Guillaume. There is also a brief but sound introduction.

*34 Charlier, C. 'Une édition du *Couronnement de Louis*, du *Charroi de Nîmes* et de la *Prise d'Orange* d'après le manuscrit Royal 20 D XI du British Museum (B^1), avec les variantes du manuscrit 24.369–70 de la Bibliothèque Nationale (B^2)' (thesis, Université de Liège, 1959–60).

35 *Guillaume d'Orange: Four Twelfth-Century Epics*, trans. by Joan M. Ferrante, Records of Civilization, Sources and Studies, 92 (New York: Columbia UP, 1974) 311 pp.
A translation into English verse, which reads oddly at times, of *CL*, *PO*, *Al*, and *MonG1*. A lengthy introduction (61 pp.) offers some interesting comments on the poems and their historical context.
Rev.: .1 P. Rogers, *Humanities Association Review*, 26 (1975), 250–52.
.2 David P. Schenck, *FR*, 49 (1976), 408.
.3 Anne Iker-Gittleman, *RPh*, 31 (1977-78), 670–73.

36 *William, Count of Orange: Four Old French Epics*, trans. by Glanville Price, Lynette Muir, and David Hoggan, Everyman's University Library, 1367 (London: Dent, 1975) xviii + 221 pp.
Very competent and readable prose renderings of *CL*, *CN*, *PO*, and *ChG*, with notes on textual difficulties and an index of proper names. The introduction, by Lynette Muir, is brief but informative.
Rev.: .1 Glyn Burgess, *FS*, 31 (1977), 439–40.
.2 Diana Teresa Mériz, *Olifant*, 5 (1978), 307–13.
.3 Joseph Gildea, *CCM*, 23 (1980), 403.

*37 *A Translation of the Cycle of William of Orange*, with an historical introduction by Jon N. Sutherland, trans. by Guérard Piffard, Monograph

Publishing on Demand. Sponsor Series (Ann Arbor, MI: University Microfilms International for San Diego State University Press, 1977), xx + 622; vi + 646; vi + 532 pp.
Rev.: .1   Joseph J. Duggan, *RPh*, 31 (1977-78), 441–43.

38   Frances Sikola Chevalier, 'A Critical Edition of the *D* Redaction of the *Couronnement de Louis* and the *Charroi de Nîmes* with a Translation in Modern English' (PhD thesis, Rutgers, The State University of New Jersey, 1995) iv + 210 pp.
The ed. and accompanying translation, which are competent but not without problems, treat the two poems as one. The lengthy introduction is an extensive scholarly exercise in manuscript and linguistic description.

39   *Le Cycle de Guillaume d'Orange, anthologie*, ed. Dominique Boutet, Livre de Poche, Lettres Gothiques, 4547 (Paris: Librairie Générale Française, 1996) 672 pp.
The volume contains extracts with facing translations into modern French from existing eds of *EnfG*, *CL*, *CN*, *PO*, *EnfV*, *ChV*, *Al*, *BL*, *MonR*, *MonG*, and *ChG*. Not all extracts are from the best eds, e.g. *EnfG* is based on Perrier (480), *CL* on Langlois (420) and *Al* on Guessard and Montaiglon (162). The introduction considers a number of problems of literary criticism, including the mythico-legendary background to the poems, their socio-political context, and the evolution of the poems into cyclic manuscripts.

Rev.: .1   R. Deschaux, *Perspectives Médiévales*, 23 (1997), 27.

(ii) *Studies*

40   Adler, Alfred, 'Guillaume et son cercle dans *Raoul de Cambrai*', *Rom*, 93 (1972), 1–19.
The author sees parallels between the structures of the CycG and *Raoul de Cambrai* as a composite poem.

41   Andrieux, Nelly, 'Variante ou variance? Approche d'un intertexte épique', in *Mélanges Louis* (1982), pp. 649–59.
Taking examples from *CN*, *EnfV*, and *EnfG* the author argues for the production of synoptic eds allowing full rein to the variability of the epic, and putting an end to the hegemony of the concept of the base text from which others deviate at specific points.

42   Andrieux-Reix, Nelly, 'Pré-dire un cycle: textes d'*Enfances* et architectures narratives dans les manuscrits cycliques de la geste de Guillaume d'Orange', in *Cyclification* (1994), pp. 143–44.

A densely argued paper designed to provoke discussion. *EnfG* and *EnfV* are given as prime examples of the way *enfances* poems mirror and re-create the structures of the cycles into which they are inserted.

43 ———, '*Des Enfances Guillaume* à la *Prise d'Orange*: premier parcours d'un cycle', *BEC*, 147 (1989), 343–69.
The analysis of the articulation of the core poems of CycG, predominantly in MS *D*, announced as essentially semantic in its study of the concepts of joy and honour and of their *loci* within the texts, is in fact based on the principles of Vladimir Propp's *Morphology of the Folk Tale*, 2nd ed. rev. and ed. by Louis A. Wagner and Alan Dundes (Austin: University of Texas Press, 1968), as the material links and boundaries between poems are associated with the dynamics of the satisfaction of lack or loss which defines the encyclopedic narrative constructed in the MS.

44 ———, 'Écriture d'un cycle. Écriture de geste. L'exemplarité d'un corpus', *Rom*, 108 (1987), 146–64.
A study of the lexeme |joi-| in the core poems of CyG shows the writing to be typical of French epic in general, the added dimension of cyclic writing representing a particular distillation of epic vocabulary.

45 Aubailly, Jean-Claude, 'Guillaume à Orange ou la quête de l'Autre Monde', in *De l'étranger à l'étrange* (1988), pp. 33–43.
A Jungian reading of CycG, assuming achronological structuring and taking no account of the conditions of production of the poems.

46 ———, 'Mythe et épopée dans la geste de Guillaume', *Olifant*, 12 (1987), 221–45.
A systematically Jungian reading of four of the five core poems of *CycG* plus *ChG*, predicated on the untenable thesis that they were composed in the order *CL*, *CN*, *PO*, *ChG*, *MonG* to provide a consistent psycho-mythic biography of the hero.

47 Augier, Michelle, 'Remarques sur la place du marchand dans quelques chansons de geste', in *Rencesvals 6* (1974), pp. 747–60.
This study of the character attributed to the merchant in a number of epics, but predominantly in *EnfV* and *EnfR*, suggests that the portrait of merchants given in thirteenth-century poems, whatever the attitude of the noble hero, was close to the social reality of the time.

48 Batany, Jean, '*Les Moniages* et la satire des moines aux XIe et XIIe siècles', in *Guillaume d'Orange III* (1983), pp. 209–37.

The article first refers to Claude Gaignebet's work on carnival, particularly in *Le Carnaval: essais de mythologie populaire* (Paris: Payot, 1974), then sets *MonG* and *MonR* into the tradition of European anti-monastic satire, suggesting that only *MonG* offers a solution by its invocation of eremitism.

49   Becker, Philipp-August, 'Der sechssilbige Tiradenschlussvers in altfranzösischen Epen', *ZrPh*, 18 (1894), 112–24.
Mistakenly argues against Nordfelt (499) that the versions of poems in CycG with the *vers orphelin* are more primitive than those without the short line. He bases much of his argument on relationships between MSS, but is mostly led astray by accepting the now discredited view that *MonG1* is older than *MonG2* (cf. 593).

50   ——, *Der südfranzösische Sagenkreis und seine Probleme* (Halle: Niemeyer, 1898) 81 pp.
The author considers the manuscript tradition, the development and historical background of the core poems of CycG, the Narbonnais sub-cycle and related legends. He concludes that the cycles were conceived as such, that they were not casual compilations, and that the current cycles result from the uniting of a northern (Guillaume) and southern (Vivien, Aimeri) cycles. A very sound book for its period taking full account of the fictitious nature of most of the material, which suffers only in inclining to increase the age of some poems, notably of *CL*, which the author sees as the kernel of CycG.

51   ——, *Das Werden der Wilhelm- und der Aimerigeste: Versuch einer neuen Lösung*, Abhandlungen der Philosophischen-historischen Klasse der sächsischen Akademie der Wissenschaften zu Leipzig, 44, 1 (Leipzig: Hirzel,1939) iv + 208 pp.
The work presents studies of Guillaume de Toulouse as archetype of *Guillaume d'Orange*, *ChG*, the cyclic poems, the Aliscans sub-cycle, the Narbonnais sub-cycle, and other poems. The origin of CycG is considered to have been a primitive *PO* (which Becker calls 'La Chanson de Tiébaut') invented as part of a dispute between monasteries associated with St William of Gellone. Although such arguments are superseded the relationships between the various songs are generally carefully plotted. The main thesis of the work is the link between poems and specific noble houses, which remains unproven. Despite some weaknesses the book remains a valuable overview of the cycle.

Rev.: .1   Stefan Hofer, *ZrPh*, 61(1941), 553–69.

52 ——, 'Das Urlied der Wilhelmgeste', *RF*, 56 (1942), 400–02.

A largely rhetorical article in reply to Hofer's review of *Das Werden* (51.1), in which Becker re-affirms his belief that the legend of Guillaume was first encapsulated not in *ChG* but in what could be seen as a version of *PO*.

53 ——, *Der Liederkreis um Vivien*, Sitzungsberichte der Akademie der Wissenschaften in Wien, Philosophisch-historische Klasse, 2231 (Munich: Brünn; Vienna: Rudolph M. Rohrer, 1944) 58 pp.

Studies the group of songs in which Vivien appears. Considers *ChG* (*G1*) to be the work of a folk-poet, imitated by *Al* (ll. 1–3000) in a more courtly manner. His division of *Al* into two parts (the second an imitation of *G2* by another folk-poet) cannot be sustained. The essay is essentially an abridgement of *Das Werden* (51) in which the author develops a systematically precise dating of the poems by historical allusion, which cannot be defended.

54 ——, 'Über die altfranzösische Epik', *RF*, 58–59 (1947), 201–07.

A response to Ernst Robert Curtius (72) in which Becker re-affirms on stylistic grounds the essential unity of composition, and probable unity of author, of *CL-CN-PO*. Such a view of the relationships between these poems is no longer tenable.

55 ——, *Der Quellenwert der Storie Nerbonesi; Wilhelm Korneis; Mönch Wilhelm* (Halle: Niemeyer, 1898) 75 pp.

A collection of three short pieces. The first studies systematically the sources of Andrea da Barberino's *Storie Nerbonesi* and concludes that all are known from extant cyclic poems; the second and third are translations into modern German of episodes from the *Karlamagnús saga* and Ulrich von dem Türlîn.

56 Bédier, Joseph, *Les Légendes épiques: recherches sur les origines des chansons de geste*, I, *Le Cycle de Guillaume* (Paris: Champion, 1908) 16 + 429 pp.

The first vol. of the fundamental four-volume study which established 'individualism' (also called 'bédiérisme') as a school within Romance epic studies. A reaction to Romantic views of the epic, which related French *chansons de geste* to Germanic epic, the nationalist aim of this work between the Franco-Prussian War and the First World War was to establish French epic as a neo-classical literary form derived only from native materials. The classic formulation 'à l'origine était la route' sought to define French epic poetry as a collaboration between clerics and *jongleurs* along pilgrim routes. Vol. 1 contains studies of St William of Gellone, Count William of Toulouse, the formation of the various sub-cycles contributing to CycG, *CL*, and *EnfV*.

Rev. (Vol. 1): .1   Wilhelm Cloetta, *ZfSL*, 34,2 (1909), 6–25.
.2   G. Huet, *MA*, sér 2, 12 (1908), 339–45.
.3   Hermann Suchier, *ZrPh*, 32 (1908), 734–42.
.4   Jean Acher, *RLR*, 57 (1914), 411–13 (review of 2nd ed.).

57   Bennett, Philip E., 'Le refus d'aide; déni de justice', in *Rencesvals 11* (1990) I, 55–64.
Discusses the feudal and legal background to the literary presentation of the king in *CN*, *EnfV*, *FC*, *MAN*.

58   —— 'Hétéroglossie et carnaval dans le cycle de Guillaume', in *Mélanges Fourquet* (1999), pp. 135–49.
Exploits the work of Mikhail Bakhtin to explore the ways poets of CycG establish stylistic tensions and contrasts to renew epic writing while questioning the ideological bases of the genre.

59   ——, *'La Chanson de Guillaume'* and *'La Prise d'Orange'*, Critical Guides to French Texts, 121.i (London: Grant & Cutler, 2000) 134 pp.
The introduction considers the different natures of the surviving poems as documents to be studied, together with the problems they pose for the student; one chapter is devoted to each of *ChG* and *PO*, dealing with problems specific to the particular poems; a final chapter considers lessons that can be drawn from a comparison of the two poems for the evolution of French epic in the twelfth century.

60   Bezzola, Reto R., 'Les neveux', in *Mélanges Frappier* (1970), pp. 89–114.
A carefully incisive study of the significance of the uncle-nephew relationship in CycG. It also considers the same relationship in other texts (notably in the Roland tradition).

61   Bomba, Andreas, '"France" in den altfranzösischen Chansons de geste: Sprachgebrauch und Verständnis eines komplexen Begriffs' in *Pragmantax: Akten des 20. Linguistischen Kolloquiums Braunschweig 1985*, ed. Armin Burkhardt and Karl-Hermann Körner (Tübingen: Niemeyer, 1986), pp. 383–92.
The paper studies the semantic content of the word 'France' in CycG from the point of view of contextual pragmatics.

62   ——, *Chansons de geste und französisches Nationalbewußtsein im Mittelalter: Sprachliche Analysen der Epen des Wilhelmszyklus*, Text und Kontext, 5 (Wiesbaden: Steiner Verlag, 1987) 330 pp.

Uses reception theory to explore ways in which the poems of CycG reflect 'instinctively' the *mentalités* of what is seen as an undifferentiated audience of knights. The semantic content of the words 'François' and 'France' is analysed to demonstrate how both represent a politico-philosophical ideal as well as a regional and 'national' designation. While it is true that the poems show a great respect for the principle of hereditary monarchy, the idealized portrait of Louis which the author finds in CycG is more questionable.

Rev.: .1   Kurt Kloocke, *Historische Zeitschrift*, 249 (1989), 155–56.
    .2   Patricia Black, *Olifant*, 16 (1991), 99–105.
    .3   F. Löfstedt, *VoxRom*, 49–50 (1990–91), 596–98.

63   Boutet, Dominique, 'Le rire et le mélange des registres', in *Plaisir de l'épopée*, ed. Gisèle Mathieu-Castellani, Créations Européennes (Paris: Presses Universitaires de Vincennes, 2000), pp. 41–53.
Denying the proposition of Micheline de Combarieu du Grès in her article 'Le héros épique peut-il être un héros burlesque et dérisoire?', in *Burlesque et dérision* (1995), that the epic hero cannot be comic, the article offers a brief survey of scholarship indicating different sorts of comedy and humour in CycG.

64   Brault, Gerard, J., 'The Cult of Saint Peter in the Cycle of William of Orange', *French Forum*, 6 (1981), 101–08.
Argues on slim evidence (especially formulaic invocations of saints which often are conveniences for assonance) that the cult of St Peter is particularly important in the CycG, reflecting Cluniac influence on twelfth-century piety.

65   Buschinger, Danielle, 'La réception du cycle des Narbonnais dans la littérature allemande du Moyen Age', in *Il Ciclo di Guglielmo d'Orange* (1997), pp. 404–20.
A study of the way the Middle High German poems *Willehalm*, *Arabel*, and *Rennewart* adapt their sources, concluding that the *Rennewart* in particular is a patch-work of material drawn from the 'Rainouart' cycle, intended purely as entertainment.

*66   Caufields, Amian B., 'A Thematic and Formulaic Comparison of the *Chanson de Guillaume* and the *Chanson d'Aliscans*' (PhD thesis, Catholic University of America, 1965). DAI, 27(1966–67), 3833–34.

67   Cazanave, Caroline, '*Du Siège de Barbastre à Beuvon de Commarchis*: Une avancée dans le cycle de Guillaume d'Orange' (Doctorat de 3ᵉ cycle, Université de Provence, centre d'Aix-en-Provence, 1991) 1034 pp.
A minutely detailed study of SB in all its MS variations and of BC, laying emphasis on the intertextual relations of both poems. Abstract in *Perspectives Médiévales*, 18 (1992), 118–19.

Rev.:   .1   Bernard Guidot, *RF*, 103 (1991), 479–82.

68   Clara Tibau, Josep, 'La révolte d'Aissó en Catalogne et son reflet dans les chansons de geste', in *Rencesvals 12* (1993), pp. 417–22.
A brief survey of the history of the establishment of the County of Barcelona at the end of the eighth and beginning of the ninth centuries and of the identifications to be made between historical characters and characters from CycG leads to the suggestion that the Borrel of the 'Hague Fragment' and elsewhere would be Borrell of Ausona, who supported the cause of the Goths against the Frankish take-over of Catalonia.

69   Cloetta, Wilhelm, 'Grandor von Brie und Guillaume von Bapaume', in *Bausteine zur romanischen Philologie: Festgabe für Adolfo Mussafia zum 15. Februar 1905* (Halle a.d. Saale: Verlag von Max Niemeyer, 1905), pp. 255–75.
The article distinguishes two redactions of the Aliscans sub-cycle poems (*Ars + C* vs *E + D + AB*) finding some inept editing in the former to allow linkage to *FC*. The same redactor, who is seen as introducing the vers orphelin into the poems, would have produced a matching version of *MonG* (= *MonG1*). The author considers the other redaction to be an early-thirteenth-century reworking by Guillaume de Bapaume of a version of the Rainouart Cycle (*Al*, *BL*, and *MonR*) produced in Sicily by Grandor (Graindor) de Brie for King William II of Sicily (1166–89). Only *BL* and *MonR* are given as original works by Graindor, added to a revision of *Al*.

Rev.:   .1   Philipp-August Becker, *ZrPh*, 29 (1905) 744–50.
In this long review, which is really an excuse for an independent article, Becker considers 'li rois Guillaume' to be Guillaume de Bapaume himself, and, while approving Cloetta's separation of *BL* and *MonR* from *Al* in Graindor's production, he sees the versions of the entire Vivien-Aliscans cycle known to Graindor as already including the *vers orphelin*. In his opinion the two extant broad cyclic groupings of these poems as identified by Cloetta descend independently from Graindor's work.
          Becker's heading to his review gives the incorrect information that this contribution by Cloetta to the *Festgabe Adolfo Mussafia* and his review of Lipke in *ZfSL* (620) are identical and have the same title.

70   Contini, Gianfranco, 'La canzone della *Mort Charlemagne*', in *Mélanges Delbouille II* (1964), pp. 105–26.
A study and ed. of the closing lines of a Franco-Italian poem conserved in Bodleian Library MS Canonici 54, dealing with the death and last testament of Charlemagne. The poem is shown to depend heavily on poems of CycG (not just

on *CL* in MS *D*), in versions known to *StNerb*. The author describes the poem as being more concerned with Guillaume than with Charlemagne.

71   Crist, Larry S., 'Remarques sur la structure de la chanson de geste *Charroi de Nîmes-Prise d'Orange*', in *Rencesvals 7* (1978), pp. 359–72.
The author applies Vladimir Propp's concepts of the structural analysis of folktales to *CN* and *PO*, as presented in the AB redaction; the study concludes, from the accomplishment at the end of *PO* of the narrative programme set out in the opening sequence of *CN*, that the two poems were received as one text by medieval audiences.

72   Curtius, Ernst Robert, 'Über die altfranzösische Epik (Mittelalterstudien XVIII)', *ZrPh*, 64 (1944), 233–320.
Part of a long series of articles exploring questions similar to those dealt with in Curtius's book *Europäische Literatur und lateinisches Mittelalter* (Bern: Francke, 1948). This section offers a general survey of the place of French epic in medieval Latin and vernacular traditions. The core Guillaume epics (*ChG*, *CL*, *CN*, *PO*, and *MonG2*) are dealt with from the point of view of style and use of topoi on pp. 286–306.

73   Dembowski, Peter F., 'Old French Epic and the Cyclical Treatment', *MPh*, 68 (1970–71), 71–75.
The article is an extended review of Madeleine Tyssens, *La Geste de Guillaume d'Orange dans les manuscrits cycliques* (22), stressing the importance of the book to studies of CycG. It also considers the literary vs oral controversy in epic studies, declaring it to be a non-problem, because of the tendency of participants to confuse the genetic with the structural analysis of texts.

74   Drzewicka, Anna, 'Le procédé de l'adaptation parodique du style formulaire: le cas de la formule "Qui don veïst..." ', in *Rencesvals 10* (1987), pp. 445–59.
Studies the formula in *CN* and *MonG*, considering variations in vocabulary of following expressions as well as the placing of the formula in the *laisse*, but does not clearly distinguish between humour, comedy, and parody. Judgements tend to be subjectively aesthetic.

75   Dubost, Francis, 'L'emploi du mot "géant" dans les chansons de geste', in *Mélanges de philologie romane offerts à Charles Camproux* (Montpellier: Centre d'Études Occitanes de l'Université Paul Valéry, 1978), pp. 299–313.
Studies Loquifer, Rainoart, Maillefer, Ysoré (*BL*, *MonR*, *MonG2*) to show that the term *géant* is applied only to the enemy; a tailpiece traces the usage in

Rabelais and Hugo to show how the term became valorized as a synonym for 'hero'.

*76   Farrell, Alan F., 'A Traditional Epic Art in the Iliad and the Cycle of William of Orange' (PhD thesis, Tufts University, 1972). Abstract in *Olifant*, 1,3 (Feb. 1974), 41–42.

77   Fassò, Andrea, 'Le petit cycle de Guillaume et les trois péchés du guerrier', in *Il Ciclo di Guglielmo d'Orange* (1997), pp. 421–40.
Argues a priori that in the three poems *CL*, *CN*, and *PO* the hero commits the 'three sins of the warrior' as defined in Georges Dumézil's trifunctional anthropology, but does not consider other possible mythico-legendary sources for the material.

78   Flori, Jean, 'Le héros épique et sa peur (du *Couronnement de Louis à Aliscans*)', in *Le Héros épique II, PRIS-MA*, 10 (1994), pp. 27–44.
The study shows that, while fear can belong to the comic mode or have ideological significance, it also has an important place in the moral portrait of the chivalric warrior hero, relating to *sapientia* rather than to *fortitudo*.

79   Frappier, Jean, *Les Chansons de geste du cycle de Guillaume d'Orange*, 2 vols (Paris: SEDES, 1955–65) 310 + 319 pp.
Vol.1 contains fundamental studies of the constitution of the cycle, the MSS and a number of historical, philological, and literary problems as well as *lectures continues* of *ChG*, *Al* and *ChV*; vol. 2 (2nd ed. rev. 1967) offers some brief methodological reflexions, then studies *CL*, *CN*, and *PO*. A third vol. containing Frappier's study of *MonG* (605) was published posthumously.

Rev. (Vol.1):	.1	Horst Baader, *RF*, 68 (1956), 195.
	.2	J. Bourciez, *RLR*, 72 (1956), 281–83.
	.3	Marcel Françon, *Speculum*, 31 (1956), 508.
	.4	Alfred Adler, *Symposium*, 10 (1956–57), 351.
	.5	Ronald N. Walpole, *RPh*, 10 (1956–57), 381.
	.6	Anon., *Neophil*, 41 (1957), 308.
(Vol. 2):	.7	Jeanne Wathelet-Willem, *MR*, 15 (1965), 124–28.
	.8	Anon., *Rom*, 87 (1966), 284–85.
	.9	R. de Cesare, *SF*, 29 (1966), 320–22.
	.10	Marcel Françon, *MLJ*, 50 (1966), 231.
	.11	Mario Mancini, *CN*, 26 (1966), 293–99.
	.12	Frederick Whitehead, *FS*, 20 (1966), 389–90.
	.13	C. Meredith Jones, *Speculum*, 42 (1967), 736–39.
	.14	Anne Iker-Gittleman, *RPh*, 21(1967-68), 342–51.
	.15	Alberto Vàrvaro, *CCM*, 10 (1967), 229–30;
	.16	L. P. G. Peckham, *RR*, 59 (1968), 213–14.

80   Garnier-Hausfater, Marie-Gabrielle, 'Mentalités épiques et conflits de générations dans le Cycle de Guillaume d'Orange', *MA*, 93 (1987), 17–40.

A largely descriptive and narrative article, taking brief examples from all poems of CycG, with little discussion of the family, feudal, or chivalric causes of conflict between generations in epic poems.

81   Goecke, Walter, *Die historischen Beziehungen in der geste von Guillaume d'Orange* (Halle, 1900) 60 pp.

A modest *état présent* of Guillaume studies at the end of the nineteenth century.

Rev.: .1   Anon., *Rom*, 29 (1900), 639.

82   Gouiran, Gérard, 'Entre Sarrasins et chrétiens', *in Le Cheval dans le monde médiéval*, Senefiance, 32 (Aix-en-Provence: Publications du CUER MA, Université de Provence, 1992), pp. 236–55.

Studies the varying relationships of the Christian and Saracen warrior to his horse in a number of texts, focusing on *ChG, EnfG, MonG, Al*.

*83   Grisward, Joël-Henri, 'Naissance d'Aymerides. L'idéologie des trois fonctions dans le cycle des Narbonnais' (Doctorat d'État, Université de Paris-Sorbonne, 1979). Abstract in *Perspectives Médiévales*, 6 (mai, 1980), 18–21.

An anthropological and mythological study of the Narbonnais based on Georges Dumézil's theories of trifunctionality, extending also into Arthurian literature and the *Voyage de Charlemagne*. The essence of the thesis was published with revisions in 635.

84   Guidot, Bernard, 'Le combat épique: permanence et évolution. Comparaison du combat "Guillaume-Corsolt" dans le *Couronnement de Louis* et du combat "Garin-Narquillus" dans les *Enfances Garin de Monglane*', *MR*, 25, 1–2 (1975), 49–69.

Features of the presentation of Narquillus and of the description of the duel in the *Enfances Garin* which might be considered burlesque or parodic are put down to romance influence, although many do not correspond to romance types. The duel in *CL* is really used as a control. The conclusion, that the epic duel is maintained by convention but has no clearly defined place in a late-thirteenth- or fourteenth-century work, is artificial and not wholly tenable.

85   ——, 'L'image du Juif dans la geste de Guillaume d'Orange', *Revue des Études Juives*, 137 (1978), 3–25.

A general study, showing that CycG followed the fashion of the age in referring to the Jews' 'deicide', but revealing more complex portraits of individual Jews in *MAN* and *GV*.

86   ——, *Recherches sur la chanson de geste au XIIIe siècle d'après certaines œuvres du cycle de Guillaume d'Orange*, 2 vols (Aix-en-Provence: Université de Provence, 1986) xxxii + 1207 pp.
A thesis for the Doctorat d'État offering a detailed and exhaustive study of the literary aspects of the poems of CycG composed after 1200, showing the evolution of taste in the last major period of epic production.

Rev.:   .1   Gerard J. Brault, *Olifant*, 11 (1986), 256–58.

87   ——, 'Mesure du temps et flou chronologique dans quelques chansons de geste du XIIIe siècle', in *Actes du colloque organisé par le Centre de recherche sur la littérature du Moyen Âge et de la Renaissance de l'Université de Reims (nov. 1984)*, ed. Yvonne Belenger (Paris: Nizet, 1986), pp. 55–70.
The analysis, based on a number of epics from CycG, concludes that time in the *chansons de geste* is imprecise and symbolic.

88   ——, 'Verbe et révolte: la dérision et l'Autre dans le Cycle de Guillaume et ailleurs', in *Rencesvals 12* (1993), pp. 423–35.
Despite its title this article is a very general study of the satirical presentation of the Lombards in the *chanson de geste*, nor is much reference made to CycG.

89   ——, 'Encore le *vers orphelin*: intérêt stylistique et originalité au treizième siècle', in *Keller Studies* (1993), pp. 97–116.
A detailed study of the themes and vocabulary of *vers orphelins*, compared with decasyllabic laisse closures in thirteenth-century poems of CycG, shows them to be a more specific focus for the 'vers de conclusion' than full lines, except in the very late *Enfances Garin de Monglane*, where they have become an undistinguished alexandrine hemistich.

90   ——, 'La fantaisie souriante dans le cycle d'Aymeri', in *Il Ciclo di Guglielmo d'Orange* (1997), pp. 241–75.
Argues that the comic and parodic features of the cycle do not constitute aggressive criticism, even when Saracen religion or the corruption of the court is in question, because the stability of the poetic community is maintained at all times.

91   ——, 'Constitution de cycles épiques: étude de quelques jalons', in *Sommes et cycles (XIIe – XIVe siècles), Actes des colloques de Lyon (mars 1998 et mars 1999)*, ed. M.-E. Bely, J.-R. Valette, and J.-Cl. Vallecalle (Lyon: Université Catholique de Lyon, 2000), pp. 25–47.
A comparison of CycG with the Lorraine cycle, which considers the evolution of the ethos depicted in the cycles as well as their collection in cyclic MSS, leads to the conclusion that the pleasure of the audience is the principle guiding the

coherent construction of epic cycles rather than an overarching plan by an 'architect' imposing a vision on the material.

92   Hausfater, Marie-Gabrielle, 'Les Conflits de générations dans les chansons de geste du cycle de Guillaume d'Orange' (Doctorat de 3e cycle, University of Paris III, 1984). Abstract in *Perspectives Médiévales*, 11(1985), 71–73.

A useful study of social conflict between fiefholders and non-fiefholders, but vitiated in its primary aim of depicting generation conflict by assuming modern interpretations for a number of medieval terms.

93   Heinemann, Edward A., 'Mémoire, répétition, système esthétique dans la chanson de geste', in *Jeux de mémoire*: *aspects de la mnémotechnique médiévale*, ed. Bruno Roy and Paul Zumthor, Etudes Médiévales (Montréal; Paris: Presses de l'Université de Montréal; J. Vrin, 1985), pp. 23–33.

A metrical study of formulaic repetition and echo, mostly based on poems from CycG. This material was later assimilated into the monograph *L'Art métrique* (96).

94   ——, 'Measuring Units of Poetic Discourse: Analogies between Laisse and Verse in the *Chanson de geste*', in *Romance Epic* (1987), pp. 21–34.

Investigates the rhythms imposed on narration by the varying ways in which units of versification (hemistich, line, laisse) and units of discourse (clause, sentence, paragraph) relate to each other. With the exception of a few examples from the *Chanson de Roland*, all examples are taken from poems of CycG (*MonR*, *CN*, *PO*).

95   ——, 'On the Metric Artistry of the *Chanson de Geste*', *Olifant*, 16 (1991), 5–59.

A general study of metrical questions, later incorporated in his book (96). Most of the material in this study is drawn from CycG.

96   ——, *L'Art métrique de la chanson de geste*, Publications Romanes et Françaises, 205 (Geneva: Droz, 1993) 336 pp.

Using the methodology established in a series of articles and papers on the same topic, the author seeks to demonstrate the artistic excellence, from the point of view of their manipulation of epic metrics, of *CN* and *PO*. The book shares with the articles which have preceded and followed it the weakness of assuming that the MS redactions of the poems that we possess represent authorial intention as far as metrical composition is concerned.

Rev.: .1   Jean Marcel Paquette, *CCM*, 37 (1994), 378.

.2 Wolfgang G. van Emden, *FS*, 49 (1995), 321.
.3 Michel Zink, *Rom*, 113 (1992–1995), 253–55.
.4 P. Uhl, *Scriptorium*, 50 (1996), 43*–44*.

97 ——, 'The Art of Repetition in the Short Cycle of "William of Orange" (The Printed *AB* Version)', *Olifant*, 19 (1994–95), 177–206.
A brief account of repeated expressions in *CL*, *CN*, and *PO*, in relation to laisse and episode construction, leading to impressionistic value judgements on the comparative 'brilliance' of the various poems. Examples of echo are gathered together in a series of appendices with graphs representing lengths of *laisses*. No attempt is made to quantify metric significance, despite its importance as a concept in the author's work, while the echoes are subjected to neither rhetorical nor discourse analysis.

98 ——, 'Patterns of Narrative and Poetic Organisation in the Kernel William Cycle', in *Reading around the Epic* (1998), pp. 249– 67.
Applying the methods elaborated in his monograph (96) and in various other studies of epic metrics, the author produces an aesthetic study of *CL*, *CN*, and *PO* which demonstrates the sophistication of the literary technique of these works.

99 ——, 'Fréquence lexicale et rythmes du vers dans les présentations de discours', in *Mélanges Suard* (1999), pp. 387–94
Analyses the frequency of use and placing in the line or hemistich of various *verba dicendi* in *CL*, *CN*, and *PO*.

100 Heintze, Michael, 'Les techniques de la formation de cycles dans les chansons de geste', in *Cyclification* (1994), pp. 21–58.
Based on part 4 of Heintze's thesis, published as *König, Held und Sippe* (Heidelberg: Winter, 1991), the paper offers a view of cycle-building centred on the project of Bertrand de Bar-sur-Aube in *GV*.

101 Hendrickson, William L., 'Geste de Guillaume ou de Garin de Monglane?', in *Mélanges Ménard* (1998), pp. 667–77.
Attributes to Bertrand de Bar-sur-Aube in *GV* and also to *AN* (whether by Bertrand or not) the establishment of the usage *geste* = epic cycle which becomes generalized in the later Middle Ages, but which, according to the author, was unknown in the twelfth century.

102 Herbin, Jean-Charles, 'Guichardet / Begonnet: une rencontre entre le Cycle de Guillaume et la Geste des Loherains?', in *Il Ciclo di Guglielmo d'Orange* (1997), pp. 276–95.
Studies the similarities of presentation in the episodes in which young heroes acquire arms in *ChG*, *ChV*, and *Hervis de Metz*. Apart from a tentative suggestion

that the arming of Guichardet in *ChV* may reflect *Hervis de Metz* rather than *ChG*, no coherent conclusions are drawn from the exercise.

103 Hofer, Stefan, 'Die *Chanson de Guillaume* und ihre Stellung zu der Fortsetzungen *Covenant Vivien*, "Chanson de Rainoart", *Aliscans*', *ZfSL*, 43,2 (1915), 252–69.
A series of careful textual comparisons lead to the conclusions that modifications to the legends of Guillaume and Vivien were conscious, not haphazard, and that the key to modifications of the data of *ChG* by *ChV* is the dominant place that *Al* came to occupy in CycG

104 Hoggan, David G., 'La biographie poétique de Guillaume d'Orange', 2 vols (Doctorat de l'Université de Strasbourg, 1953).
A fundamental study of the central poems of CycG (*EnfG*, *CL*, *CN*, *PO*, *Al*, and *MonG*) focusing on the unifying personality of the hero. The most important study of CycG never to be published.

105 ——, 'The Version of *Aliscans* Known to the Author of *Foucon de Candie*', *MAe*, 26 (1957), 74–89.
A comparison of significant episodes in *ChG* (G2), *Al*, and *FC* indicates a common source rather than borrowing between extant poems. Hoggan refers to this source not as a 'Chanson de Rainouart' but as a primitive *Al*.

106 ——, 'La formation du noyau cyclique: *Couronnement de Louis-Charroi de Nîmes-Prise d'Orange*', in *Rencesvals 5* (1977), pp. 22–44.
Reviews arguments originally made in the author's thesis (104) to suggest that the first part of *CN* along with original *PO* dates from pre-1125, while the second part of *CN* belongs to the 1190s with extant *PO*. This also implies redating *CL* to pre-1125, which is hard to justify.

107 ——, 'L'isotope C38 dans la composition des poèmes du cycle de Guillaume', in *Rencesvals 6* (1974), pp. 563–82.
An analysis of a variety of textual features in the poems *EnfG*, *CL*, *CN*, and *PO* leads to the conclusion that the archetype of the surviving MSS in all redactions was constructed of quaternions with double columns of 38 lines. This hypothetical MS would have contained all four poems composed with the physical constraints of page layout in mind. The use of the composite Langlois ed. (419 / 420) to provide data from *CL* raises questions about some of the conclusions reached.

108 Hoyer, Richard, *Das Auftreten der Geste 'Garin de Monglane' in den chansons der anderen Gesten*, Beilage zum Jahresbericht der

Oberrealschule der Franckeschen Stiftung (Halle: Buchdruckerei des Waizenhauses, 1901) 42 pp.
A brief study of characters belonging to CycG appearing at least by name in poems outside the cycle.

109   Ihata, Anne C., 'Humour in the Old French Epic (Cycle de Guillaume)', *English Research Association of Musashino Women's University*, 15 (1982), 113–28.
A summary presentation, heavily reliant on previous scholarship, of comic techniques of narration and character portrayal in *CL*, *CN*, and *PO*.

110   Jeanroy, Alfred, 'Études sur le cycle de Guillaume au court nez: II *Les Enfances Guillaume, Le Charroi de Nîmes*; rapport de ces poèmes entre eux et avec la *Vita Willelmi*', *Rom*, 26 (1897), 1–33.
A study of literary relationships which still has some significance. The theory of an Occitan origin for *PO* is not without interest, although the attribution of it to the ninth century is no longer valid. The relationships discerned between *PO*, *CL*, and *CN* are also based on a model no longer generally accepted.

111   Kindrick, Robert L., 'Battles and Quarrels in the Cycle of William of Orange', in *Studia in honorem prof. M. de Riquer*, vol. 4 (Barcelona: Quaderns Crema, 1991), pp. 439–454
An interesting attempt to study the distinction between individual quarrel and professional, chivalric combat in CycG. Unfortunately it suffers from frequent misunderstandings and misrepresentations of the texts being exploited.

112   Klapötke, A., 'Das Verhältnis von *Aliscans* zur *Chanson de Guillaume*' (doctoral dissertation, University of Halle-Wittemberg, 1907).
Offers a simple description of corresponding passages of the two poems.

113   Koss, Ronald G., *Family, Kinship and Lineage in the 'Cycle de Guillaume d'Orange'* (Lewiston, NY: Edwin Mellen Press, 1990) 217 pp.
A superficial study of selected poems from CycG, including *ChG*, tending to a narrative approach, which largely ignores anthropological and sociological considerations. Surprisingly no reference is made to Wathelet-Willem, *Recherches* (348).

114   Krappe, Alexander Haggerty, 'The Origin of the Geste Rainouart', *NM*, 24 (1923), 1–10.
After giving very brief résumés of Rainouart's role in *EnfV* and *Al*, makes a list of motifs linking him to the two story types of 'The Bear's Son' and 'Strong

John'. The author considers that this folktale hero was introduced into poems of CycG 'to relieve the monotony of the average *chanson de geste*'.

115   Lejeune, Rita, 'Le problème de l'épopée occitane', *Cahiers de Saint-Michel de Cuxa*, 3 (1972), 147–79.
Surveys the evidence for the existence in Occitan of lost originals for poems about Garin d'Anseüne, Aimeri de Narbonne, and Aïmer le Chétif.

116   Lot, Ferdinand, 'Études sur les légendes épiques françaises. IV: le cycle de *Guillaume d'Orange*', *Rom*, 53 (1927), 449–73.
A reply to Bédier, *Légendes épiques* I (56), studying *ChG*, stressing that only late poems are related to pilgrim routes and sanctuaries; Lot reaffirms the importance of oral tradition in the elaboration of the earliest OF epics.

117   McMahon, Kathryn Kristine, 'Narrative and Direct Discourse in Three Old French Epics' (PhD thesis, Cornell University, 1976) v + 353 pp.
Studies the ways in which direct speech is deployed within the narrative structures of *ChG*, *CL*, and *PO*.

118   McMillan, Duncan, '*Les Enfances Guillaume* et les *Narbonnais* dans les manuscrits du grand cycle: observations sur la fusion du cycle de Narbonne avec le cycle de Guillaume', *Rom*, 64 (1938), 313–27.
A careful codicological and palaeographic study of MSS B^1 and B^2 shows the revised version of the ending of *Narb* to be the work of a late interpolator, not part of the original conception of the *grand cycle*.

119   ——, 'Les *Narbonnais* et le *Siège de Barbastre*: fragment d'un ms. cyclique', *Rom*, 67 (1942–43), 91–103.
An ed. of the fragment from the University of Chicago library, which the author considers independent of all other known redactions.

120   ——, 'Notes sur quelques clichés formulaires dans les chansons de geste de *Guillaume d'Orange*', in *Mélanges Delbouille II* (1964), pp. 477–94.
The article shows a strictly individualist approach to the analysis of formula, pointing out the role of assonance in determining the appearance of certain 'clichés', by stressing the relative fixity from manuscript to manuscript of formulæ in various poems. Considering the *chansons de geste* to be the product of individual authors, the main purpose of similar studies would be to determine whether the authorship of surviving versions was single or multiple. The author is at pains to point out the dangers of undertaking statistical analyses of textual material in the absence of fully reliable editions of all manuscript versions of poems to be studied.

121   Maddox, Donald, and Sara Sturm-Maddox, 'Intertextual Discourse in the William Cycle', *Olifant*, 7 (1979–80), 131–48.
The article appeals to an eclectic set of theories of textual construction and reception to demonstrate that the intertextual and intratextual references out of which cyclical coherence is generated are of an inherently conservative nature. No account is taken of elements tending to question inherited material.

122   Mandach, André de, 'La genèse du *Guide du pèlerin de Saint-Jacques*, Orderic Vital et la date de la geste de Guillaume', in *Mélanges Lejeune* (1969), pp. 811–27.
Dates the first poems of CycG to just before the composition of the *Guide* (pre-1129).

123   Martin, Jean-Pierre, 'De la *Chanson de Guillaume à Aliscans*: l'emploi des motifs rhétoriques', in *Rencesvals 13* (1995), pp. 471–79,
The main mark of *Al* as a rewriting of the common ancestor *Y* which links it to *G2* is its supple use of *amplificatio* by which motifs typical of epic narrative composition are linked in sequences. The only real point of comparison between *Al* and *ChG* exploited is that of the death scene of Vivien.

124   ——, 'De la *Chanson de Guillaume à Aliscans*: l'emploi des motifs narratifs', in *Mélanges Subrenat* (2000), pp. 367–77.
The article demonstrates how traditional motifs are deployed in the service of *amplificatio* in the reworking of material common to *ChG* and *Al*.

125   Meneghetti, Maria Luisa, 'Le butin, l'honneur et le lignage: la carrière d'un héros épique', in *Rencesvals 8* (1981), pp. 335–44.
Rejecting the approaches of Eugene Dorfman, *The Narreme in Medieval Romance Epic* (Toronto: Toronto UP, 1969), and Alfred Adler, *Epische Spekulanten* (Munich: Fink, 1975), this study of narrative motifs in *CN*, *PO*, and the *Poema de mio Cid* considers the development of heroic biography from a basis of socio-political ideology, concluding that *CN* and *PO* in particular reflect the reaction of the minor feudal nobility to the centralizing policies of Philippe Auguste.

126   Moisan, André, 'Guillaume et Rainouart sous l'habit monacal: une rencontre singulière du spirituel et de l'humain', in *Burlesque et dérision* (1995), pp. 93–110.
The article takes a narrative approach to presenting the themes of the hero's vocation, his continued status as knight, the clash of the spiritual and the human and anti-monastic satire. The conclusion, which is not totally convincing, suggests a serious didactic intent of encouraging monastic reform behind the comic façade.

127 ——, 'L'abbé Henri et ses moines dans le *Moniage Guillaume* et le *Moniage Rainouart*, ou la perfidie dans l'état monastique', in *Le Clerc au Moyen Âge*, Senefiance, 37 (Aix-en-Provence: Publications du CUER MA, Université de Provence, 1995), pp. 435–47.
Considers the two *Moniages* as virulent attacks on perversions of the Rule of St Benedict rather than on monasticism *per se*, concluding that despite their satire both poems are optimistic in that the heroes manage to combine the ideals of chivalry and sanctity in their final days. Owes much to the arguments of Jean Subrenat (612).

128 ——, 'De l'illusion à la magie dans la geste de Rainouart', in *Magie et illusion* (1999), pp. 351–63.
A superficial account of the opponents of Rainouart in the various songs of his sub-cycle, stressing the animalistic aspects of their grotesque portraits, in which the element of illusion is asserted without demonstration. The hero's career as monk is treated as a form of wish-fulfilment. The magical elements refer mainly to Rainouart's stay in Avalon in *BL*.

129 Mölk, Ulrich, 'La liturgie de saint Guillaume et la geste de Guillaume aux XIe et XIIe siècles', in *Rencesvals 8* (1981), pp. 353–57.
In a study intended to undermine further the *bédiériste* link between pilgrimage sites and the generation of *chansons de geste*, a close consideration of the hagiographic and liturgical texts associated with the cult of St William of Gellone indicates that while from the second quarter of the twelfth century there is some traffic from the epic to the hagiographic the converse is never true, since liturgical texts always maintain their independence from secular tradition.

*130 Nichols, James Robinson III, 'Heroes and Clowns: a character study in the Old French William epic' (PhD thesis, University of Michigan, 1971) 201 pp. *DAI*, 32 (1971–72), 1523.

131 Payen, Jean-Charles, 'L'emploi des temps dans le *Charroi de Nîmes* et la *Prise d'Orange*', in *McMillan Essays* (1984), pp. 93–102.
A careful analysis of tense-usage in *CN* and *PO*, particularly with regard to the opposition Present vs Past Historic, reveals *CN* to be much more conservative than *PO*, which is closer to romance models. This confirms the independent origins and authorship of the poems despite their often unified presentation in CycG MSS.

*132 Pemberton, Lyn, 'Story Structure: a narrative grammar of nine chansons de geste of the Guillaume d'Orange Cycle' (PhD thesis, University of Toronto, 1985). *DAI*, 46 (1985–86), 1275.

133   Rajna, Pio, 'Una rivoluzione negli studi intorno alle *Chansons de geste*', *Studi Medievali*, 3 (1910), 331–91.
A study of CycG which is effectively a critical response to and rebuttal of the individualist theories of vol. 1 of Bédier's *Légendes épiques* (56).

*134   Reinhard, A. F., 'Die Quellen der Nerbonesi' (doctoral dissertation, University of Altenburg, 1900).

135   Riquer, Martín de, '"Li quons Willame ert a Barzelune"', in *Rencesvals 11* (1990), I, pp. 15–20.
Acting as a general introduction to the conference proceedings, this short paper gives an overview of the reception of French epic, as well as of other forms of literature, in twelfth-century Catalonia.

136   Röll, Erich, *Untersuchungen über das Verhältnis des "Siège de Barbastre" zum "Bueves de Commarchis" von Adenet le Roi, und die Stellung der Prosafassung* (Greifswald: Buchdruckerei Hans Adler, 1909) 101 pp.
The relationship of *BC* to *SB* is traced through lengthy quotation and brief commentary. Röll finds that the first and last thirds of *BC* remain close to *SB* with the central portion more freely adapted. The *RomG* consistently shows more freedom in its adaptation of *SB* than Adenet does in his reworking. Variants are given at the foot of each page for the passages quoted, but there is no discussion of the methods of linguistic or textual adaptation employed, only broad narrative developments being considered.

137   Runeberg J., *Études sur la geste Rainoart* (Helsingfors: Aktiebolaget Handelstryckeriet, 1905) 174 pp.
The studies analyse the MSS and their relationships, problems of versification including the *vers orphelin*, give résumés of the poems, and analyse the folklore elements in the poems (the most interesting part of the work today). Runeberg also discusses the dates of the poems and relationships between them, but never disguises his lack of appreciation of the poems, showing little understanding of how cycles were elaborated.

*138   Schenck, David P., 'Towards a Re-Interpretation of the William of Orange Cycle' (PhD thesis, Pennsylvania State University, 1971) 242 pp. *DAI*, 33 (1972–73), 286.
Examines the artistic unity of the five 'core' poems of CycG and considers the theme of land acquisition as the vital structuring feature. Cf. 321 note 5.

139   ——, 'Le mythe, la sémiotique et le cycle de Guillaume', in *Rencesvals 7* (1978), pp. 373–81.

A very general and superficial paper which mentions in no great detail a number of contemporary literary theories which might be applied to the poems of CycG to provide a structuralist and mythographic reading, but offers no significant analyses of the primary texts in support of the proposed thesis.

140 ——, 'Le comique et le sérieux dans le *Moniage Guillaume* et le *Moniage Rainouart*', in *Guillaume d'Orange III* (1983), pp. 239–60.
Studies the incongruity of the union of monk and knight within the hero and its potential for ironic humour within a serious framework.

141 ——, *The Myth of Guillaume: Poetic Consciousness in the Guillaume d'Orange Cycle* (Birmingham, AL: Summa Publications, 1988) 144 pp.
The book deals in six chapters with what is predicated before any analysis as 'the myth of Guillaume'. Discussions of terms such as 'myth', 'image', 'motif', and 'symbol' are confused throughout; the theoretical bases of the study are highly eclectic and poorly assimilated, the whole work giving the impression of being the product of a course on theoretical approaches to literature. There is no attempt to differentiate the poems studied (*CL, CN, PO, MonG, Al,* and *ChG*) hierarchically within the elaboration of CycG: indeed they are considered, oddly, as existing *sub specie aeternitatis*, a view which reveals the author's dependence on the highly problematic structuralist approach of Alfred Adler, *Epische Spekulanten* (Munich: Fink,1975).

Rev.: .1 Sarah Kay, *FS*, 44 (1990), 319–20.
.2 William Calin, *FR*, 64 (1991), 841–42.
.3 Joan M. Ferrante, *Speculum*, 66 (1991), 478–79.
.4 Joan B. Williamson, *Olifant*, 16 (1991), 124–28.

*142 Shen, Lucia Simpson, 'The Old French "Enfances" Epics and their Audience' (PhD thesis, University of Pennsylvania, 1982) 321 pp. *DAI*, 43, (1982–83), 2343.

143 Simoni, Fiorella, 'La tesi di Bédier e le prospettive attuali della storiografia sui pellegrinagi. III Le due France', in *Rencesvals 10* (1987) pp. 53–75.
Analyses *ChG, CL,* and *CN* to reject Bédier's theory that the pilgrimage route lies at the heart of OF epic poetry in favour of a theory that, in these poems at least, the underlying theme is that of the increasing influence of the north of France in the affairs of the south, in particular the role of the French kings in disputes between the counts of Saint-Gilles and those of Toulouse-Barcelona in the mid-twelfth century.

144 Sturm-Maddox, Sara, '*From Couronnement to Moniage*: the *jovente* and the *aage* of Guillaume', in *Rencesvals 8* (1981), pp. 491–95.

Structural parallels perceived by the author between *CL* and *MonG2* based on episodic juxtaposition and a thematics of self-sacrificing service are not totally valid, but the argument that *MonG2* hybridizes epic and hagiographic models is important. (There are spelling differences between the version of the title given in the volume's Table of Contents and that given at the head of the article.)

145   Suard, François, 'Le motif du déguisement dans quelques chansons du cycle de Guillaume d'Orange', *Olifant*, 7 (1979–80), 343–58.
A perspicacious article demonstrating how disguise is used to revalorize and reorient the hero's inherent qualities, whether or not comedy is a major factor in the depiction of the disguise.

146   ——, 'De la *Chanson de Guillaume* à *Aliscans*: quelques aspects de l'art épique au XIIe siècle', in *Comprendre et aimer* (1994), pp. 28–46.
Studies the techniques of *abbreviatio* in *ChG* and those of *amplificatio* in *Al*, stressing the lyric density of the former, but noting the literary qualities of the latter, despite its less rigorous structures.

147   ——, 'Héros et action héroïque, des batailles de Larchamp au Moniage Guillaume', in *Il Ciclo di Guglielmo d'Orange* (1997), pp. 208–40.
Despite being regularly undermined in different poems heroism remains a vital concept in CycG, embodied in various members of the Narbonnais clan, but especially in the trio Guillaume, Guibourc, and Rainouart.

148   ——, '*Vox poetæ* dans la *Chanson de Guillaume* et dans *Aliscans*', in *L'Hostellerie de pensée. Études sur l'art littéraire au Moyen Âge offertes à Daniel Poirion par ces anciens élèves*, ed. Michel Zink, Danielle Bohler, Eric Hicks, and Manuela Python, Cultures et Civilisations Médiévales, 12 (Paris: Presses de l'Université de Paris-Sorbonne, 1995), pp. 421–37.
Studies the narratorial voice in *ChG* and *Al* to show the distinction between lyric and narrative which separates the two songs. In particular the narrator of *Al* identifies himself with the *jongleur* performing the poem. Revealingly, all the examples from *ChG* establishing this distinction are found in *G1*.

149   Suchier, Hermann, *Über die Quelle Ulrichs von dem Türlîn und die älteste Gestalt der Prise d'Orange* (Paderborn: Ferdinand Schöningh, 1873) 44 pp.
An analysis of Ulrich's continuation of Wolfram's *Willehalm* which further considers its relationship to *EnfG* and *PO*, concluding that Ulrich preserves elements of *PO* earlier than the extant redaction.

150   ——, 'Recherches sur les chansons de Guillaume d'Orange', *Rom*, 32
       (1903), 353–83.
       The first part only of a study, which does not come to a conclusion, the article
       addresses a number of disparate points: the patronage by the house of
       Champagne of Bertrand de Bar-sur-Aube, historical equivalents for various
       characters from CycG, especially Aïmer le chétif, and sources for the *Sagittaires*
       in *MAN*.

151   Tyssens, Madeleine, 'Le problème du vers orphelin dans le "Cycle
       d'Aliscans" et les deux versions du *Moniage Guillaume*', in *Technique
       littéraire* (1959), pp. 429–56.
       A careful study of a complex issue, concluding that the *vers orphelin* was
       introduced to the poems by the revisor responsible for the immediate common
       ancestor of MSS *C* and *Ars*, imitating the 'Cycle d'Aimeri'. Tyssens also
       demonstrates convincingly that *MonG1* is an abridgement of *MonG2* by the same
       revisor.

152   ——, 'La composition du *Moniage Rainouart*', in *Rencesvals 6* (1974),
       pp. 585–605.
       Argues convincingly from the presence of grotesque, fantastic, and comic
       features, as well as from a predilection for rare rhymes that one author, probably
       Guillaume de Bapaume, was responsible for certain battle scenes in *Al*,
       interpolating the 'Gadifer' section in *MonR*, and composing *BL*.

153   ——, 'Jean d'Outremeuse et le cycle de *Guillaume d'Orange*', in
       McMillan Essays (1984), pp. 175–95.
       A general overview of the way in which Jean d'Outremeuse incorporated epic
       material into his chronicle, demonstrating his persistent tendency to diminish the
       importance of Guillaume and his clan in favour of Ogier the Dane and other
       members of the clan of Doon de Mayence.

154   ——, 'Relectures de la geste des Narbonnais', in *Rencesvals 10* (1987),
       pp. 163–95.
       This survey, which ultimately deals with all the poems of CycG, ranges
       chronologically from *ca* 1000, the compromise date accepted for the 'Hague
       Fragment', to 1450, the date of *RomG*. The approach is to consider the literary
       implications of the successive rewritings of the poems in various redactions, re-
       assessing critical judgements on the different versions. The conclusion, that the
       failure of CycG to be represented in popular literature from the fifteenth to the
       eighteenth century is a consequence of the weaknesses of *RomG*, gives too much
       weight to one witness to a tradition which clearly remained popular at a sub-
       textual level.

155   ——, 'Aspects de l'intertextualité dans la geste des Narbonnais', in *Il Ciclo di Guglielmo d'Orange* (1997), pp. 163–83.
Considers repeated narrative situations in the cycle and their exploitation by poets in discrete narratives to generate an integrated whole, while still acknowledging the role of revisors in effecting the same work in cyclic MSS.

*156   van Hamel, A. G., 'Guillaume d'Orange', *De Gids*, 62 (1898).
Includes a study of the origin of CycG arising from a review of the play *Guillaume d'Orange* by Georges Gourdon (Paris: Lemaire, 1896).
See *Rom*, 25 (1896), 631.

157   Wathelet-Willem, Jeanne, 'Le roi et la reine dans la *Chanson de Guillaume* et dans *Aliscans*. Analyse de la scène de Laon', in *Mélanges Lods* (1978), pp. 558–70.
A comparison of the scenes set at the royal court in *ChG* and *Al* reveals the theatricality of the former compared with the literary quality of the latter.

158   ——, '*Aliscans*, témoin de l'évolution du genre épique à la fin du XIIe siècle', in *Mélanges de langue et de littérature françaises du moyen âge et de la renaissance offerts à Monsieur Charles Foulon*, tome I (Rennes: Institut de Français, Université de Haute-Bretagne, 1980), pp. 381–92.
A comparison of *ChG* and *Al* reveals the poet of *Al* as a careful reworker of his material, who was concerned for the coherence of his poem when inventing new material. The two poems should not be judged aesthetically in the light of each other, as they really belong to different literary modes.

159   ——, 'Les Sarrasins dans le "cycle de Vivien"', in *Images et signes de l'Orient dans l'Occident médiéval*, Senefiance, 11 (Aix-en-Provence: Publications du CUER MA, Université de Provence, 1982), pp. 357–70.
The study of *ChG*, *Al*, *ChV*, *EnfV*, and *FC* shows that, with the exception of the silent anonymity of the pagans in *Gl*, the treatment of Saracens in these poems, which stress their exoticism and evil nature (both pushed to near burlesque extremes), is hardly different from that found in most *chansons de geste*.

160   ——, 'Guibourc, femme de Guillaume', in *Guillaume d'Orange III* (1983), pp. 335–55.
Starting from the brief allusions to Orable-Guibourc at the beginning of *MonG* in both redactions, the article studies first the role of Orable in *EnfG*, partly with a view to rehabilitating the poem's literary reputation, then briefly considers the evolving biography of the couple in the rest of CycG, stressing the unshakeable stability and unity of the spouses.

*161   Weeks, Raymond, '*Aliscans* and the Nerbonesi' (PhD thesis, Harvard University, 1897).
Published in various parts with revisions. See 217, 218, 219, 220, 678.

C. EDITIONS AND STUDIES OF INDIVIDUAL POEMS

ALISCANS

(i) *Editions and Translations*

162   *Aliscans*, ed. F. Guessard and A. de Montaiglon, Les Anciens Poëtes de France, 10 (Paris: A. Franck, 1870), xcvi + lxix + 327 pp.
An ed. of *Ars*, believed by the editors to be an early redaction because the MS is early, but shown by the presence of the *vers orphelin* to be late. Much of the introduction seems outdated, but pertinent comments on the chronological development of the legend of Guillaume are made, including one on Guillaume IV of Orange taking a cornet as canting arms (a pun on the sobriquet of the legendary ancestor). The editors also offer a defence of the artistic unity of the poem, which still has value. The editor remains useful as a witness to *Ars*, but should be used only in conjunction with those of Wienbeck, Hartnacke, and Rasch (164) and of Régnier (167).

163   *Aliscans, mit Berücksichtigung von Wolframs von Eschenbach Willehalm*, ed. Gustav Rolin (Leipzig, 1894).
Offers an arbitrary reconstruction of an *Ur-Al* based predominantly on *Ars*.

Rev.: .1   Anon., *Rom*, 23 (1894), 491.
       .2   Philipp-August Becker, *ZrPh*, 19 (1895), 108–18.

164   *Aliscans*, ed. Erich Wienbeck, Wilhelm Hartnacke, and Paul Rasch (Halle: Niemeyer, 1903) xlvii + 544 pp.
A 'globalist' ed. of *Al* incorporating all major redactions, made confusing since each editor had responsibility for one third of the poem and applied separate criteria to editing the text. The ed. contains extensive variants but no glossary or index. Despite its weaknesses it remains the standard ed. of *Al*.

Rev.: .1   Paul Meyer, *Rom*, 33 (1904), 315.
       .2   Raymond Weeks, *Rom*, 35 (106), 309–16.

165   *Aliscans, chanson de geste du XIIIᵉ siècle*, trans. C. Chacornac (Paris: F. Lanore, 1933) 253 pp.

A translation into modern French prose for the general reader, based on the Guessard & Montaiglon ed. (162), with some editing to remove 'unseemly' material; part and chapter divisions are added on the model of modern novels. The brief introduction is scholarly, and the notes illuminating. Illustrated with specially commissioned woodcuts.

166 *La Versione franco-italiana della 'Bataille d'Aliscans': codex Marcianus fr. VIII [= 252],* ed. by Günter Holtus, Beihefte zur *ZrPh*, 205 (Tübingen: Niemeyer, 1985) lxxiii + 273 pp.
A good critical ed. of the Franco-Italian text of *Al*, frequently considered closest to the original poem. The introduction deals exclusively with linguistic and metrical problems. The text, which indicates resolved abbreviations, incorporates occasional readings from other MSS. Rejected readings and critical notes are placed at the foot of each page. The ed. is completed by an index of proper names and a glossary. All critical material is in Italian.

Rev.: .1 Nancy Bradley-Cromey, *Olifant*, 11 (1986), 244–49.
.2 Gianfranco Contini, *SM*, 27 (1986), 189–92.
.3 Gilles Roques, *RLiR*, 50 (1986), 287–90.
.4 L. Bartolucci, *ZrPh*, 103 (1987), 460–61.
.5 E. Eusebi, *RF*, 99 (1987), 243–45.
.6 Anthony J. Holden, *MAe*, 56 (1987), 332–34.
.7 Hans-Erich Keller, *VoxRom*, 46 (1987), 251–53.
.8 F. Lebsanft, *ZfSL*, 98 (1988), 197–200.
.9 Philippe Vernay, *CCM*, 31 (1988), 276–79.
.10 Stefano Maria Cingolani, *Romanistisches Jahrbuch*, 40 (1989), 215–21.
.11 G. Ernst, *Archiv*, 226 (1989), 457–60.
.12 Alice Colby-Hall, *RPh*, 44 (1990-91), 344-47

167 *Aliscans*, ed. Claude Régnier, CFMA, 110–11 (Paris: Champion, 1990) 368 pp.
Replacing the highly complex and confusing Wienbeck, Hartnacke, and Rasch ed. (164) for most students, this ed. is a critical text of the AB redaction based on A^2. The placing of all critical apparatus at the end of the second vol. is a disadvantage. The edition is accompanied also by a detailed philological introduction, helpful notes, a copious glossary, and an index of proper names. The ed. is marred by a large number of minor errors in the text.

Rev.: .1 Günter Holtus, *ZrPh*, 107 (1991), 786–87.
.2 Wolfgang G. van Emden, *MAe*, 61 (1992), 141–42.
.3 Jean-Pierre Martin, *LRom*, 47 (1993), 104–07.
.4 Duncan McMillan, *RLiR*, 58 (1994), 577–84.
.5 Annette Brasseur, *CCM*, 37 (1994), 153–54.

168 *Aliscans*, trans. Bernard Guidot and Jean Subrenat, Traductions des CFMA, 49 (Paris: Champion, 1993) 237 pp.
An excellently lively and fluid translation into modern French prose based on Régnier's ed. (167), with a stimulating introduction (by Bernard Guidot) dealing predominantly with thematic and poetic matters, enlightening notes covering textual difficulties, and genealogical tables of French and Saracen heroes.

169 *Nos vieilles épopées, La Chanson de Roland, Les Aliscans, Huon de Bordeaux, La Chanson des Albigeois*, trans. Jules Arnoux, Collection Alcide Picard (Paris: Librairie d'Éducation Nationale, 1905), 294 pp.
A general introduction, introductions to the individual poems, and translated extracts with commentaries designed for use in *lycées*. Simplified (and variably reliable) but based on the then latest scholarship. *Al* = p. 73–130.

170 *The Song of Aliscans*, trans. Michael A. Newth, Garland Library of Medieval Literature, B85 (New York: Garland Publishing, 1992) xxxvi + 245 pp.
A brief introduction marred by over-generalization and numerous confusions, a brief bibliography, index of proper names, and translation into modern English heroic blank verse, based on the Guessard & Montaiglon ed. (162) with some reference at points not indicated to the Wienbeck, Hartnacke, and Rasch ed. (164) The translation divides the poem, on no authority, into canto-like 'parts'.

171 Tyssens, Madeleine, '*Aliscans*, fragment BN fr. n. a. 934', in *Mélanges Le Gentil* (1973), pp. 851–67.
The study of what is in fact three fragments constituting MS BN fr. n. a. 934, and an ed. of Fragment III, reveal, despite the complexity of the affiliations of variant readings, that the fragmentary text belongs to the late interpolated group of MSS including *BED*, and BNF fr. 2494 but has been subject to 'critical edition' by its redactor, intended to bring its version closer to the primitive 'Chanson de Rainouart'.

(ii) *Studies*

172 Andrieux-Reix, Nelly, '"Grant fu l'estor, grant fu la joie": formes et formules de la fête épique; le cas d'*Aliscans*', in *Mourir aux Aliscans* (1993), pp. 9–30.
A study of the semantic components of motifs in *Al* which make it, like most *chansons de geste*, the expression of a celebration unifying battle and feasting on the psychological and sociological levels.

173 ——, 'Au cœur du cycle', in *Comprendre et aimer* (1994), pp. 13–25.

The essay considers how *Al* constitutes the kernel of the Vivien-Rainouart cycle in thematic and structural as well as in narrative terms.

174   Bastide, Mario, 'Les actes de parole dans *Aliscans*', *Inf Litt*, 45, 5 (Nov.-Dec. 1993), 5–13.
The article analyses first monologues, some of which are held to give a courtly air to *Al*, then dialogues (exchanges of insults, challenges, and appeals for enemies to convert); finally narratorial interventions, including ways in which the poem actualizes and dramatizes its own recitation are considered.

175   Boutet, Dominique, '*Aliscans*: une expérience esthétique', in *Mourir aux Aliscans* (1993), pp. 31–53.
The study considers *Al* in its socio-historical context at the end of the twelfth century, particularly in relation to those poems, epics or romances, which provide its cultural context. *Al* is seen as both renewing and re-affirming the aesthetic and ideological bases of the *chansons de geste*.

176   ———, '*Aliscans* et la problématique du héros médiéval', in *Comprendre et aimer* (1994), pp. 47–62.
The article falls into three parts: the first demonstrates that the OF epic hero functions as an exemplary representative of the chivalric order; the second derives these figures from the Indo-European ideology of the three functions as expounded by Georges Dumézil; the third investigates the role of Rainouart as holy fool saving traditional society.

177   Brasseur, Annette, 'Au fil du texte, fruit de nouvelles méditations sur la rédaction A d'*Aliscans*', in *Mourir aux Aliscans* (1993), pp. 197–208.
A series of individual commentaries on points of vocabulary in *Al,* based on the Régnier ed. (167).

178   ———, 'Les parémies dans la Rédaction A d'*Aliscans*', in *Mélanges Suard* (1999), pp. 111–24.
A study of the comparatively small number of proverbs and proverbial expressions used in *Al* shows that they are used to add humanity to the personality of Guillaume, while helping to revalorize Rainouart in his advance from king's scullion to knight and feudal overlord. All passages including proverbs are quoted in full. An appendix provides a table of key words.

179   Buschinger, Danielle, 'Deux témoins de la réception des *Aliscans* en Allemagne au Moyen Âge tardif: l'*Arabel* d'Ulrich von dem Türlîn et *Die Schlacht von Alischanz*', in *Rencesvals 13* (1995), pp. 339–44.
While *Arabel* seems to have no OF antecedents, the *Schlacht* offers some literal translations of *Al*, but uses the toponym Archant more frequently than Aleschanz.

180   Combarieu du Grès, Micheline de, '*Aliscans* ou la victoire des "nouveaux" chrétiens (étude sur Guibourc et Rainouart)', in *Mourir aux Aliscans* (1993), pp. 55–77.
A subtle study of the ways in which the converted siblings are shown to be the essential vehicles for the renewal of an exhausted epic society represented by the other members of the Narbonnais clan, and by the King and Queen.

181   Crépin, André, 'L'héroïque et le romanesque: réflexions d'un angliciste à la lecture des *Aliscans*', in *Le Héros épique I, PRIS-MA*, 9 (1993), pp. 189–95.
Taken out of its cyclical context which defines it as epic, *Al* might be considered more nearly related to romance. The point of comparison is Old English epic rather than OF romance, but the conclusion holds.

182   Donnelly, Evelyna Assenova, '*Aliscans*: étude normative et esthétique' (PhD thesis, Northwestern University, 1976) 177pp. *DAI*, 37 (1976–77), 5167.
A superficial and subjective reading of Al. 'Normative' refers to the ideologies of Christianity and feudalism.   There are many basic mistakes in the discussion of the text. The reference ed. is that of Guessard and Montaiglon (162).

*183   Fischer, F. W., 'Der Stil des *Aliscans*-epos' (doctoral thesis, University of Rostock, 1930).

184   Friscia, Alberto, 'Le personnage de Rainouart au tinel dans la chanson d'*Aliscans*', *Annales de l'Université de Grenoble*, 21 (1909), 43–98.
An extract from a thesis presented at Grenoble (title and date not given), dealing with *Al* and the influence of Rainouart on later European literature. It is an unscientific eulogy of Rainouart as a precursor of the Revolution: a Voltairian representative of the People destroying *L'Infâme*.

185   Gally, Michèle, 'La chanson d'*Aliscans* ou écrire l'épopée', in *Comprendre et aimer* (1994), pp. 9–12.
A very general reflection on the position of *Al* within CycG introducing the other contributions to the vol.

*186   Gonfroy, Gérard, and P. Chatard, *Aliscans. Concordancier des formes graphiques occurentes* (Limoges: TELMOO, Université de Limoges, 1993).

187   Gros, Gérard, 'Rainouart aux cuisines ou les enfances d'un héros (*Aliscans*, laisses LXXI–LXXV)', in *Burlesque et dérision* (1995), pp. 111–22.

A close reading of the text demonstrates how the comic valorizes the character of Rainouart and turns satire against his enemies, especially the Saracens.

188   Guidot, Bernard, '*Aliscans*: structures parentales ou filiation spirituelle?', in *Les Relations de parenté dans le monde médiéval. Actes du quatorzième colloque du CUER MA (février 1989)*, Senefiance, 26 (Aix-en-Provence: Publications du CUER MA, Université de Provence, 1989), pp. 25–45.
A general review of relationships in *Al*, stressing the unity of the Narbonnais clan, but noting the potential for disruption caused by the entry of Saracens into the clan as a result of Guillaume's marriage. A particular study is made of the place of Rainouart in the clan and of the implications of his presence.

189   ——, 'Paysages d'*Aliscans*: réalités, symboles ou mythe?', in *Provinces, régions, terroirs au Moyen Âge, de la réalité à l'imaginaire (Actes du colloque international des Rencontres Européennes de Strasbourg, 19–21 septembre 1991)*, ed. Bernard Guidot (Nancy: Presses Universitaires de Nancy, 1993), pp. 299–311.
Landscape in *Al* is seen as always either symbolic — associated with the spiritual and emotional life of the characters — or linked to the specific demands of epic narrative.

190   ——, '*Aliscans*, chanson de la tendresse', *Olifant*, 18 (1993–94), 5–20.
A revealing but rather subjective evocation of non-confrontational emotional and psychological relationships between characters in *Al*, and of the tendency for such depictions to be coupled with humour. The conclusion that *Al* is a more supple, *ChG* a more rigidly hieratic song, unfortunately suggests a misreading of the latter poem.

191   ——, 'Le monde de la guerre dans *Aliscans*: horreur et humour', in *Mourir aux Aliscans* (1993), pp. 79–102.
The horrifying incantation to violence and death which *Al* is shown to share with other epics, notably with *ChG*, is also presented as being attenuated by various distancing devices, the use of exaggerated numbers and other hyperboles, repetitious deictic formulae, periphrases, and, above all, parodies.

192   ——, 'Le mythe familial de Narbonne dans la chanson des *Aliscans*: une insertion souriante', *TraLi*, 7 (1994), 9–25.
Studies the ways in which the poet of *Al* distorts the legends of Hernaut and Aïmer, undermines the character of Guillaume, but brings a sense of renewal and salvation into the song by the invention of the innocent character, Aélis. This renewal through undermining is achieved above all through the parody implied in the role of Rainouart.

193 ——, 'Aélis et Rainouart dans la Chanson d'*Aliscans*: un renouveau oblique de la famille de Narbonne', *TraLi*, 9 (1996), 21–35.
A dithyrambic meditation on the transitory nature of renewal in CycG, especially in the sub-cycle of the Narbonnais, symbolized by the union of characters representing opposite poles. Equates Rainouart with the suffering Christ.

194 Holtus, Günter, 'Zur Edition der franco-italienischen Fassung von *Aliscans*', *ZrPh*, 94 (1978), 14–26.
A concise and thorough presentation of the problems of editing the Marciana MS of *Al*, together with an appraisal of the importance of that version, as a witness to the *Al* tradition and to the acclimatization of the OF epic in northern Italy (cf. 6).

195 Huby-Marly, Marie-Noël, '*Willehalm* de Wolfram d'Eschenbach et la *Chanson des Aliscans*: matière et san du modèle français', *Études Germaniques*, 39 (1984), 388–411.
A careful analysis of the narrative, poetic, and thematic aspects of *Al*, followed by a study of how Wolfram adapts his source.

*196 Klapötke A., 'Das Verhältnis von *Aliscans* zur *Chanson de Guillaume*' (doctoral thesis, Halle, 1907).

197 Labbé, Alain, 'De la cuisine à la salle: la topographie palatine d'*Aliscans* et l'évolution du personnage de Rainouart', in *Mourir aux Aliscans* (1993), pp. 209–25.
The kitchen and the great hall provide the poles of an axis for a mythographic study of the characters of Guillaume and Rainouart, ultimately derived from Dumézil's tri-functional theories, but also influenced by the Jungian psychoanalytic criticism of Gaston Bachelard.

198 Lachet, Claude, 'Figures féminines dans *Aliscans*', in *Mourir aux Aliscans* (1993), pp. 103–19.
The study of the ways in which the presence of several female characters introduces an element of romance writing into the epic focuses particularly on Guibourc's redeeming role as 'New Eve'.

199 ——, 'Echos signifiants dans la composition d'*Aliscans*', in *Mélanges Ménard* (1998), II, 783–97.
A traditional vocabulary-formula study considering how 'echoes' unify the writing, create character, and contribute to the depiction of a heroic community.

200 Lorenz, Paul, 'Das Handschriftenverhältnis der Chanson de Geste *Aliscans*', *ZrPh*, 31 (1907), 385–431.
An extensive review of evidence for MS filiation and revisions of the text, indicating the importance of *M* as a witness to the earliest state of *Al*.

201   Martin, Jean-Pierre, 'D'où viennent les Sarrasins? A propos de l'imaginaire épique d'*Aliscans*', in *Mourir aux Aliscans* (1993), pp. 121–36.
Examines the mythographic aspects of the Orient as Other World in the presentation of Saracens in *Al*.

202   Martinet, Suzanne, 'Les *Aliscans* et la ville de Laon', in *Guillaume et Willehalm* (1985), pp. 71–80.
A slight paper equating sites in Laon with episodes in *Al*.

203   Murjanoff, Michaël, 'Note sur deux nouveaux fragments de l'*Aliscans*', *Rom*, 85 (1964), 533–38.
A brief description of the uncatalogued Leningrad fragments, accompanied by photographs and a transcription.

204   Pastré, Jean-Marc, 'Un avatar courtois de la *Bataille d'Aliscans*, le *Willehalm* de Wolfram von Eschenbach', in *Rencesvals 9* (1984), pp. 333–47.
Argues that the courtly rehabilitation of the Saracens in *Willehalm* is part of a wider programme of moral and religious reconciliation, the limits of which are already apparent in *Al*.

205   Perennec, René, 'Willehalm et Guillaume. Une non-rencontre. Analyse comparative de l'instabilité du récit dans les *Aliscans* et dans le *Willehalm*', in *Guillaume et Willehalm* (1985), pp. 111–24.
According to the author Wolfram takes a challenging view of the material he adapts. *Al* offers a structure setting lineage and war against each other as themes; Wolfram exaggerates this by emphasizing the Trinitarian aspects of the Narbonnais clan, but uses Gyburg (Guibourc) to call in question the crusade.

206   Rasch, Paul, *Verzeichnis der Namen der altfranz. Chanson de Geste 'Aliscans'*, Progr. des kgl. Domgymnasiums Magdeburg (Magdeburg: Carl Friese, 1909) 44 pp.
An index of proper names in *Al* with cross-references to *ChG* and Wolfram von Eschenbach's *Willehalm*.

      Rev.:   .1   R. Weeks, *RR*, 1 (1910), 451–53. (A highly critical review, but not without its own errors.)

207   Ribémont, Bernard, 'Le héros épique: un homme à cheval (l'exemple d'*Aliscans*)', in *Le Héros épique II, PRIS-MA*, 10 (1994), pp. 45–58.
Considers the symbolic implications of the relationship between the hero and his mount, suggesting that Guillaume's change of horse in *Al* forms part of the hero's transition from defeat to victory.

208   Rocher, Daniel, 'Wolfram von Eschenbach, adaptateur de la chanson
      d'*Aliscans*', in *Rencesvals 10* (1987), pp. 959–73.
      A general introduction for *romanistes* to Wolfram's work, stressing its
      complexity and sophistication; the importance of pacifism is emphasized, as is
      the union of pagan and Christian, symbolized by Gyburc and Rennewart.

209   Saly, Antoinette, 'La prière dans *Aliscans*', in *Le Héros épique II, PRIS-
      MA*, 10 (1994), pp. 59–69.
      Considers the *prière du plus grand péril* as a device similar to the *deus ex
      machina* contributing to the dramatic nature of the epic.

*210 Schneider, Karl, *Die Charakteristik der Personen im Aliscans*
      (Waidhofen: Henneberg, 1901).

*211 Spencer, Sonia B., 'The Aliscans: A Focal Point of Late Epic Themes'
      (PhD thesis, Duke University, 1974). DAI, 35 (1974–75), 5365.
      Abstract in *Olifant*, 2 (1974–75), 296–97.

212   Stäblein, Patricia Harris, 'La trace de l'envers: le bonheur, le carême et le
      carnaval dans la typologie d'*Aliscans*', in *L'Idée de bonheur au Moyen
      Age. Actes du colloque d'Amiens de mars 1984*, ed. Danielle Buschinger,
      Göppinger Arbeit zur Germanistik, 414 (Göppingen: Kümmerle Verlag,
      1990), pp. 225–33.
      A structuralist reading of *Al*, incorporating an exploitation of Bakhtin's notion of
      carnival as subversion to reveal *Al* as an essentially disruptive text.

213   Suard, François, 'Le temps épique dans *Aliscans*', in *Mourir aux Aliscans*
      (1993), pp. 137–61.
      Starting from the premise that *Al* offers a unique conjunction of time, grief, and
      pain posited by a pre-existing text, this carefully argued article shows how time
      and its poetic manipulations are the dominating characteristic of the song.

214   Subrenat, Jean, 'Les forces militaires en présence aux *Aliscans*', in
      Mourir aux Aliscans (1993), pp. 163–75.
      Analyses the symbolic, politico-sociological, and epic-heroic implications of the
      ways in which the sizes of armies are presented by the poet in *Al*, with emphasis
      on the way in which the heroes are portrayed as isolated individuals facing
      innumerable, inorganic hosts of enemies.

215   ——, 'Le heurt des religions dans *Aliscans*', in *Comprendre et aimer*
      (1994), pp. 87–105.
      While emphasizing the traditional theme of the irreconcilable conflict between
      Islam and Christianity as central to *Al*, the article argues that the conversion of

Rainouart calls in question at least tentatively the ideology of conflict which seeks to eliminate rather than assimilate the Other.

216 Vallecalle, Jean-Claude, 'Aspects du héros dans *Aliscans*', in *Mourir aux Aliscans* (1993), pp. 177–95.
Self-doubt and demoralization are seen as essential features of the crisis of heroism in *Al*, represented by the failures of Vivien and Guillaume. The situation is recuperated, however, by the integration of Rainouart into heroic society, which the author presents as a symbol of the redirection of energies necessary to the saving of that society.

217 Weeks, Raymond, 'Études sur *Aliscans* (I)', *Rom*, 30 (1901), 184–97.
Lists the internal illogicalities and self-contradictions of the plot of *Al*, as well as incoherences between *Al* and other songs of the cycle, especially *ChV* and *FC*. The conclusion, invalidated by later discoveries (especially the publication of *ChG*), is that *FC* represents the primitive legend of the battle of *Aliscans*.

218 ——, 'Études sur *Aliscans* (II)', *Rom*, 34 (1905), 237–77.
The main object of this article, exploiting numerous epics and chronicles, is to demonstrate that the original site of the battle of L'Archamp-Aliscans was in Spain. The new article contains a long section on *ChG* and its incoherences, as well as on its contribution to the cyclic tradition. Conclusions about the chronology of the shift of the battle site to near Orange, as well those about the poems associated with that displacement, are no longer valid, although much of the rest of the argument is.

219 ——, 'Études sur *Aliscans* (III)', *Rom*, 38 (1909), 1–43.
The conclusion to the series of articles suggests that *Al* is the product of the fusion of *ChG*, and two lost songs: 'Le Siège d'Orange' and 'Renoart'. The author accepts that his conclusions are only provisional, and asserts that the point of his articles was to provoke debate on problematic features of the poems which had previously been ignored.

220 ——, 'The Messenger in *Aliscans*', in *Studies and Notes in Philology and Literature*, 5 (Boston, MA: Ginn, 1897) pp. 127–50.
A discussion of narrative inconsistencies in *Al* giving mistaken weight to *StNer* as preserving primitive material.

Rev.: .1   Gaston Paris, *Rom*, 27 (1898), 322.

221 Wiesmann-Wiedemann, Friederike, *Le Roman du Willehalm de Wolfram d'Eschenbach et l'épopée d'Aliscans: étude de la transformation de l'épopée en roman*, Göppinger Arbeiten zur Germanistik, 190 (Göppingen: Kümmerle, 1976) 275 pp.

The book studies in turn the structure, ideology, and characters of *Al* and *Willehalm*, concluding that Wolfram is more concerned with complex structuring, narratorial-authorial distance, and didacticism than his French source.

Rev.: .1   Sidney M. Johnson, *Olifant*, 5 (1978), 313–17.
.2   Carl Lofmark, *MLR*, 73 (1978), 225.

222   ——, 'Les rapports entre la structure, les personnages et la matière d'*Aliscans*', in *Voices of Conscience: Essays on Medieval and Modern French Literature in Memory of James D. Powell and Rosemary Hodgins*, ed. Raymond J. Cormier (Philadelphia: Temple UP, 1977), pp. 61–77.
A frankly subjective study of the aesthetic qualities of *Al*, considered as being determined by the need to please an audience concerned with immediate effects, not with overall structural consistency.

AYMERI DE NARBONNE

(i) *Editions and Translations*

223   [Bertrand de Bar-sur-Aube], *Aymeri de Narbonne, chanson de geste publiée d'après les manuscrits de Londres et de Paris*, ed. Louis Demaison, SATF, 2 vols (Paris: Firmin Didot, 1887) cccxxxiv + 281 pp.
The very long introduction (vol. 1) is effectively a monograph covering a variety of aspects of the legend of Aymeri. While it still has some pertinent features, and the basic philological work is sound, much of the historical and literary historical material is now outdated. Vol. 2 contains a composite critical ed. based principally on *R*, a glossary, and a table of proper names.

Rev.: .1   Gaston Paris, *Rom*, 17 (1888), 330.
.2   Maurice Wilmotte, *MA*, 1 (1888), 268–70.

224   Bertrand de Bar-sur-Aube, *Aymeri de Narbonne*, [ed. L. Demaison], trans. by C. Chacornac (Paris: F. Lenore, 1930) 205 pp.
Described by the translator as intended for the general reader, the *Avant-propos* gives an overview of CycG and résumé of the poem. The translation is into clear, simple modern French prose, following the original closely; it is divided into 'Parts' and 'Chapters', each of which notes the corresponding line numbers of the SATF ed. The work is completed by 25 pages of notes explaining archaic terms or elucidating literary and historical problems for the new readership. The notes are sober and accurate. The book contains original woodcuts by Y. Lenore.

225   Bogdanow, Fanni, 'Un nouveau fragment d'*Aymeri de Narbonne*', *Rom*,
       84 (1963), 380–89.
       The ed. of a 160-line fragment from a paste-down in a binding in the Roxbourne
       Library. The fragment is closely related to A^2.

(ii) *Studies*

226   Calin, William, 'The Woman and the City: Observations on the Structure
       of *Aymeri de Narbonne*', *RoNo*, 8 (1966), 116–20.
       A résumé of Ch. 1, 'The Quest for the Woman and the City', in Calin's *The Epic
       Quest* (Baltimore: The Johns Hopkins Press, 1966). This article stresses the
       importance of a hierarchically ordered sequence of ordeals establishing Aymeri
       within the heroic and feudal communities.

227   ——, 'Aspects of Realism in the Old French Epic: *Aymeri de Narbonne*',
       Neophil, 50 (1966), 33–43.
       While correctly arguing that realism is a culturally conditioned aesthetic
       phenomenon, some of the evidence for realism in *AN*, e.g. the fascination with
       numbers present in armies, is at best ambiguous, while the presentation of
       caricatural ethnic stereotypes is, by the author's admission, a counter-argument
       for realism in the poem.

228   Kibler, William W., 'Bertrand de Bar-sur-Aube, Author of *Aymeri de
       Narbonne*?', *Speculum*, 48 (1973), 277–92.
       Pours cold water on previous studies which use stylistic evidence to identify
       Bertrand as author of *AN*, but lacks a sound statistical base for stylistic comments
       made to suggest that *AN* and *GV* must be by different hands. Evidence not
       obviously supporting the author's case tends to be manipulated to minimize its
       importance.

229   Paris, Gaston, 'Sur un épisode d'*Aymeri de Narbonne*', *Rom*, 9 (1880),
       515–46.
       Traces the various forms of the tale of walnuts used for fuel and cloaks used for
       seats by Aymeri's ambassadors across many European poems and chronicles
       from the eleventh to the sixteenth century. However, the obvious conclusion that
       this is widely diffused folk material is ignored in favour of the theory of an
       original in a lost French epic, transmitted to the rest of Europe by the Normans.

230   Weiske, H. [Johannes], 'Quellengeschichtliches zu *Aimeri de Narbonne*',
       Archiv, 107 (1901), 129–34.
       Argues from inconsistencies in the extant *AN* that the original comprised two
       poems ('The Capture of Narbonne'; 'The Winning of the Bride') and that the
       latter episode is also built of two conflated versions.

LA BATAILLE LOQUIFER

(i) *Editions and Translations*

231 Graindor de Brie, *La Bataille Loquifer, I, édition critique d'après les manuscrits de l'Arsenal et de Boulogne*, J. Runeberg, Acta Societatis Scientiarum Fennicae, 38,2 (Helsingfors: Imprimerie de la Société de Littérature Finnoise, 1913) 76 pp.

The ed. has neither introduction nor glossary but has an index of names and an index of rhymes; rejected readings, variants, and critical notes are at the foot of each page.

*232 R. Raelet, '*La Bataille Loquifer*, édition critique d'après les manuscrits de la Vulgate' (thesis, Université de Liège, 1962–63).

233 *La Bataille Loquifer*, ed. Monica Barnett, Medium Ævum Monographs, 6 (Oxford: Blackwell, 1975) 194 pp.

A very brief introduction dealing with MS matters is followed by the text of MS *D*, with variants at the foot of each page. A series of appendices give passages unknown to *D*. There are also an index of proper names and a very perfunctory glossary.

    Rev.: .1   Glanville Price, *MAe*, 45 (1976), 214–17.
           .2   Emmanuèle Baumgartner, *RPh*, 31 (1977–78), 455–57.
           .3   P. B. Grout, *MLR*, 72 (1977), 677–78.
           .4   Wolfgang G. van Emden, *FS*, 3 (1979), 521.
           .5   Jeanne Wathelet-Willem, *CCM*, 25 (1982), 140–43.

(ii) *Studies*

234 Andrieux, Nelly, 'Arthur et Charlemagne réunis en Avalon: la *Bataille Loquifer* ou l'accomplissement d'une parole', in *Rencesvals 9* (1984), pp. 425–34.

A highly speculative article which considers the implications of differing cyclic structures among the MSS collections of CycG, and suggests that the Avalon episode of *BL* represents a closure of encyclopedic writing, as opposed to the biographical closure offered by *MonG* and *MonR*.

235 Lecouteux, Claude, 'Note sur Isabras (*Bataille Loquifer I*)', *Rom*, 103 (1982), 83–87.

The author argues that the description of Isabras in *BL* derives purely from the learned tradition of Latin texts dealing with oriental wonders extant in the late twelfth century, with no reference to vernacular epic models.

236   Rossi, Marguerite, 'Sur Picolet et Auberon dans la *Bataille Loquifer*', in
       Mélanges Wathelet-Willem (1978), pp. 569–91.
       The first part of the study establishes that Picolet has no special character in *BL*.
       The literary shortcomings of the poet are adduced as proof that he will not have
       invented Auberon, Picolet's brother, from which it is further deduced that the
       poet of *Huon de Bordeaux* and Jean Bodel, in *Le Jeu de Saint Nicolas*, were both
       probably exploiting the same popular late-twelfth-century text in which Auberon
       figured as did the poet of *BL*.

237   Suard, François, 'La *Bataille Loquifer* et la pratique de l'intertextualité au
       début du XIIIe siècle', in *Rencesvals 8* (1981), pp. 497–503.
       An analysis of *BL*, leads to a comparison of the Avalon section with both
       romance and later epic texts. The conclusion emphasizes the exploitation of
       motifs and techniques allowing an intergeneric as well as an intertextual reading
       of the episode.

238   Wathelet-Willem, Jeanne, 'La *Bataille Loquifer* dans la version D: une
       "mervaillose chanson"', in *Studies in Medieval French Language and
       Literature presented to Brian Woledge in Honour of his 80th Birthday*,
       ed. Sally Burch North (Geneva: Droz, 1988), pp. 235–52.
       A detailed analysis of *BL* in the Barnett ed. (233) reveals the tightly knit structure
       of the exploitation of many themes and motifs borrowed from CycG. Even if the
       marvels referred to in the poem's prologue allude strictly to the Avalon episode,
       the term 'mervaillose' may also be held to characterize the artifice of *BL*'s
       composition.

BEUVES DE COMMARCHIS

(i) *Editions and Translations*

239   Adenet le Roi, *Bueves de Commarchis par Adenés li Rois, chanson de
       geste publiée pour la première fois*, ed. Auguste Schéler (Bruxelles:
       Matthieu Closson et Cie, 1874) xvi + 186 pp.
       The introduction is limited to a plot summary, but the notes are copious, dealing
       predominantly with linguistic and textual matters, the table of proper names is
       extensive, while the glossary, which is a consolidated, if selective, lexicon for all
       of Adenet's works, contains some detailed discussion of problematic cases; the
       text is soundly edited from *Ars*.

       Rev.:   .1   G[aston] P[aris], *Rom*, 5 (1876), 117–19 (as part of a longer
                        review of the three vols of Adenet's works published by Schéler).

240 Adenet le Roi, *Les Œuvres d'Adenet le Roi; II, Buevon de Conmarchis*, ed. Albert Henry, Rijksuniversiteit te Gent. Werken uitgegeven door de Faculteit van de Wijsbegeerte en Letteren, 115 (Bruges: De Tempel, 1953) 223 pp.
The introduction comprises a synopsis of the plot and a study of the relationship of *BC* to *SB*. The ed. is completed by detailed notes on linguistic usage, a lexicological and grammatical index, and a table of proper names.

Rev.: .1 Robert Bossuat, *MA*, 60 (1954), 202–03.
.2 Alfred Ewert, *RBPH,* 32 (1954), 1147–48.
.3 Edward B. Ham, *RPh,* 8 (1954–55), 59–61.
.4 John Orr, *MLR*, 49 (1954), 233–34.
.5 A. H. Diverres, *MAe*, 23 (1955), 122–24.
.6 Martín de Riquer, *RLitt*, 7 (1955), 234–36.
.7 E. A. Robson, *FS*, 9 (1955), 256–57.

(ii) *Studies*

241 Essert, Otto, *Beuves de Commarchis, chanson de geste par Adenet le Roi*, Königsberg Löbenichtschen Höheren Bürgerschule Programme, 24 (Königsberg in Preussen: Buchdruckerei von R. Leupold, 1890) 18 pp.
A brief account of the life and works of Adenet is followed by a synopsis of the plot of *BC*, considered to be the weakest of Adenet's productions, a short study of the historical background to the poem, and a sketchy analysis of its language.

LA CHANSON DE GUILLAUME

(i) *Editions and Translations*

242 *La Chancun de Willame*, ed. [George Dunn] (London: Chiswick Press, 1903) [114 pp.]
This is a semi-diplomatic, limited edition for a bibliophile audience. The work is totally anonymous, being prepared by the collector who purchased several parts of the Edwardes codex from Christies in 1901. The volume includes two facsimiles of the MS, now British Library Add. 38663: f. 1 recto – top half; f. 25 recto – full page. The volume is not paginated, but has quires labelled a–t.

Rev.: .1 Paul Meyer, Rom, 32 (1903), 597–618.
This review gives a detailed account of the poem, and explores relationships between it and other poems of CycG.

243 *L'Archanz (La Chançun de Willelme)*, ed. G. Baist (Freiburg im Breisgau: A. Wagners Universitäts Buchdruckerei, 1904 [1908]) 99 pp.

Effectively a pirate ed. of 242, with introductory material in German, but indicated as available on subscription only.

244   *La Chançun de Guillelme. Französisches Volksepos des XI. Jahrhunderts*, ed. Hermann Suchier, Bibliotheca Normannica, 8 (Halle: Niemeyer, 1911) lxxvi + 195 pp.
A detailed introduction studying the MS, verse form, and a selection of philological problems is followed by an edition of *G1*, since the editor considers *G2* to be an independent poem entitled 'La Chanson de Rainouart'. The edited text is normalized to eliminate Anglo-Normanisms of language and prosody, but the volume also includes a diplomatic transcription of the same section of the poem taken from Dunn's ed. (242). It also has a glossary.

Rev.:   .1   Jean Acher, *RLR*, 54 (1911), 335–46.
        .2   Philipp-August Becker, *Archiv*, 127 (1911), 237–43.
        .3   Ernest Langlois, *BEC*, 72 (1911), 154–58.
        .4   Raymond Weeks, *RR*, 5 (1914), 276–84.

245   *La Chançun de Willame, an edition of the unique manuscript of the poem*, ed. Elizabeth Stearns Tyler, Oxford French Series (New York: Oxford University Press, 1919) xvii + 173 pp.
The brief introduction deals mostly with editorial technique; rejected readings and critical notes are placed at the foot of each page; further editorial interventions are in brackets in the text. The ed. does not distinguish i/j, u/v according to modern convention but otherwise offers a critical text. There is a brief glossary and an index of proper names.

246   *La Chanson de Guillaume*, ed. Duncan McMillan, SATF, 2 vols (Paris: Picard, 1949–50) 147 + 193 pp.
Vol. 1 contains a very conservatively edited text, which at the time was controversial by maintaining the *laisses* of mixed assonance apparently indicated in the MS, and an index of proper names. Vol. 2 contains the introduction justifying the edition and dealing with the textual problems raised by the poem, as well as a detailed glossary and bibliography. The first attempt to edit rather than reconstruct the MS, it remains the reference edition of the poem.

Rev.:   .1   Ernst Robert Curtius, *ZrPh*, 68 (1952), 454–56.
        .2   Omer Jodogne, *LR*, 6 (1952), 70–72.
        .3   Jeanne Wathelet-Willem, *MA*, 58 (1952), 172–76.
        .4   Brian Woledge, *MLR*, 47 (1952) 588–89.
        .5   Jean Frappier, *RLR*, 72 (1955), 281.

247   *The Song of William (La Chançun de Guillelme) Translated into Verse*, [ed. Elizabeth Stearns Tyler], trans. E. N. Stone (Seattle: University of Washington Press, 1951) xvii + 109 pp.

A reasonably competent translation. *G1* and *G2* are treated separately as 'The Song of William' and the 'Song of Rainoart' respectively, on the basis of Suchier's division of the text (cf. 244).

Rev.: .1   Duncan McMillan, *MLR*, 47 (1952), 236–37.

248   *La Chançun de Willame*, ed. Nancy V. Iseley, UNCSRLL, 13 (Chapel Hill: University of North Carolina Press, 1952) xix + 128 pp. 2nd ed. UNCSRLL, 35 (Chapel Hill: University of North Carolina Press, 1961) xxii + 211 pp.
An inadequate introduction and a conservative ed. marred by a number of misreadings of the MS. The 2nd ed. has minor modifications to the introduction, corrections to the text, and an etymological glossary by G. Piffard, which has its own detailed annotations and further notes, in general very useful but not without error.

Rev. [2nd ed.]: .1   Claude Régnier, *Rom*, 83 (1962), 411–12.
                 .2   Duncan McMillan, *RPh*, 19 (1965–66), 629–37.

249   *Chanson de Guillaume, übersetzt, eingeleitet und mit Anmerkungen versehen*, ed. Beate Schmolke-Hasselmann, Klassische Texte des Romanischen Mittelalters in zweisprachigen Ausgaben, 20 (München: Wilhelm Fink Verlag, 1983) 301 pp.
The ed. prints and translates into modern German prose Wathelet-Willem's 1975 hypothetical text (348), adding a brief introduction, some corrections to Wathelet-Willem's text, and an index of proper names.

Rev.: .1   P. Cockshaw, *Scriptorium*, 41 (1987), 24*.
       .2   Gert Pinckernell, *Archiv*, 224 (1987), 446–47.
       .3   Gilles Roques, *RLiR*, 51 (1987), 641–43.
       .4   F. Olef-Krafft, *ZrPh*, 104 (1988), 147–48.

250   *La Chanson de Guillaume*, ed. François Suard, Classiques Garnier (Paris: Bordas, 1991) 307 pp.
Contains a conservatively edited text and translation into modern French prose as well as notes, glossary, and an index of names. While not separating mixed *laisses* the ed. uses (a), (b) etc., following Wathelet-Willem's *laisses* divisions (see 348). The Introduction deals briefly but thoroughly with the problems raised by the extant text.

Rev.: .1   Philip E. Bennett, *CCM*, 36 (1993), 328–30.
       .2   Philippe Verelst, *MA*, 99 (1993), 361–63.
       .3   Roger Bellon, *Perspectives Médiévales*, 20 (1994), 123–24.

251   *La Chanson de Guillaume*, trans. Teruo Sato, in *Corpus poétique du monde*, 1, Antiquité et Moyen Age (Tokyo: Heibonsha, n.d.), pp. 227–63.

Translates *G1* only into Japanese.

252 *La Canzone di Guglielmo*, ed. Andrea Fassò, Biblioteca Medievale, 47 ([Parma]: Pratiche Editrice, 1995) 357 pp.
Gives the McMillan text of *ChG* (246) with minor corrections, a translation into modern Italian, an introduction largely concerned with a social-anthropological reading of the text based on the theories of Georges Dumézil as elaborated by Joël Grisward (635), and predominantly philological notes.

Rev.: .1   Philip E. Bennett, *CCM*, 41 (1998), 386–88.
       .2   A. Callewaert, *LR*, 52 (1998), 185–86.

253 *Cantar de Guillermo*, trans. Joaquín Rubio Tovar, Clásicos Medievales, 5 (Madrid: Gredos, 1997) 197 pp.
This translation into modern Spanish is eclectic, being based primarily on the McMillan ed. (246) but incorporating renderings derived from other eds. The introduction deals broadly with the poetic and cultural context of the poem, while the explanatory notes are aimed predominantly at Spanish-speaking university students.

254 *La Chanson de Guillaume (La Chançun de Willame)*, ed. Philip E. Bennett, Critical Guides to French Texts, 121.ii (London: Grant & Cutler, 2000) 209 pp.
A conservative ed. with a running translation at the foot of each page, intended for English-speaking students. The ed. has a brief introduction, rejected readings, and explanatory notes, but no glossary or index of proper names.

255 Rechnitz, Franz, *Prologomena und 1.Teil einer kritischen Ausgabe der Chanson de Guillaume* (Bonn: E. Eizele, 1909) viii + 105 pp.
A philological study and ed. of *ChG* ll. 1–1002, based as normal at this period on Dunn's transcription rather than on a fresh reading of the MS.

Rev.: .1   Philipp-August Becker, *Archiv*, 127 (1911), 237–43.
Becker uses this review as an excuse to set out again at length his own views on *ChG* and CycG.

*256 Willem, Jeanne, '*La Chançun de Willame*. Édition du manuscrit unique' (doctoral thesis, University of Liège, 1941–42).
The ed., with modifications of approach, was eventually published in vol. 2 of the author's *Recherches sur la Chanson de Guillaume* (348).

(ii) *Studies*

257 Acher, Jean, 'A propos d'un doute sur le livre de Chiswick', *RLR*, 55 (1912), 60–72.
This article begins as a review of Tron (331), whose opinions Acher systematically refutes. It then gives a history of scholarship on the Edwardes codex (from which *ChG* was extracted) up to 1912, indicating that until palaeographical and codicological work was done directly on the MS, it was unsafe to assume that a new *chanson de geste* had been discovered. Since Tyler worked only on photographs for her ed. (245), it was not until Wathelet-Willem did her work for 256 and McMillan his for 246 that Acher's plea was truly answered.

258 Adler, Adolf, 'Rainouart and the Composition of the *Chanson de Guillaume*', *MPh*, 49 (1951–52), 160–71.
A study of antecedents and parallels for burlesque and popular characters in high epic is followed by an essentially socio-psychological reading of *ChG*. The article attempts to demonstrate the inherent unity of the poem as presented in the London MS; the author deems necessary the presence of Rainouart to the poem's overall message. The conclusion is that the poem as constituted in BL Add. 38663 should be regarded as a timeless literary artefact, not as the accidental product of compilation.

259 ——, 'Guillaume, Vivien et Rainouart, le souillé et le pur', *Rom*, 90 (1969), 1–13.
The article applies the structuralist socio-anthropological theories of Claude Lévi-Strauss to the analysis of *ChG* without properly applying his method. It does show that there is a confusion of categories in *G1*, but comes to no firm conclusions about G2. The author calls for more studies of OF epic adopting this sort of theoretical approach.

260 Alexander, Douglas, 'A Note on the *Chançun de Willame*', *RoNo*, 10 (1968–69), 379–83.
A totally misguided article which manages to misinterpret both words, *drue* and *nurreture*, on which the argument depends.

261 Appel, Carl, 'Zur *Chançun de Willelme*', *ZrPh*, 42 (1922), 426–57.
An intelligent discussion of the state of research into *ChG* in the early 1920s. The most interesting part of the article today is the defence of the song's oral style by comparison with the Anglo-Scots ballad tradition.

262   Ashby-Beach, Genette, 'La structure narrative de la *Chanson de Guillaume* et de quelques autres poèmes apparentés du Cycle de Guillaume', in *Rencesvals 9* (1984), pp. 811–28.
Analyses *ChG*, *Al* and *ChV* using Greimas's semiotic model to show that *ChG* is a complete, unified poem, but begs the question of compilation-substitution in the assembly of the extant *ChG*.

*263   Baumgart, P. H., 'Wort- und Gedankenschatz in der *Chanson de Guillelme*' (doctoral thesis, University of Breslau, 1915).

264   Bennett, Philip E., '*La Chanson de Guillaume*, poème anglo-normand?', in *Rencesvals 10* (1987), pp. 259–81.
A statistical analysis of the versification of the poem suggests that the Girart-Guischard and Gui episodes of *G1* were probably the work of an Anglo-Norman poet, while the rest of the poem including *G2* was probably of continental origin, although much altered by Anglo-Norman scribes.

265   Black, Patricia Eileen, 'The Couple in the *Chanson de Guillaume*' (PhD thesis, Cornell University, 1985) 185 pp. *DAI*, 46 (1985–86), 1935.
Focusing primarily on Guibourc and her relationships with other characters, the thesis studies the importance of the couple, and above all of the spoken word in strict dialogue, in structuring *ChG*. Such dialogue between couples is seen to empower women at the expense of men. A rather narrow set of comparisons between *ChG*, *Al*, and *Erec et Enide* by Chrétien de Troyes, reveals *ChG* as being a borderline text between epic and romance.

266   Blons-Pierre, Catherine, 'L'expression de la rapidité dans la *Chanson de Roland* et la *Chanson de Guillaume*: une manière d'établir une distinction entre Francs et Sarrasins', in *Rencesvals 13* (1995), pp. 111–20.
A comparative study, notably of vocabulary associated with attitudes in battle, leads to the suggestion that *ChG* offers a less monolithic and more humane picture of the Frankish warrior and his fate than the *Roland*, and that by allowing characters to express fear *ChG* increases the impression of their courage.

267   Brault, Gerard J., 'La *Chanson de Roland* et la *Chanson de Guillaume*: à propos de l'aspect littéraire de deux chansons de geste', in *Rencesvals 8* (1981), pp. 57–62.
The study starts from strictly individualist premises, referring to the Roland as the model of *ChG*, suggests inspiration from symbolism in St Paul's Epistles, from iconographic schemes, and from folktale motifs, but comes to no definable conclusions.

268 Buhr, Wilhelm, *Studien zur Stellung des Wilhelmsliedes innerhalb der ältesten altfranzösischen Epen* (Hamburg: s.n., 1963) 168 pp.
Doctoral thesis. The introduction is a survey of scholarship. The thesis accepts traditionalist views for the pre-history of *ChG*, but is individualist in positing the direct literary influence of the *Chanson de Roland* and *Gormont et Isembart* on *ChG*, which is considered to be a unified whole. A chapter also considers *ChG* in relation to *chansons de toile* and their refrains. There is an extensive bibliography.

269 Burger, André, 'La mort de Vivien et l'épisode de Gui', in *Mélanges Rychner* (1978), pp. 49–54.
Basing the argument on Vivien's death as an *imitatio passionis Christi*, the author argues that the 'resurrection' scene in which Guillaume discovers Vivien in *G2* must belong to the original scheme of *ChG*. On the other hand the humoristic tone of the Gui episode marks it out as an interpolation.

270 Castellani, Arrigo, 'Osservazioni su alcuni passi *della Canzone di Guglielmo*', *CN*, 25 (1965), 167–76.
Proposes a number of corrections to the text of *ChG*, based on philological reasoning, in cases where, according to the author, it is obvious that the MS does not faithfully reproduce the original. The result is inevitably hypothetical, begging the question of what constituted the original to which the MS is being compared.

271 Cingolani, Stefano Maria, 'Carlomagno e Guglielmo d'Orange. Vecchiaia, giovinezza e morte alle origini della letteratura in francese', *SM*, 3rd ser., 34, 1 (1993), 341–63.
The study of age in the two poems reveals the major contrast between the transcendental aspirations of the *Roland*, and the purely human realism of *ChG*, which finds its consolation in the experience of age and in human relationships (between Guillaume and Guibourc) rather than in a spiritual salvation ethic.

272 Clifton, Nicole, 'Adolescent Knights in *The Song of William*', *Olifant*, 20 (1995–1996) [2000], 213–33.
A positivist attempt to analyse the psychology of youthful characters in *ChG*, as if they belonged to realist fiction. Misguided in many of its comments on the literary creations involved, it also relies on an inadequately intuitive psychology of adolescence.

273 Crosland, Jessie, 'The Diction of the Earliest Chansons de Geste', *MLR*, 12 (1917), 64–68.

Places the diction of *ChG* into a context of traditional epic language to refute Wilmotte's claim (358) that the poet of *ChG* was simply plagiarizing the *Chanson de Roland*.

*274   Dauer, Hedwig, 'Der Kunstcharakter der *Chançon de Willelme*' (doctoral thesis, University of Munich, 1932).

275   Fernández Jiménez, Juan, 'Cowardice in Two Epic Poems: *La Chançun de Willame* and *Poema de Mio Cid*', in *Literary and Historical Perspectives of the Middle Ages: Proceedings of the 1981 SEMA Meeting*, ed. Patricia W. Cummins, Patrick W. Conner, and Charles W. Connell (Morgantown: West Virginia University Press, 1982), pp. 38–51.
The theme of cowardice, represented by the flight of Tedbald de Burges and Esturmi in *ChG* and by the Infantes de Carrión in the *Cid*, is studied to re-affirm the independence of Castilian from French epic, and the common descent of the two traditions from Germanic stock.

276   Flutre, L.-F., and Duncan McMillan, 'Sur l'interprétation du texte de la *Chanson de Guillaume*', *Rom*, 77 (1956), 361–82.
A discussion over Flutre's proposed corrections to McMillan's ed. (246), with particular reference to the glossary.

277   Foerster, Wendelin, 'Zu *Willame* v. 2649', *ZrPh*, 34 (1910), 90–91.
Corrects MS *traineals* to *trumeals*, suggesting that palaeographic errors lie behind the wrong reading.

278   Frappier, Jean, 'Le caractère de la mort de Vivien dans la *Chanson de Guillaume*', in *Coloquios de Roncesvalles* (1956), pp. 229–43.
The main purpose of this study of the death of Vivien in its two versions is to underscore the division between *G1* and *G2*. Incidentally, while claiming to approve Hoepffner's view that *ChG* is a literary imitation of *La Chanson de Roland* (286 & 287), the author demonstrates the extent and the grandeur of the independent poetic creativity evident in *ChG*, particularly in *G1*.

279   Frey, Leonard H., 'Monday in the Evening: Refrain and Formula in the *Chanson de Guillaume*', *FSB*, 60 (1996), 1–4.
Returns, without showing any knowledge of previous work in the field, to the idea, long abandoned because it has no relevance to warfare against enemies of the faith, that the refrain in *ChG* structures the poem's symbolic messages around the ideology of the Truce of God.

280   Gay, L. M., '*La Chanson de Roland* and *La Chançun de Willame*', *University of Wisconsin Studies in Language and Literature*, 20 (1924), 21–44.

A surgical demolition of Wilmotte's article (358) which also reveals some of the richness of expression of *ChG*.

281   Grillo, Peter R., 'A Note on the *Chançon de Willame*', *Archiv*, 205 (1968–69), 41–43.
Confirms the identification of Corberan d'Oliferne (*ChG* l. 2300) with the hero of *Les Chétifs* and consequently the double provenance of *G1* and *G2*, an argument relying on a now discredited early date for the extant *G1*.

282   Grunmann, Minette Helen, 'Temporal Patterns in the *Chanson de Guillaume*', *Olifant*, 4 (1976–77), 49–62.
A perceptive analysis of the use of tenses and of various temporal markers to create a sense of monumental stasis in *ChG*, although the analysis really concerns *G1* only, reference to *G2* being limited to the death of Vivien in relation to the same episode in *G1*.

283   Györy, Jean, 'Le refrain de la *Chanson de Guillaume*', *CCM*, 3 (1960), 32–41.
Associates the refrain with the restrictions on combat imposed by the Truce of God, but fails to notice that these did not apply to battles against the Infidel.

284   Haegawa, Yô, 'Sur le problème de la répartition des refrains dans la *Chanson de Guillaume*', *Bulletin de la Section Régionale de Chubu de la Société Japonaise de Langue et Littérature Françaises*, 7 (1983), 2–12.
Japanese text: Argues that the refrains tie the poetic text of *ChG* to song, taken in a lyric sense.

285   Hamilton, Theodore Ely, *The Cyclic Relations of the Chanson de Willame*, The University of Missouri Studies, Literary and Linguistic Series, 2 (Columbia: University of Missouri, 1911) 301 pp.
Gives résumés of texts reflecting material found in *ChG* (*Al*, *ChV*, *EnfV*, *FC*, *StNerb*) with a general and now superseded analysis of the elaboration of the material in cyclic form.

286   Hoepffner, Ernest, 'Les rapports littéraires entre les premières chansons de geste', *SM*, ns, 4 (1931), 233–58.
A misguided article which treats *chansons de geste* as if they were modern or classical literary artefacts. The conclusion of the comparison between *ChG* and the *Chanson de Roland* is that the poet of *ChG* is an original poet of genius, who none the less constantly plagiarizes the *Roland*.

287   ——, 'Les rapports littéraires entre les premières chansons de geste', *SM*, ns, 6 (1933), 45–81.

As in his previous article the comparison now extended to *Gormont* et *Isembart* is based on modern literary perceptions. Confusingly the author appeals in his conclusion both to the longstanding traditions of the epic with its 'clichés' and to the close literary relationships between the earliest extant poems, despite their very disparate origins. The *Roland* is seen as the fount of OF literary epic composition, imitated with free inspiration by *ChG* and servile dullness by *Gormont et Isembart*, with *ChG* acting as intermediary in the chain of descent.

288   Hofer, Stefan, 'Bemerkungen zur Datierung der *Chanson de Guillaume*', *ZrPh*, 60 (1940), 62–68.
Taking a strictly individualist stance the author dates *ChG*, defined as the entire poem contained in the London MS, to the first half of the twelfth century on the basis of perceived borrowings from other texts. The decision to compose a poem about Vivien's death is attributed to an unidentified ecclesiastical institution.

289   Jonin, Pierre, 'L'or dans la *Chanson de Roland*', in *L'Or au Moyen Âge (monnaie-métal-objets-symbole)*, Senefiance, 12 (Aix-en-Provence: Publications du CUER MA, Université de Provence, 1983), pp. 225–43.
Uses *ChG* as a comparator, arguing, not totally convincingly, that gold does not have a properly symbolic function in that poem.

290   Kvapil, Josef, 'Problèmes de style dans la *Chanson de Roland* et dans la *Chanson de Guillaume*', in *Actele celui de al XII-lea congres internațional de linguistică și filologie romanică*, ed. Alexandru Rosetti (Bucarești: Editura Academiei Republicii Socialiste România, 1971), II, pp. 621–26.
A rather superficial survey of a number of features of the *Chanson de Roland* and *ChG* which never comes to a synthesis; it is not really a stylistic study, nor even the psycho-critical study it claims to be, but a loosely Marxist account of 'popular' composition.

291   Lafont, Robert, 'Le mystère de L'Archamp', *MedRom*, 13 (1988), 161–80.
The article argues from very precise, though at times unreliable, toponymic evidence that the original of *ChG* was composed in, and about a battle for, Narbonne. The essence of the argument is that it was composed for ceremonial purposes associated with a cult of St Vezian at Fontfroide near Narbonne. Although fusion of a southern epic with the legend of Vivien of Tours and the battle of AD 851 is acknowledged, the implications of this fusion for aspects of the topographical argument are ignored.

292   Lefèvre, Yves, 'Les vers 2802–2806 de la *Chanson de Guillaume* et le sens du mot *vers*; *Ai ore* dans la *Chanson de Guillaume*', *Rom*, 77 (1956), 499–505.
There are actually two articles — pp. 499–502 & 502–505 respectively: i) interprets *vers* as 'story' / 'fable', associating it with the *Premier Vers* of Chrétien's *Erec et Enide*; ii) takes *ahi* as a separate exclamation meaning approximately 'well then!' and *ore* as 'come on!'.

293   Legros, Huguette, '"Seignur barun", "vavassur onuré". Le discours mobilisateur dans la *Chanson de Guillaume*', *MA*, 89 (1983), 41–62.
The article analyses Guillaume's discourses (*ChG* ll. 1569ff. & 1592ff.) in terms of the representation of the stratifications of feudal society; the author comes to the unwarranted conclusion that *ChG* (with no distinction of its constitutive elements) must date from between 1130 and 1150, being a faithful reflection of its age.

294   Lejeune, Rita, 'Le camouflage de détails essentiels dans la *Chanson de Guillaume*', *CCM*, 3 (1960), 42–58.
Studies textual details in passages showing repetition in *ChG* to conclude that a revisor consciously changed details to provide a new geographical location for the action of *G1*, or translated or glossed words foreign to his normal vocabulary.

295   ——, 'Le troubadour Arnaut Daniel et la *Chanson de Guillaume*', *MA*, 69 (1963), 347–57.
Identifies the allusion to the hunger of St Guillaume's nephew in a *canso* by Arnaut Daniel as being specifically to Gui in *G1*, concluding that *G1*, complete with the Gui episode, must have been in circulation in Occitanie by 1180–87 at the latest (cf. 788 & 798).

296   Mandach, André de, 'Sur les traces du site originaire de la "Bataille de Larchant" de Guillaume et Vivien: une énigme de la *Chanson de Guillaume* résolue par la *Chanson de Roland*', in *Keller Studies* (1993), pp. 49–71.
Starting from a literalist reading of the Latin *flumen* in chronicle accounts of Guillaume of Toulouse's battle of AD 793, the author refuses to accept the identification of the site with the Orbieu, proposing instead the town of Llardecans on the Ebro as the appropriate site of the battle both in history and in *ChG*.

297   Martin, Jean-Pierre, 'Le motif de l'adoubement dans le Cycle de Guillaume', in *Il Ciclo di Guglielmo d'Orange* (1997), pp. 333–61.
A general analysis of the formulaic content of the motif of dubbing, and its relationship to the more general motif of arming for battle, leads to a study of

three cases of dubbing in *ChG*, although the conclusion that all three (those of Girart, Guiot, and Reneward) are parodic simplifies and decontextualizes them.

298   Meyer, Paul, '*La Chançun de Willame*', *Rom*, 32 (1903), 597–618.
Officially a review of the Dunn diplomatic ed. (242), the article actually presents the newly discovered *ChG* to the readers of *Rom*. Footnotes offer a number of corrections to Dunn's readings. The article opens with some very astute comments on the poem which still have validity. The bulk of the article provides a commented résumé of *ChG*, with particular emphasis on its relationship to *ChV* and *Al*, including a number of extracts in semi-critical edition.

299   Moisan, André, 'La fuite de Charles le Chauve devant les Bretons d'Erispoé (22–24 août 851) et la mort héroïque du comte Vivien de Tours', in *Mélanges Louis* (1982), pp. 85–100.
Although the underlying thesis, that one of the models for Vivien was the lay abbot of Tours, is indisputable, many of the parallels adduced by the author between the chronicle accounts of the battle of AD 851 and the first part of *ChG* are highly speculative and not subjected to rigorous demonstration.

300   Muir, Lynette, 'Est-ce qu'on peut considérer Vivien comme un "anti-Roland"?', in *Rencesvals 4* (1969), pp. 238–44.
The paper correctly views *ChG*, especially *G1*, as being influenced by the thought of St Bernard, but takes a no longer tenable position in believing Vivien to be a literary riposte to the character of Roland.

301   Nichols, Stephen G., Jr., 'The Rhetoric of Recapitulation in the *Chanson de Guillaume*', in *Studies in Honor of Tatiana Fotitch*, ed. Josep M. Solá-Solé, Alessandro Crisafulli, and Siegfried Schulz (Washington, DC: Catholic University of America Press, 1972), pp. 79–92.
The author sees recapitulation, actually the recounting at length by a character of an incident the poet has presented briefly or vice versa, as a unifying element in *ChG* and as proof that the entire work in its current form is due to one poet carefully manipulating discourse as well as the rhetoric of *abbreviatio* and *amplificatio* for artistic ends.

302   Niles, John D., 'Ring Composition in *La Chanson de Roland* and *La Chanson de Willame*', *Olifant*, 1 (1973–74), 4–12.
The article seeks to demonstrate the presence of cyclic 'ABCBA' structures at all levels of the composition of the *Chanson de Roland* and *ChG*, the corollary being the necessary completeness of these poems as oral compositions. None of these aims is achieved.

303   ——, 'Narrative Anomalies in *La Chançun de Willame*', *Viator*, 9 (1978), 251–64.
A seriously flawed article which misuses both oral-composition theory and Vladimir Propp's theory of folktale morphology in an attempt to demonstrate the essential unity of *ChG* in the London MS.

304   Nogués Aragonés, Juan, 'La fecha de la *Chanson de Guillaume*', *Romanistisches Jahrbuch*, 11 (1960), 54–59.
Argues from the presence of the reference to Almoravids in *ChG*, l. 2442 that the text as constituted in the London MS must have existed before 1170, since by that date the memory of the Almoravids was fading. This is to put too much weight on a single allusion in the history of the development of *ChG*, which was both protracted and complex.

305   Okada, Machio, '*se laissed* au vers 632 de la *Chanson de Guillaume*: un emploi pronominal inconnu ou mal connu du verbe laissier et de son équivalent occitan laissar', *Études de Langue et Littérature Françaises* (published by La Société Japonaise de Langue et Littérature Française, Tokyo), 70 (1997), 3–15.
The author argues, mostly using parallels in Occitan poetry, that *se laissed* should be accepted as a correct reading. The argument is undermined by a number of forms in the *ChG* MS in which e + cons = es + cons.

*306   Piffard, Guérard, 'Philological Considerations of *La Chanson de Willame*' (PhD thesis, Stanford University, 1959). *DAI*, 19 (1959–60), 2085.

307   Pope, M. K., 'Four Chansons de Geste: A Study in Old French Epic Versification', *MLR*, 8 (1913), 352–67; 9 (1914), 41–52.
The second study (pp. 360–67) deals with *ChG*, which is found to be rough, popular epic, akin to the ballad, and an image of what a pre-Oxford *Roland* might have been. In the continuation of the article *Al* receives rather superficial treatment, indicating differences in approach from *ChG* at pp. 41–45.

308   Raamsdonk, I. N., 'La Chanson de Rainoart', *MLR*, 16 (1921), 173.
Offers a correction to ll. 2405–09 of the Tyler ed. of *ChG* (245).

309   ——, 'A Source of the *Chançun de Willame*', *Neophil*, 14 (1929), 168–70.
Accepting Wilmotte's view (358) that the poet of *ChG* was a plagiarist and basing the argument on the similarity of some phrases in *ChG* with phrases in Old Testament texts, the author concludes that the poet must have known and exploited the two books of Maccabees.

310   Rechnitz, Franz, 'Der Refrain in der unter dem Namen *Chançun de Willame* veröffentlichen Handschrift', *ZrPh*, 32 (1908), 184–230.
A detailed but ultimately misguided attempt to reconstruct a logical chronology for the narrative of at least *G1* on the basis of the refrains and other data. The article ends with a hypothetical reconstruction of all passages of *ChG* including a refrain.

311   ——, *Prolegomena und erster Teil einer kritischen Ausgabe der Chançon de Guillelme* (Bonn, 1909), viii + 105pp.
In this doctoral thesis for the University of Bonn Rechnitz gives ll. 1–1001of *ChG* in reconstructed Francien. He argues that *G1* has a logical unity and sees *ChG* as oldest witness to Guillaume and Vivien material.

Rev.:   .1   Willy Schulz, *ZfSL*, 35, 2 (1910), 61–70.
Much of Schulz's review re-emerges in his later article (323).

312   Reichenkron, Günter, 'Textkritisches zum *Wilhelmslied*', in *Festschrift für Walter Hübner*, ed. Dieter Riesner and Helmut Gneuss (Berlin: Erich Schmidt Verlag, 1964), pp. 16–25.
The article is critical of many of Suchier's reconstructions in his ed. of *ChG* (244) and studies in detail the language of the first 200 lines of the poem. However, the analysis is based not on a new reading of the MS, but on the editions of McMillan (246) and Iseley (248). A promised study of the complete text was never published.

313   Richthofen, Erich von, 'Katalonien im französischen *Wilhelmslied*. Vorbemerkungen', in *Mélanges de linguistique et de littérature romanes à la mémoire d'Istvan Frank, offerts par ses anciens maîtres, ses amis et ses collègues de France et de l'étranger*, Annales Universitatis Saraviensis, 6 (Saarbrücken: Philosophischen Falkultät der Universität des Saarlandes, 1957), pp. 560–72.
According to the author the original location of the action of *ChG* was Catalonia as evidenced by a number of place names, hence 'terre certeine' (*ChG*, l. 229 etc.) is to be identified with Cerdagne. The problem of relating the underlying tradition to the extant redaction for interpreting the surviving text remains unaddressed.

314   Robertson, Howard S., *La Chanson de Willame: A Critical Study*, UNCSRLL, 65 (Chapel Hill: University of North Carolina Press, 1966) 52 pp.
An often misguided study which takes an ultra-individualist view of the poem. Robertson has an unscientific approach to the question of parody in early

literature, being too ready to take twentieth-century prejudices for a universal norm.

Rev.: .1   D. J. A. Ross, *MLR*, 64 (1969), 419–20.
       .2   Jeanne Wathelet-Willem, *CCM*, 12 (1969), 195–97.

315   Ruiz-Domènec, José Enrique, 'La *Chanson de Guillaume*: relato de frontera', in *Il Ciclo di Guglielmo d'Orange* (1997), pp. 496–506.
A suggestive article which sees in the account of wars on the border between Christendom and pagandom a metaphoric or symbolic account of the uncertainties of social and political change in the twelfth century; the author also argues convincingly that such narratives provide an exploration of the mythic bases of the development of the European psyche.

316   Rychner, Jean, 'Sur la *Chanson de Guillaume*', *Rom*, 76 (1955), 28–38.
A comparison of *G1* and *G2* with *A1* suggests that both parts of *ChG* were reworked by the same revisor, whom the author considers 'heavy-handed'.

317   Salverda de Grave, J. J., 'Observations sur le texte de la *Chanson de Guillaume*', *Neophil*, 1 (1916), 1–18 & 181–92.
The criticisms levelled at all scholars not accepting the fundamental unity of composition of *ChG* are essentially negative, as the author refuses to accept any sort of inconsistency or contradiction in the text as infallible proof of multiple origin or authorship. The same approach is maintained in denying any possibility of correcting the text of the London MS to produce a more primitive state of the song, and of using the refrains to establish a chronology for the narrative.

*318   Sauciuc, B., 'L'emploi du participe passé dans la *Chanson de Guillaume*', *Mélanges de l'École Roumaine en France*, 2 (1924), 39–78.
The reference to this article in *ZrPh*, Supplementheft, 44, Bibliographie, 1924 (Halle: Niemeyer, 1927), p. 69 (#2269) is faulty: the volume indicated does not contain the article referred to. I have been unable to locate it in other vols of the same periodical or elsewhere.

*319   Schad, Georg, 'Die Wortstellung in der *Chanson de Guillaume* und ihre Fortsetzung der "Chanson de Rainoart"' (doctoral dissertation, University of Halle-Wittemberg, 1911).

320   Scheludko, Dimitri, 'Über das *Wilhelmslied*', *ZfSL*, 50 (1927), 1–38.
A strange article which first traces the origins of *ChG* through oral epic to a memory of the Moorish invasion of France in AD 732, then argues for a purely clerical origin of the song, while depreciating the poet's compositional powers. The reflections on the date of the two parts of *ChG* are totally superseded.

321   Schenck, David P., 'The Finite World of the *Chanson de Guillaume*', *Olifant*, 1 (1973–74), 13–20.
Sees contained, defined space as the attribute of Christian-Frankish heroes set against the formless void of the Other.

322   ——, 'The Refrains of the *Chanson de Guillaume*: a spatial parameter', *RoNo*, 18 (1977), 135–40.
A purely subjective assessment of what constitutes the main theme of a *laisse* in which a refrain occurs is used to back up the author's previous thesis (321) that definitions of space dominate the thematics of *ChG*.

323   Schulz, Willy, 'Beiträge zur Entwicklung der *Wilhelmslieder*', *ZfSL*, 44 (1917), 1–68 & 189–210.
The two parts are quite distinct. The first takes a very positivist, indeed a rather misguided view, looking for the 'real' site of L'Archamp, trying to determine the 'real' age of Vivien, and map his 'real' epic career by comparing evidence from the whole range of poems and from *RomG*. The conclusion is by contrast remarkably sound: that topography and similar concrete matters in the poems belong solely to rhetoric. The second part is an extended review of Schuwerack (325) aimed at demonstrating that *ChG* is the work of one poet, and that significant parts of the poem are reworkings of the flight of Tedbald de Burges. Schuwerack's views are more soundly based.

324   Schurfranz, Barbara, 'Thiebaut du Plesseïs in *Garin le Loheren*: An Echo of *La Chanson de Guillaume*?', *RoNo*, 21 (1980–81), 243–47.
Argues that the rise and fall of the popularity of *ChG*, at least in Picardy and Champagne, can be plotted by a *remanieur*'s addition of the characters Thiebaut and Estourmi to an earlier version of *Garin le Lorrain*, and by the way they are marginalized in later redactions and in *Gerbert de Metz*.

325   Schuwerack, Joseph, *Charakteristik der Personen in der altfranzösischen 'Chançun de Guillelme'. Ein Beitrag zur Kenntnis der poetischen Technik der ältesten Chansons de geste*, Romanistische Arbeiten, 1 (Halle: Niemeyer, 1913) xviii + 138 pp.
A doctoral dissertation for Kiel based on Suchier's ed. (244), treating the 'Chanson de Rainouart' as a separate poem. Each main character is presented, versification and characterization techniques of the poem are considered, and comparisons made with other epics. Conclusions are impressionistic, but a cogent case is made for attributing Vivien and Girart-Guischard-Gui material to different hands. The satirical intent of the Gui episode, and the importance of the role of Guibourc, are also correctly stressed.

Rev.:   .1   Anon., *Rom*, 42 (1913), 625.

.2   Willy Schulz, *ZfSL*, 43 (1915), 157–61.

.3   Ernst Hoepffner, *ZrPh*, 38 (1917), 255.

326   Seidenspinner-Núñez, Dayle, 'William and Rainouart: Comic Renewal in the *Chançun de Willame*', *Olifant*, 7 (1979–80), 3–21.

Studies the *ChG* as comic structure, stressing, as others have done, the importance of renewal, social and literary. While appositely criticizing Howard S. Robertson (314) for his misreadings, this article also begs the question of the relationships of various parts of *ChG* to each other, allowing by circularity of argument the conclusion that Rainouart is necessary to the thematic wholeness of the extant poem.

327   Silver, Barbara Levy, 'The Death of Vivien in *La Chançun de Willame*', *NM*, 71 (1970), 306–11.

The scene in *G2* in which Guillaume finds Vivien and administers the *viaticum* is considered as a 'revivification miracle' confirming Vivien's sanctity. In support of this is cited the 'odour of sanctity' which emanates from the young warrior when his uncle finds him. The thrust of the argument is to deny any prior independent existence of *G1* and *G2*. The article does not take into account evidence from any other poem of CycG in reaching this conclusion.

328   Smith, Hugh Allisson, 'The Composition of the *Chanson de Willame* (I)', *RR*, 4 (1913), 84–111; 'The Composition of the *Chanson de Willame* (II)', *RR*, 4 (1913), 149–65.

In the first part of the article Smith argues convincingly that the sections with the refrains 'lores fu mecresdi' and 'joesdi al vespre' are the work of a late compiler. A weakness is the presumed early date of *ChV*. The second part offers a reconstruction of what the author considers to be a 'lost original version' of *ChG* based on comparisons with *Al* and *ChV*.

329   Studer, Paul, 'The "Chançun de Rainoart". Material for a Critical Edition', *MLR*, 15 (1920), 41–48.

Effectively a review of Tyler's ed. of *ChG* (245), in which the first part (the ed. of ll. 1–1980) is by implication treated as having been plagiarized from Suchier (244). The ed. of ll. 1981–3554 is regarded as quite inadequate, numerous corrections are suggested to Tyler's readings, and numerous additions to the glossary are proposed.

330   Suard, François, 'La *Chanson de Guillaume* et les épopées de la révolte', in *Rencesvals 12* (1993), pp. 437–47.

While not totally convincing on the announced theme of revolt, the paper does offer a subtle and penetrating analysis of the shifting dynamics of the role of the overlord-commander and his relationships to feudal and military followers across the whole of *ChG*.

331   Tron, Emil, *Trouvaille ou pastiche? Doutes exprimés au sujet de la 'Chançun de Willame'* (Bari: Joseph Laterza et Fils, 1909) 16pp.
A brief pamphlet by a non-specialist offering a series of unsupported suppositions about the London MS of *ChG* which is presented as a forgery.

Rev.:   .1   Raymond Weeks, *RR*, 1 (1910), 453–54.

332   Tyler, Elizabeth Stearns, 'Notes on the *Chançun de Willame*', *RR*, 9 (1919), 396–429.
A prologomenic article anticipating her ed. of *ChG* (245). A large number of corrections to Suchier's readings are listed, and there is detailed discussion of his approach to correcting the MS in 244. In addition to problems relating to the MS the article considers the versification and refrain of *ChG*, and implications for the cyclic relationships of the poem.

333   Tyssens, Madeleine, 'Deux passages suspects dans la *Chanson de Guillaume*', in *Hommage Delbouille* (1973), pp.107–21.
Proposes corrections to ll. 2270 and 2495 of *ChG* to eliminate infractions of the 'loi de Bartsch'.

334   Valtorta, Bruna, '*La Chanson de Willelme*', *Studi Romanzi*, 28 (1939), 19–140.
The first part of this book-length study reviews very competently the evidence for seeing *ChG* as two poems, arguing for *G2* being a conscious sequel to *G1*. The stylistic elements of the study are based on Giuseppe Chiri's view that the OF epic depends predominantly on Latin models (*L'epica latina medioevale e la Chanson de Roland* (Genoa: Emiliano Degli Orfini, 1936). The case for *G1* being an organic and artistic whole is unconvincing. The second part examines the relationship of *ChG* to the cyclic poems. Its conclusion that *G1* dates from the eleventh century and lies with *CL* at the root of CycG is unsound.

335   van Emden, Wolfgang G., '"E cil de France le cleiment a guarant": Roland, Vivien et le thème du garant', in *Rencesvals 6* (1974), pp. 31–61.
The study of the commander's role as protector of his men, designed to show that Roland's change of heart is a feudo-chivalric matter not a theological one, uses Vivien, in *ChG*, as an extensive comparator, since his role has explicit Christian overtones.

336   Vàrvaro, Alberto, 'La *Chanson de Guillaume* et l'histoire littéraire du XIIᵉ siècle', in *Il Ciclo di Guglielmo d'Orange*, pp. 184–207.

Reviews critically the literature dealing with the dating and composition of *ChG*. The reflexions tend to be impressionistically subjective.

337   Waltz, Matthias, *Rolandslied, Wilhelmslied, Alexiuslied; zur Struktur und geschichtliche Bedeutung* (Heidelberg: Carl Winter, 1965) 207 pp.
A series of three discrete studies based on Erich Köhler's socio-political theory of medieval literary production, and on early notions of reception aesthetics. *ChG* (*G1* only) is dealt with pp. 158–78. The study errs in considering *ChG in toto* to be an early-twelfth-century poem and in taking no account of the complex history of the poem's development. It is less concerned with audience(s) than with the depiction of a knighthood supposedly more motivated by inner truth than by concrete reality.

Rev.:   .1   André Burger, *MAe*, 35 (1966), 240–48.
         .2   Martha G. Worthington, *RPh*, 22 (1968–69), 329–33.
         .3   Jean-Charles Payen, *MA*, 75 (1969), 323–30.
         .4   Cesare Segre, *ZrPh*, 87 (1971), 414–19.

338   Warren, F. M., 'On the Date and Authorship of the *Chanson de Guillaume*', *MPh*, 29 (1931–32), 385–89.
The author bases his approval of the date and provenance of *ChG* suggested by Ferdinand Lot, 'Études sur les légendes épiques françaises', *Rom*, 53 (1927), 449–73, on the arbitrary identification of certain characters with historical personages associated with the Anglo-Norman court at the end of the eleventh century.

339   Wathelet-Willem, Jeanne, 'Prolégomènes à une nouvelle édition de la *Chançun de Willame*', *RBPH*, 24 (1945), 47–72.
The detailed study of the language and versification of *ChG* clearly shows the work of an Anglo-Norman scribe. The study is aimed at refuting, if not the whole idea of Bédier's insistence on adherence to the text of the MS being edited, at least its applicability in the case of *ChG*. On the other hand the author rejects here what will ultimately be the logical outcome of her approach in her published ed. (348), the reconstruction of an original version, in favour of a presentation making clear on the published page what belongs to the scribe, and what can be attributed to the poet.

340   ——, '*La Chançun de Willame*. Le problème de l'unité du ms. British [Museum] add. 38663', *MA*, 58 (1952), 363–77.
The study of the vocabulary, style, and versification of *ChG* reveals it to be constructed of two major units by different poets. However, the fact that these parts were assembled, for whatever reason, in the Middle Ages requires that *ChG* be edited and studied as a single entity. This article effectively consecrates the

designation of the two parts of *ChG* as *G1* and *G2* (although here the abbreviations W I and W II are used).

341   ——, 'Sur la date de la *Chançun de Willame*', *LR*, 7 (1953), 331–49.
The article is effectively a detailed review of McMillan's work on the versification and language of *ChG* in his ed. (246). Based predominantly on an analysis of the handling of enclitic pronouns, a date of *ca* 1140 is proposed for *ChG* in its current form (containing both *G1* and *G2*).

342   ——, 'Sur deux passages de la *Chanson de Guillaume*', *MA*, 65 (1959), 27–40.
The first part of the article criticizes and corrects the punctuation offered by both Suchier (244) and McMillan (246) for ll. 252 ff. of *ChG*; the second part seeks to demonstrate that Vivien does not die in *G1* and suggests that it was the revisor responsible for incorporating the primitive 'Chanson de Vivien' into *ChG* who suppressed the explicit description of the death to take account of the situation at the beginning of *G2*.

343   ——, 'Les refrains dans la *Chanson de Guillaume*', in *La Technique littéraire* (1959), pp. 457–83.
A highly complex article which starts by reviewing scholarship on the refrains in *ChG*, then considers the refrains in their several narrative and poetic contexts; it finally compares *ChG* and *ChV* from the point of view of archaism, before concluding that *ChG* is a poem to the glory of youth inserting the episodes of Girart, Guischard and Guiot to emphasize the theme. Only the refrain *lunsdi al vespre* can be held to belong to the archaic form of the poem: the other refrains, *joesdi al vespre* and *lores fu mecresdi*, were invented by the interpolators on the model of the original.

344   ——, 'A propos de la géographie dans la *Chanson de Guillaume*', *CCM*, 3 (1960), 107–15.
A study of the problems posed by the form of the name and the identification of the site of L'Archamp in *ChG*, which concludes that the poem reveals strata of recomposition by different poets with different perspectives.

345   ——, 'Guillaume, mari ridicule et complaisant?', in *Mélanges d'histoire littéraire, de linguistique et de philologie romane offerts à Charles Rostaing par ses collègues, ses élèves et ses amis*, ed. Jacques de Caluwé, Jean-Marie d'Heur, and René Dumas (Liège: Association des Romanistes de Liège, 1974), pp. 1213–33.
A detailed and convincing refutation of Robertson's (314) and Alexander's (260) interpretations of *ChG* as essentially parodic in all its episodes, including that of the death of Vivien.

346   ——, 'A propos de la technique formulaire dans les plus anciennes chansons de geste', in *Mélanges Delbouille II* (1964), pp. 705–27.

In part a rebuttal of Wilmotte's thesis that *ChG* plagiarized the *Chanson de Roland* (358), the article reveals a flexibility of use in *ChG* as well as in the *Roland* and *Gormont et Isembart* within the fixity of formulaic usage which assures the independence of each poetic creation. As a corollary to the study the author suggests that the octosyllable was probably the original metre of the *chanson de geste*.

347   ——, 'La vérité psychologique d'un héros épique secondaire. Le jeune Gui de la *Chanson de Guillaume*', in *Mélanges Le Gentil* (1973), pp. 881–98.

A conventional character study, which fails to take account of the parodic aspects of the Gui episode of *G1*, while offering very pertinent remarks on the poetic and narrative structures of the episode and its relationship to other poems, as well as to other parts of *ChG*. The conclusion, that the episode may have been composed to please a particular patron by offering the portrait of a young hero, lacks conviction.

348   ——, *Recherches sur la Chanson de Guillaume, études accompagnées d'une édition*, Bibliothèque de la Faculté de Philosophie et Lettres de l'Université de Liège, 210, 2 vols (Paris: Les Belles Lettres, 1975) 1301 pp.

A fundamental and encyclopedic study of the problems relating to *ChG*. Vol. 1 contains a series of studies of the London MS — its origins, provenance and date, its language, its versification — and of the poem: its structure, its relationships to other poems of CycG, personal and place names, and general vocabulary. Vol. 2 contains a diplomatic transcription of the MS, a highly controversial reconstruction of a hypothetical original text, a translation into modern French, critical apparatus including palaeographic and textual notes, an exhaustive glossary, an index of proper names, an index to problems discussed in vol. 1, and an extensive bibliography.

Rev.:   .1   Emmanuèle Baumgartner, *Rom*, 98 (1977) 121–29.
     .2   Gerard J. Brault, *FR*, 51 (1977), 110.
     .3   Bernard Guidot, *RF*, 89 (1977), 115–18 & 121–28.
     .4   David P. Schenck, *Olifant*, 5 (1977–78), 125–34.
     .5   W. M. Hackett, *MLR*, 73 (1978), 179–81.
     .6   Kurt Kloocke, *ZfSL*, 88 (1978) 273–76.
     .7   Gilles Roques, *ZrPh*, 95 (1979), 165–68.
     .8   Philip E. Bennett, *RBPH*, 60 (1982), 641–46.
     .9   Beate Schmolke-Hasselmann, *VoxRom*, 41 (1982), 280–84.

349   ——, 'L'enseignement du vocabulaire (étudié par les méthodes modernes
        ou par les procédés traditionnels) dans la recherche de la structure de la
        Chanson de Guillaume', in *Actes du XIIIe congrès international de
        linguistique et philologie romane*, 2 vols (Québec: Les Presses de
        l'Université Laval, 1976), II, pp. 811–23.
        This analysis of the vocabulary of *ChG* is concerned less with establishing the
        structure of the poem by means of statistical analyses than with demonstrating the
        shortcomings of such approaches to medieval texts. Studies of individual items of
        vocabulary are sensitive and informative.

350   ——, 'Réflexions sur la *Chanson de Guillaume*', in *Mélanges Louis*
        (1982), pp. 607–21.
        Some interesting thoughts on the nature of epic composition and diffusion in the
        twelfth century are followed by a perceptive and subtle analysis of the major
        components of *ChG* and their relationship to other parts of the cycle.

351   ——, 'Vivien et le héros "al corb nez" dans la *Chanson de Guillaume*', in
        Symposium Riquer (1984), pp. 463–76.
        The study of various characters of *ChG* — Vivien, Tedbalt de Burges, and
        Guillaume — indicates that the poem does preserve the memory of real historical
        personages, places, and events.

352   ——, 'Le héros "au courbe nez" dans la *Chanson de Guillaume*', in
        Guillaume et Willehalm (1985), pp. 145–57.
        A brief commented synopsis of *ChG*, not particularly centred on Guillaume,
        aiming to demonstrate the unity of the assembled poem.

353   Weeks, Raymond, 'The Newly Discovered *Chançun de Willame*', MPh, 2
        (1904-05), 1–16 & 231–48; 3 (1905–06), 211–34.
        An analysis of the content of *ChG* based on Dunn's transcription (242) leads to
        some pertinent conclusions about the construction of the extant poem, and on the
        ballad-like nature of much of the style of *G1*. However, attempts to determine
        what must have been in the original poem and in the original of *Al*, based on
        comparisons with other poems of CycG, are frequently misguided because they
        depend on erroneous preconceptions of the history of OF epic. The continuation
        of the study contains the author's assessment of problematic passages in *ChG*,
        though some are problematic only because he applies to the MS readings criteria
        of 'objective realism'. The description of difficulties such as the resuscitation of a
        number of heroes from *G1* to *G2*, the confusions between Gui and Guischard, the
        repetition of the feast motif are good, but the conclusions, based on the idea that
        modifications are due either to scribal incompetence or to attempts to reconcile
        genuinely conflicting traditions, are frequently invalid.

354   ——, 'The *Chançun de Willame*', *The Library*, 6 (1905), 113–36.
An elegantly erudite presentation of *ChG* for the cultivated general reader.

355   Williamson, Joan B., 'L'unité idéologique de la *Chanson de Guillaume*', in *Rencesvals 10* (1987), pp. 1139–52.
Argues that *ChG* offers an artistically unified ideology based on a Christian view of the acceptance of suffering. The article reveals a number of misunderstandings of the text, including misreading as a *credo épique* ll. 2156–57 from which the argument starts.

356   ——, 'Structural Unity in the *Chanson de Guillaume*: The Role of Rainouart', *South Atlantic Review*, 52 (1987), 15–24.
Arguing from the essential unity of *ChG* in the London MS, sees the presence of Rainouart as necessary to the structure of the poem, as he compensates for the lacks inherent in the other characters, whether the heroes of *G1* or Louis in *G2*.

357   ——, 'The *Chanson de Guillaume*: Why Warriors Wage War', in *Rencesvals 11* (1990), II, pp. 359–72.
Argues cogently enough that the motivation for heroism in the *ChG* is a mixture of Christian and non-Christian elements. Unfortunately the article is marred by a number of misreadings or misrepresentations of the poetic text.

358   Wilmotte, Maurice, 'La *Chanson de Roland* et la *Chançun de Willame*', *Rom*, 44 (1915–17), 55–86.
Offering an interesting mixture of individualism (that it was the product of an original author) and traditionalism (that it was generated by oral diffusion accounting for the poor state of the poem in the London MS) the study considers *ChG* as a literary imitation of the *Chanson de Roland*, based on a performer's memory of that poem. Much of the evidence adduced for the imitation is highly tendentious.

LA CHANSON DE RAINOUART: SEE *LA CHANSON DE GUILLAUME*

LE CHARROI DE NÎMES

(i) Editions and Translations

359   *Le Charroi de Nîmes, chanson de geste du XIIe siècle*, ed. J.-L. Perrier, CFMA, 66 (Paris: Champion, 1931) viii + 77 pp.
An inadequate critical ed. based on the AB redaction, with a brief introduction, scanty notes, and minimal glossary. Now superseded by McMillan (365).

360   *Le Charroi de Nîmes, altfranz. Epos, Handschrift D*, ed. E. Lange-Kowal
      (Berlin: Verlag Arthur Collignon, 1934) 77 pp.
      An edition of *D* marred by several misreadings of the MS. The introduction is
      very brief; the notes provide a linguistic analysis of the *D* version. There are also
      an index of proper names and a brief glossary.

      Rev.:   .1   J. Dvořák, *Casopis pro Moderní Filologii*, 21 (1935), 347.
              .2   Alfred Jeanroy, *Rom*, 61 (1935), 112–14 (Gives an extensive list
                      of errors in the ed.).
              .3   K. Sneyders de Vogel, *Neophil*, 21 (1935), 49.

361   *Le Charroi de Nîmes, an English Translation with Notes*, trans. by Henri
      J. Godin (Oxford: Basil Blackwell, 1936) viii + 55 pp.
      A trans. of the Perrier ed. (358) with extensive linguistic notes designed to make
      the vol. a teaching aid for OF language.

362   *Il Carriaggio di Nîmes, canzone di gesta del XIIe secolo*, ed. Giuseppe E.
      Sansone (Bari: Dedalo Libri, 1969) 201 pp.
      Reprints Perrier's ed. (359) with new notes on problematic passages and a
      translation into Italian prose.

      Rev.:   .1   C. Guerrieri-Crocetti, *Paideia*, 25 (1970), 272–73.
              .2   Lawton P. G. Peckham, *RR*, 61 (1970), 219.
              .3   Duncan McMillan, *Rom*, 91 (1970), 114–15.
              .4   Frederick Kœnig, *RPh*, 25 (1971–72), 135–37.

363   *Le Charroi de Nîmes*, ed. G. de Poerck, R. van Deyck, and R. Zwaenen-
      poel, Textes et Traitement Automatique, 1, 2 vols (Saint-Aquilin-de-
      Pacy: Mallier, 1970) 116 + 227 pp.
      Vol. 1 contains a composite text of the A family MSS, making it neither
      diplomatic nor critical, exhaustive variants of the A family for the first 500 lines,
      a concordance of proper names, a list of assonances (in which there are some
      errors), and a list of repeated hemistichs. Vol. 2 contains the full concordance and
      a repertoire of morphological features. Again there are some omissions and
      errors. A useful tool for approaching *CN* if used with caution.

      Rev.:   .1   Duncan McMillan, *ZrPh*, 86 (1970), 554–63.
              .2   Jeanne Wathelet-Willem, *MR*, 20 (1970), 139.
              .3   William W. Kibler, *FR*, 45 (1971), 547–48.
              .4   Giuseppe di Stefano, *SF*, 43 (1971), 117.
              .5   Suzanne Hanon, *Revue Romane*, 8 (1973), 421–23.
              .6   Ian Short, *RPh*, 28 (1974–75), 239–41.
              .7   Oriel C. L. Redmond, *Olifant*, 4 (1976–77), 125–26.

364 *Le Charroi de Nîmes*, [ed. J.-L. Perrier], trans. Fabienne Gégou, Traductions des CFMA, 11 (Paris: Champion, 1971) xiii + 97 pp.
A sound but uninspiring line-by-line rendering of the poem, based principally on Perrier's ed. (359), but with corrections taken from commentaries by Régnier (397) and McMillan (362.3). Some useful linguistic and textual notes are appended.

Rev.: .1   Duncan McMillan, *CCM*, 16 (1973), 71–72.
     .2   John L. Grigsby, *RPh*, 35 (1981–82), 534–35.

365 *Le Charroi de Nîmes, chanson de geste du XIIe siècle*, ed. Duncan McMillan, Bibliothèque Française et Romane, Série B: Éditions Critiques de Textes, 12 (Paris: C. Klincksieck, 1972) 169 pp.
This ed. replaces Perrier's totally inadequate one (359), giving the text of AB based on A^2. There is a detailed, predominantly philological, introduction; critical apparatus is at the foot of each page. The ed. is completed by extensive notes, a glossary, and an index of proper names.

Rev.: .1   Giuseppe di Stefano, *SF*, 49 (1973), 110.
     .2   Kurt Kloocke, *ZfSL*, 83 (1973), 285–86.
     .3   Jean-Charles Payen, *MAe*, 42 (1973), 279–81.
     .4   Ruggero M. Ruggieri, *SM*, 14 (1973), 1195–96.
     .5   Glyn S. Burgess, *ZrPh*, 90 (1974), 313–15.
     .6   Giuseppe E. Sansone, *Studi Mediolatini e Volgari*, 22 (1974), 311–14.
     .7   Guy Raynaud de Lage, *MA*, 81 (1975), 326–27.
     .8   Wolfgang G. van Emden, *FS*, 29 (1975), 61–62.
     .9   Jeanne Wathelet-Willem, *MR*, 25 (1975), 130–32.
     .10   Alfred Foulet, *RPh*, 29 (1975–76), 571–72.
     .11   Jean Rychner, *VoxRom*, 35 (1976), 243–46.
     .12   Mario Mancini, *CCM*, 22 (1979), 306–08.
     .13   R. van Deyck, *RBPH*, 60 (1982), 653–54.

2nd ed. Paris, 1978.
Rev.: .14   David G. Hoggan, *FS*, 33 (1979), 60–61.
     .15   Glyn S. Burgess, *ZfSL*, 90 (1980), 71–72.
     .16   L. Fontanella, *SF*, 24 (1980), 315.
     .17   M. Bossard, *VoxRom*, 41 (1982), 284–86.
     .18   Claude Régnier, *RLiR*, 46 (1982), 212–15.
     .19   Jean-Claude Thiolier, *CCM*, 26 (1983), 179–81.

366 *Le redazioni C e D del Charroi de Nîmes*, ed. Salvatore Luongo, Romanica Neapolitana, 28 (Naples: Liguori, 1992) 432 pp.
A sound ed. of each of the MSS, *C* and *D*, representing families not edited by McMillan (365). It is a traditional philological ed. in the Italian manner,

indicating resolved abbreviations, with an extensive introduction and notes concerned purely with linguistic, palaeographic, and editorial matters. The glossary and table of proper names render into Italian.

Rev.: .1 Günter Holtus, *ZrPh*, 110 (1994), 769–70.
.2 Philip E. Bennett, *MLR*, 90 (1995), 993–94.
.3 Stefan Dörr, *VoxRom*, 54 (1995), 281–82.
.4 G. M. Roccati, *SF*, 117 (1995), 516.
.5 François Suard, *CCM*, 38 (1995), 386.
.6 Larry S. Crist, *Olifant*, 20 (1995–96), 291–98.

(ii) Studies

367 Adler, Alfred, 'A propos du *Charroi de Nîmes*', in *Mélanges Frappier* (1970), pp. 9–15.
Considers *CN* as a product of folklore, and, like Jean-Charles Payen (393), considers the essential structural opposition of the poem to be that of the poverty and ingratitude of the king vs the wealth and devotion of the vassal.

368 Brault, Gerard J., 'The Road Not Taken in the *Charroi de Nîmes*', in *McMillan Essays* (1984), pp. 15–21.
A loosely ordered piece that asserts the primacy of the hero's dramatic gesture of refusing fiefs as the key to the interpretation of *CN*, in which the decision to invade 'Spain' is seen as the product of an heroic boast made out of an aristocratic sense of the need for personal display.

369 Burgess, Glyn S, 'The *Charroi de Nîmes*: Some Recent Scholarship', *Olifant*, 4 (1976–77), 97–99.
A simple research checklist of material on *CN* published between 1970 and 1975 with no critical comment.

370 Drzewicka, Anna, 'La scène du vilain dans le *Charroi de Nîmes* et le malentendu sociopsychologique', *Kwartalnik Neofilologiczny*, 23 (1976: *Mélanges H. Lewicka*), 95–103.
Sets the scene of Guillaume's conversation with the peasant in *CN* in a series of comic episodes in which misunderstanding based on the sociocultural ambiguity of key terms gives rise to humour.

371 ——, 'Guillaume narrateur. Le récit bref dans le *Charroi de Nîmes*', in *Narrations brèves. Mélanges de littérature ancienne offerts à Krystyna Kasprzyk*, ed. Piotr Salva and Ewa Dorota Zoliewska, Publications de l'Institut de Philologie Romane (Warsaw: University of Warsaw; Geneva: Droz, 1993), pp. 5–16.

A study of the seven occasions within *CN* on which Guillaume acts as narrator, invoking psychological motivation for the presence of the device of retrospective narrative by the hero, which is here considered unusual.

372 Fox, J. H., 'Two Borrowed Expressions in the *Charroi de Nîmes*', *MLR*, 50 (1955), 315–17.
Discusses the expressions *tenir le chief* and *torner le vermeil de l'escu*, which are held to be borrowed from Occitan.

373 Galmés de Fuentes, Álvaro, '*Le Charroi de Nîmes* et la tradition arabe', *CCM*, 22 (1979), 125–37.
An article in three parts, the first and third of which seek to demonstrate the Hispano-Arabic source of much OF epic; the second part considers *CN* particularly as based on a Perso-Arabic tale-type of warriors disguised as merchants. Finally the author proposes that Guillaume's epithet 'al cort nes', which he considers earlier than 'al corb nes', must derive from Islamic penal practices. Unfortunately the article, which is less than rigorous in dealing with relative chronology, makes unverifiable assumptions about modes of transmission.

374 Girault, Marcel, 'L'itinéraire du *Charroi de Nîmes*. Chemin de Saint-Gilles et Chemin de Regordane', in *Mélanges Louis* (1982), pp. 1105–16.
Supplementing the comments by Joseph Bédier on the *Via Tolosana* (56, pp. 353–64) with particular reference to *CN*, places mentioned in each of the MS versions of the episode are identified and commented on.

375 Gregory, Stewart, 'Pour un commentaire d'un passage obscur du *Charroi de Nîmes*', *Rom*, 109 (1988), 381–83.
The article argues that the essence of the misunderstanding between Guillaume and the peasant (*CN*, ed. McMillan [364], ll. 902–29) lies in the ambiguity of *estres* (l. 908).

376 Heinemann, Edward A., 'Aperçu sur quelques rythmes sémantiques dans les versions *A*, *B* et *D* du *Charroi de Nîmes*', in *Rencesvals 8* (1981), pp. 217–22.
A detailed analysis of a short passage of *CN* (*AB*, ll. 384–94; *D*, ll. 450–58) reveals how the use and placing of tool words, as well as that of semantically full words, creates rhythms within the epic *laisse* which contribute to the overall aesthetic message.

377 ——, '"Composite Laisse" and Echo as Organizing Principles: The Case of Laisse I of the *Charroi de Nîmes*', *RPh*, 37 (1983–84), 127–38.

As with the song as macro-structure, so with the composite *laisse* of many
chansons de geste as micro-structure, echo is seen as a unifying principle. The
long opening *laisse* of *CN* is taken as an example of the phenomenon.

378   —— 'Le jeu d'échos associés à l'hémistiche "non ferai, sire" dans le
Charroi de Nîmes', *Rom*, 112 (1991), 1–17.
The study of this formula and some that provide a context for it leads to the
conclusion that the poet used the formula as part of his strategy to undermine
characters and song. He is represented as addressing an ideal audience, which we
are coming close to replicating with computer analyses of the text.

379   ——, 'Line-Opening Tool Words in the *Charroi de Nîmes*', *Olifant*, 17
(1992–93), 51–64.
The main purpose of this short study was to run a test on text-analysis software.
The lack of significance of the work for epic poetics is not only admitted by the
author but is apparent in an uncharacteristic lack of rigour in some of the
discussion.

380   ——, 'Mapping Echoes with TACT in the Old French Epic the *Charroi
de Nîmes*', *Literary and Linguistic Computing*, 8 (1993), 191–202.
This prologomenic article sets out the way in which the author will use the
software TACT to trace complex verbal echoes with variations across *CN* of
which a brief study is included as a test case. The system will be the basis for all
his researches in this area.

381   ——, 'The Peculiar Echo in Laisse XXV of the *Charroi de Nîmes*',
Olifant, 18 (1993–94), 205–19.
A detailed analysis of verbal parallelisms in ll. 641–55 of *CN* leads to a not
always coherently connected series of other reflections on parallelism and echo in
the poem. The article comes to no specific conclusions but draws attention to the
complexity of poetic composition in *CN*.

382   ——, 'L'art métrique de la chanson de geste: un exemple
particulièrement réussi, le *Charroi de Nîmes*, et l'apport de
l'informatique', in *La Chanson de geste. Écritures, intertextualités,
translations*, ed. François Suard, Littérales, 14 (Paris: Université de Paris
X-Nanterre, 1994), pp. 9–39.
A detailed study of verbal echoes in *CN* designed to demonstrate the excellence
of the entire metrical structure of the poem, including that of the *laisses*. No ed. is
cited as the basis for the study; this gives the unwarranted impression that the text
we read is the product of a poet's intention. In fact the McMillan ed. (365) is

used, so that the text analysed is that of MS A^2. Pp. 28–39 present a series of appendices discussing the computerized analysis of the text.

383 ——, 'Existe-t-il une chanson de geste aussi brillante que le *Charroi de Nîmes?*', in *Rencesvals 13* (1995), pp. 461–69.
A close study of metrical and poetic patterns in *CN*, on the same lines as the author's other studies, but which goes further than them in supposing that existing MS versions represent original authorial intention.

384 Hunt, Tony, 'L'inspiration idéologique du *Charroi de Nîmes*', *RBPH*, 56 (1978), 580–606.
Starting from an analysis of the ideology of *CL*, seen as reflecting the political situation of the mid-1130s, Hunt argues that the same pro-monarchic ideology drives *CN*, which should be seen as belonging to the same period, pre- Second Crusade. However, as the analysis refers only to the first part of *CN*, which adopts and adapts *CL*, there is a certain circularity in the argument.

385 Kaehne, Michael, 'Trobadorlyrik (Bernart von Ventadorn) und Wilhelmsgeste (*Charroi de Nîmes*): zwei Versuche einer dichterischen Lösung des gleichen Problems', in *Festschrift für Rupprecht Rohr zum 60. Geburtstag, gewidmet von seinen Kollegen, Schülern und Mittarbeitern*, ed. Wolfgang Bergerfurth, Erwin Diekmann, and Otto Winkelmann (Heidelberg: Julius Gross Verlag, 1979), pp. 211–30.
A Marxist reading of the economic position of poor knights in the later twelfth century, based on the theories of Georges Duby and Erich Köhler. A general essay, touching only briefly on *CN*, to conclude that the escape from the economic and social constraints of the court projected in the conquest of 'pagan' lands was rarely achieved in reality.

386 Lot, Ferdinand, 'Le *Charroi de Nîmes*', *Rom*, 26 (1897), 564–69.
A brief but not altogether clear account of the genesis of *CN*, deriving the poem from an incident in the Continuation of the Chronicle of Fredegarius and an exploit attributed to Rustam in *Shahnameh*.

387 Luongo, Salvatore, 'Il *Charroi de Nîmes* nel ms. fr. 1448: un caso di restituzione memoriale?', *MedRom*, 16 (1991), 285–321.
A detailed analysis of *CN* in context with the treatment in *D* of *CL* and *PO* leads to the conclusion that all three are the product of one singer's memory rather than one scribe's attempts to deal with poor copies.

388 McMillan, Duncan, 'Le *Charroi de Nîmes*, déstemmatisation et délocalisation des manuscrits', *CN*, 56 (1996), 411–33.

A polemical and highly critical review of the methods and findings of Lene Schoesler (16 & 401) with regard to the MS stemma and the dialect origins of *CN*. The author believed that attempting to reduce textual criticism to a mathematical formula applied with the aid of a computer was perceptually flawed as a project.

389   Mancini, Mario, 'L'édifiant, le comique et l'idéologie dans le *Charroi de Nîmes*', in *Rencesvals 4* (1969), pp. 203–12.
A Marxist reading of the poem which is at pains to reduce any element of religious motivation and to stress, in standard terms of infrastructure, the importance of the feudal in the formulation of an epic ideology in *CN*, which recuperates the comic.

390   ——, *Società feudale e ideologia nel 'Charroi de Nîmes'*, Università di Padova, Pubblicazioni della Facoltà di Lettere e Filosofia, 49 (Firenze: Leo S. Olschki Editore, 1972) viii + 208 pp.
A Marxist reading of *CN*, deriving essentially from the theoretical works of Erich Köhler and Hans-Robert Jauß. The first four chapters consider developments in feudal and chivalric society, the loss of the sacral in depictions of Guillaume and Vivien, the threat to feudal and chivalric society from the bourgeoisie, and the place of the *bacheler* in the feudal and chivalric hierarchy. The last two chapters emphasize the role of the comic and of parody in the poem as means of challenging received ideology.

Rev.: .1   Paolo Merci, *SM*, 13 (1972), 1116–18.
       .2   Louis Chalon, *MA*, 79 (1973), 553–54.
       .3   Roberto Crespo, *MedRom*, 1 (1974), 423–31.
       .4   Friedrich Wolfzettel, *ZfSL*, 84 (1974), 369–72.
       .5   Giuseppe E. Sansone, *ZrPh*, 91 (1975), 435–39.
       .6   Alfred Foulet, *RPh*, 29 (1975–76), 571–72.
       .7   Duncan McMillan, *MAe*, 47 (1978), 119–22.

391   Mantou, Reine, 'Notes sur les vers 548–579 du *Charroi de Nîmes*', in *Mélanges Horrent* (1980), pp. 275–78.
This study of the 'Dame de St-Gilles' episode of *CN* concludes by proposing that *celier* (l. 558) should be interpreted as an underground passage leading some distance from the *vavasor*'s castle and its peaceful surroundings to a separate tower from which the Saracens' depredations are witnessed. This is a rather prosaic and positivist reading of the poem; for a symbolic interpretation of the same lines see Bennett (725).

392   Owen, D. D. R., 'Structural Artistry in the *Charroi de Nîmes*', *Forum for Modern Language Studies*, 14 (1978), 47–60.

Considers echo techniques and the exploitation of audience recall in the structuring of *CN*.

393   Payen, Jean-Charles, '*Le Charroi de Nîmes*, comédie épique?', in *Mélanges Frappier* (1970), pp. 891–902.
An interesting reading of *CN* as neo-Classical comedy, considering burlesque and realist elements, but most importantly treating the poem as a comedy of character in the confrontation of the powerless king, Louis, and the rich *bacheler*, Guillaume.

394   Perfetti, Lisa R., 'Dialogue of Laughter: Bakhtin's Theory of Carnival and the *Charroi de Nîmes*', *Olifant*, 17 (1992–93), 177–95.
The application of Bakhtin's notion of carnival to *CN* is used to explain various features of the poem's humour, and to draw the conclusion that comedy reinforces its feudal ideology, assuring its unity as a literary product.

395   Press, A. R., '"Sen a un ris gité" in the *Charroi de Nîmes*', *Forum for Modern Language Studies*, 12 (1976), 17–24.
Studies the way in which the author uses the formula to structure his poem.

396   ——, '"Sen a un ris gité" in the *Charroi de Nîmes*: a Further Note', *Forum for Modern Language Studies*, 14 (1978), 42–46.
Extends the original investigation (395) to a number of other formulæ in *CN*.

397   Régnier, Claude, 'À propos de l'édition du *Charroi de Nîmes*', *InfLitt*, 20 (1968) 32–33.
A brief presentation of OF epic as oral literature, with less than flattering comments about the taste and rigour of audiences, singers, and scribes alike, precedes a scathing critique of Perrier's ed. (359), which includes a list of readings and glosses requiring correction.

398   ——, 'Encore le *Charroi de Nîmes*', in *Mélanges de philologie romane offerts à Charles Camproux* (Montpellier: Centre d'Études Occitanes de l'Université Paul Valéry, 1978), pp. 1191–97.
Offers some textual and linguistic commentaries on *CN* with reference to the McMillan ed. (365).

399   Saccone, Antonio, 'Formule e produzione del testo nello *Charroi de Nîmes*', *Annali dell'Istituto Orientale di Napoli, Sezione Romanza*, 29 (1987) 195–207.
A structural linguistic approach to formula analysis, which relates classification of formulæ to the deep structures of the utterances. Groups of lines reflecting the

same deep structure are considered formulaic even when showing variations in surface structure.

400   Sansone, Giuseppe E., and Duncan McMillan, 'Precisazioni sul *Carriaggio di Nîmes*', *Rom*, 91 (1970), 419–23.
A reply by Sansone to McMillan's review of his translation (362.3), criticizing the lack of supporting evidence in the review; McMillan retorts that Sansone should have known better than to base his work on Perrier's very unreliable ed.

401   Schoesler, Lene, 'New Methods in Textual Criticism: The Case of the *Charroi de Nîmes*', in *Medieval Dialectology*, ed. Jacek Fisiak, Trends in Linguistics, Studies and Monographs, 79 (Berlin: Mouton de Gruyter, 1995), pp. 225–76.
Using as a sample the lines appearing in fragment *Af*, Schoesler attempts to establish a revised stemma for *CN* and to establish the dialect of the original composition by computerized analysis of readings. The methodology is not without flaws, and the application at times unsystematic. See McMillan's critique (388).

402   Suard, François, 'Les petites *laisses* dans le *Charroi de Nîmes*', in *Rencesvals 6* (1974), pp. 651–67.
Studies both the way in which *laisses* are grouped within the poem and the functions of different types of *laisses* according to broad categories of length. An interesting analysis of the contribution of the *laisse* to the poetics of the epic, partially undermined by a lack of rigour in separating *laisse* types.

403   Szabics, Imre, 'Procédés expressifs dans le *Charroi de Nîmes*', *Annales Universitatis Scientiarum Budapestiensis de Rolando Eötvös Nominatae, Sectio Philologica Moderna*, 4 (1973), 23–36.
A number of stylistic features, notably verbal tenses, as well as rhetorical features (repetition, antithesis) are studied for their expressivity, although some alternations studied (e.g. past historic ~ present) are non-operative in epic.

LA CHEVALERIE VIVIEN (LE COVENANT VIVIEN)

(i) *Editions and Translations*

404   *La Chevalerie Vivien, chanson de geste, I: Textes*, ed. A.-L. Terracher (Paris: Champion, 1909) viii + 287 pp.

A very brief introduction plus the texts of *C* and *D*, the first 125 lines of *E*, and the prose text. The promised vol. 2 (full introduction etc.) was never published (see 417, p. vi).

Rev.: .1   Anon., *Rom*, 38 (1909), 630.
.2   Willy Schulz, *ZfSL*, 35, 2 (1910), 61–70 & 169–84 (really a review-article with some very pertinent comments on the poem and its MSS).

405   *Chevalerie Vivien, facsimile prototypes of the Sancti Bertini Manuscript of the Bibl. mun. de Boulogne-sur-Mer*, ed. Raymond Weeks, The University of Missouri Studies: Literary and Linguistic Series, 1 (Columbia: University of Missouri, 1909) 12 pp. + 24 plates.
A publication in facsimile of the text of the MS on which Weeks had intended to base his own ed. of *ChV* until pre-empted by Terracher (404). The brief introduction is mostly concerned with idiosyncratic passages inserted by the Picard redactor of MS *C*, which increase the 'clearness and reasonableness of the poem'; it closes with a few corrections to Terracher's readings.

406   *La Chevalerie Vivien, édition critique des Mss S, D, C, avec introduction, notes et glossaire*, ed. Duncan McMillan, completed by Jean-Charles Herbin, Jean-Pierre Martin, and François Suard, Senefiance, 39–40 (Aix-en-Provence: Publications du CUER MA, Université de Provence, 1997) 748 pp.
A highly competent semi-synoptic ed. of *ChV*, presenting the texts of *D* and *S* facing each other in vol. 1, and that of *C* together with idiosyncratic passages of *D* and *E* in vol. 2. The ed. is completed by an extensive glossary, an index of proper names, critical notes, concordances of line numbers between different editions and between the various redactions, and a solid and extensive philological introduction.

407   Busby, Keith, 'Some Unpublished Epic Fragments', *Olifant*, 10 (autumn, 1982– winter, 1985), 3–23.
Includes the text of a fragment of *ChV* from the binding of Cambridge University Library MS Additional 2751 (7). A plain edition with gaps filled from Terracher's ed. (404).

(ii) *Studies*

408   Barbero, Alessandro, 'Il problema del coraggio e della paura nella cultura cavalleresca', *L'Immagine Riflessa*, 12 (1989: *Forme dell'identità cavalleresca: Actes du colloque de Bagni di Lucca 4–7 juin 1987*), 193–215.

This contribution looks at Vivien in *ChV*, concluding that the depiction of fear, or the absence of it, forms an essential part of the overall presentation of heroism. Vivien's lack of hesitation in *ChV* distorts the image given of him in *ChG*.

409   Bennett, Philip E., 'Le jeu de l'intertextualité dans la *Chevalerie Vivien*', in *Mélanges Suard* (1999), pp. 57–68.
A close study of passages offering allusions to other poems of CycG and to the *Chanson de Roland* leads to the conclusion that redactions SAB, and *D* become confused in trying to maintain references in the archetype of *ChV* to *ChG*, while *C* eliminates such allusions to bring *ChV* closer to *EnfV*. It would also appear from allusions in *ChV* that by the late thirteenth century Roland was a more familiar figure to epic audiences than was the Guillaume of *ChG*.

410   Labbé, Alain, '"A cel chastel ancïen et rebelle..." Une silhouette castrale dans la *Chevalerie Vivien*', in *Mélanges Suard* (1999), pp. 503–14.
The study emphasizes the poetic aspects of the tower in which Vivien and his troop take refuge in *ChV*, its links to a mythical, classical, and chthonic past; its role as an enclosed psychological space provides a refuge from the open menace of the battlefield, which is a sterile site from which the hero proceeds to his death.

411   McMillan, Duncan, '*La Chevalerie Vivien*, projet d'édition des textes en vers', in *Rencesvals 10* (1987), pp. 1253–55.
A very brief announcement, justifying and describing the programme of work for the edition of *ChV* (406).

412   Roussel, Claude, 'Tradition épique et innovation romanesque: remarques sur deux versions de la *Chevalerie Vivien*', *LR*, 37 (1983), 3–30.
Analyses the versions of MSS *D* and *C* in the Terracher ed. (404) to show that *D* remains firmly epic in outlook, but that *C* by its treatment of the narrator, of the chronology of narration, and of the fictive universe as autonomous and self-generating belongs to romance mode.

413   Schoesler, Lene, and Pieter van Reenen, 'Le désespoir de Tantale ou les multiples choix d'un éditeur de textes anciens: à propos de la *Chevalerie Vivien* éditée par †Duncan McMillan', *ZrPh*, 116 (2000), 1–19.
This article is really an extended apologia for the authors' project to mount an ed. of *CN* on the web. The article contains a number of criticisms of McMillan's approach to describing the dialects of the MSS of *ChV* (406) and of *CN* (365) from the point of view of scientific dialectologists. It also contains a positive assessment of much of the rest of McMillan's editorial work.

*414   Schulz, Willy, 'Das Handschriftverhältnis des Covenant Vivien' (doctoral thesis, University of Halle-Wittemberg, 1908).

Terracher describes the work as 'conscientious', but indicates a reliance on faulty manuscript transcriptions (415, p. v).

Rev.: .1 Raymond Weeks, *RR*, 1 (1910), 219–22 (a highly critical review reinforcing Terracher's view of the poor quality of the transcriptions on which the study is founded).

415 ——, 'Der *Covenant Vivien* und der gegenwärtige Stand der Forschung', *ZfSL*, 38 (1911), 196–230.
A discursive critical bibliography of work on Vivien, Guillaume, and Rainouart up to 1911, with, as a conclusion, a synoptic view of the evolution of their epic legends.

416 Suard, François, 'La *Chevalerie Vivien* comme prologue à *Aliscans*', in *Mélanges Subrenat* (2000), pp. 497–509.
The study of the way *ChV* adapts received material in generating itself as the necessary prologue to *Al* reveals how the lyricism of the older poems was replaced by dramatic narrative.

417 Terracher, A.-L., *La Tradition manuscrite de la 'Chevalerie Vivien'* (Paris: Champion, 1923) vi + 82 pp.
Originally printed as the author's *thèse complémentaire de doctorat* in 1914, this is a highly detailed and meticulous study of the MSS of *ChV*, including a sound assessment of the place of *S* in the tradition; it is still the reference study.

Rev.: .1 Mario Roques, *Rom*, 43 (1914), 479.

418 Weeks, Raymond, 'The Boulogne Manuscript of the *Chevalerie Vivien*', *MLR*, 5 (1910), 54–67.
The study of specific passages of *ChV* in the *C* redaction (especially ll. 129–242 and 950–1075) convinces the author that this redaction is the work of a single revisor working in Picardy. He makes no distinction between *C* and the other redactions in regard of the prime source for *ChV* being *ChG* (*G1*).

LE COURONNEMENT DE LOUIS

(i) *Editions and Translations*

419 *Le Couronnement de Louis, chanson de geste publiée d'après tous les manuscrits connus*, ed. Ernest Langlois, SATF (Paris: Firmin-Didot,1888) clxvii + 236 pp.

Still regarded by many as the definitive ed. of *CL* , this fully critical ed. has the disadvantage of presenting a reconstructed text with readings from different redactions. Editorial intervention is not always clearly signalled.

420 *Le Couronnement de Louis, chanson de geste du XIIe siècle*, ed. Ernest Langlois, CFMA, 22 (Paris: Champion, 1920) xvii + 169 pp.
An interventionist text based on AB, but showing a number of reconstructed readings. Contains a brief introduction, critical notes, and glossary. A simplified ed. for students and general readers derived from 419.

Rev.: .1 Anon, *Rom*, 46 (1920), 454.

Revised ed. 1984
Rev.: .2 Richard Trachsler, *VoxRom*, 53 (1994), 324.

421 *Le Couronnement de Louis*, trans. André Lanly, Traductions des CFMA, 6 (Paris: Champion, 1969) 149 pp.
A very usable line-by-line translation of 420, including a brief introduction and notes on technical vocabulary as well as on some of the poem's characters.

Rev.: .1 Charles Brucker, *RLiR*, 33 (1969), 436–37.

422 *Les Rédactions en vers du 'Couronnement de Louis'*, ed. Yvan G. Lepage, TLF, 261 (Geneva; Paris: Droz, 1978) 521 pp.
A semi-synoptic ed., giving critical texts of *C* and AB (based on *A^2*) facing each other, and the text of *D* in an appendix. The weakness of the ed. is that it corrects each critical text with the help of other redactions. Critical apparatus is at the foot of each page. There are also a glossary and an index of proper names. The ed. is distinctly more useful than Langlois's composite text.

Rev.: .1 André de Mandach, *Bibliothèque d'Humanisme et Renaissance*, 41 (1979), 659–61.
.2 Gilles Roques, *ZrPh*, 95 (1979), 664–65.
.3 Nelly Andrieux, *Rom*, 101 (1980) 402–09.
.4 H. H. Christmann, *RF*, 92 (1980), 392–93.
.5 L. Fontanella, *SF*, 24 (1980), 315.
.6 Omer Jodogne, *Scriptorium*, 34 (1980), 181.
.7 Jean Subrenat, *MA*, 86 (1980), 275–79 (review-article).
.8 David G. Hoggan, *FS*, 35(1981), 424.
.9 H. S. Kay, *RPh*, 34 (1980–81), 274–79.
.10 L. Löfstedt, *VoxRom*, 40 (1981), 327–29.
.11 Glyn S. Burgess, *ZfSL*, 92 (1982), 65–66.
.12 Andrea Fassò, *CCM*, 25 (1982), 67–69.
.13 Geneviève Hasenohr, *BEC*, 140 (1982), 259.
.14 P. Verhuyck, *RBPH*, 62 (1984), 643.

423 Hoepffner, Ernest, 'Un fragment du Couronnement de Louis', *Rom*, 61 (1935), 90–94.
A study and ed. of the thirteenth-century Picard Mulhouse fragment, equivalent to *C* ll. 2392–2410 & 2444–62 (cf. 434).

424 Paris, Gaston, 'Les vers 1–378 du Couronnement de Louis d'après le manuscrit de Boulogne', *Bulletin de la Société des Anciens Textes Français*, 22 (1896), 51–58.
Prints the text of the idiosyncratic passage of *CL* in MS *C*, omitted by mistake from the Langlois SATF ed. (419).

(ii) *Studies*

425 Adler, Adolf, 'The Dubious Nature of Guillaume's Loyalty in *Le Couronnement de Louis*', *Symposium*, 2 (1948), 179–91.
The article presupposes that *CL* was composed during the reign of Louis VI, and depends on the Chartres School for its Neoplatonic view of *imperium*. Guillaume remains essentially loyal, despite the independence of his actions on a feudal level, because he fights for the Empire and for a Gregorian view of the Church.

426 Batany, Jean, 'Home and Rome, a Device in Epic and Romance: *Le Couronnement de Louis* and *Ille et Galeron*', *YFS*, 51 (1975), 42–60.
Aimed ultimately at explaining the structures and generic affiliations of *Ille et Galeron*, the article subjects it to a comparative study with *CL* to elucidate a series of binary oppositions, based on the concepts of Claude Lévi-Strauss, which dominate both works. There is also an attempt, using a combination of Lévi-Strauss's theories and those of Georges Dumézil, to distinguish *CL* as epic from *Ille et Galeron* as romance. Both are seen as products of the secular spirit in opposition to the *Vie de Saint Alexis*, revealing the same structures within a spiritual-clerical ideology.

427 ——, 'Propagande carolingienne et mythe carolingien: le programme de Louis le Pieux chez Ermold le Noir et dans *Le Couronnement de Louis*', in *Mélanges Louis* (1982), pp. 313–40.
A detailed textual analysis of the passages in Ermoldus Nigellus, *In honorem Hludowici Christianissimi Cæsaris Augusti* [...] *elegiacum carmen*, and *CL* dealing with the ideology of imperial kingship in the context of the coronation of Louis reveals a shift in the mythology of the ruler from transcendent ritualization of an ideal to a personal and social psychodrama.

428 Beckmann, Gustav Adolf, 'Die erste Branche des *Couronnement Louis* und die drei Typen epischer "Historizität"', *GRM*, 55, ns, 24 (1974), 385–408.

The first part of the article is a long presentation of the historical personalities involved with Louis the Pious in the ninth century, and the perpetuation of the memory of the events with which they were involved in the tenth. The second part offers detailed textual criticism of passages in the MSS of *CL* giving the names of Hernaut or Arneïs d'Orliens, concluding that whichever version of the name scholars believe to be original, it must reflect the person of Arnoldus, the first tutor of Louis in Aquitain. Arguing that neither the texts of the ninth and tenth centuries nor the historical facts of the twelfth can account for the narrative of *CL* , the article proposes that a contemporary ideology is cloaked in a historical garb, eked out by oral traditions in a poem probably composed after 1152.

429   Bennett, Philip E., 'Poetic Structures in the *Couronnement de Louis*', in *Littera et Sensus: Essays on Form and Meaning in Medieval French Literature Presented to John Fox*, ed. D. A. Trotter (Exeter: University of Exeter, 1989), pp. 17–30.
A study of the cyclic system of repetitions used to structure the poem and present its themes shows that it contains sufficient distortions and variations to call in question the assertions about the providential political system described by the author in his prologue.

430   ——, 'Des jongleurs et des rois: réflexions sur le "prologue" du *Couronnement de Louis*', in *Il Ciclo di Guglielmo d'Orange* (1997), pp. 296–312.
Analyses the role of the narrator and the rhetoric of the text in the various MS versions of the opening of *CL*, corresponding to AB *laisses* 1–5 of the Lepage ed. (422), to suggest a clerical origin for the debate on kingship enshrined in the poem.

431   Blumenfeld-Kosinski, R., 'Praying and Reading in the *Couronnement de Louis*', *FS*, 40 (1986), 385–92.
The study of the two *prières du plus grand péril* uttered by Guillaume in the Corsolt episode of *CL* leads Blumenfeld-Kosinski to conclude that the typological relationship between the contents of the two prayers suggests a way of reading the whole poem as a model of salvation history. In this the author seeks to support Stephen Nichols's interpretation of *CL* (459). It also has implications for the learning, and probable clerical status, of the author of *CL* .

432   Brault, Gerard J., 'Narrative Techniques in the *Couronnement de Louis*', in *Mittelalterstudien* (1984), pp. 68–74.
A catalogue of narrative devices used in *CL*, but with emphasis on a series of antithetical structures and on the motif (literal and metaphoric) of crowning.

433 Combarieu du Grès, Micheline de, 'La violence dans *Le Couronnement de Louis*', in *Mélanges Lods* (1978), pp. 126–52.
A study of the uses to which violence is put in the portrayal of Guillaume and other warriors in *CL*, including the chivalric duty of humbly protecting the poor, concludes by suggesting that the pusillanimity of Louis is exaggerated by the poet as a means of justifying as well as of glorifying the hero.

434 Comeau, Ivan, 'À propos de deux fragments du *Couronnement de Louis*', *Rom*, 88 (1967), 537–40.
Demonstrates that the Mulhouse fragment of *CL* (423) comes from the same MS as the Paris fragment, BNF, n. a. fr. 5094.

435 Crespo, Roberto, 'Alla ricerca di un significato: l'"arche" nel *Couronnement de Louis*', *MedRom*, 1 (1974), 337–50.
A detailed critique of the interpretations given to arche by Yves Lefèvre (453), concluding that the use of *arche* to refer to the reliquary tomb of St Peter is an indication of the clerical status of the author of *CL*. An appendix indicates in support of this view the use of *arche* in the Châteauroux text of the *Chanson de Roland* to mean 'martyr's tomb'.

*436 Decker, Eugene M., 'The Historicity and Philology of the *Couronnement de Louis*' (PhD thesis, University of Texas, Austin, 1968), 140 pp. *DAI*, 29 (1968–69), 594.

437 Dufournet, J., 'Note sur *Le Couronnement de Louis*, à propos d'un ouvrage de M. Frappier', *RLR*, 77 (1966), 103–18.
The article provides an eulogistic review of Frappier, *Les Chansons de geste* (79), based purely on the chapter devoted to *CL* . It embroiders some complementary remarks around Frappier's analyses, which the author extends, but never challenges. It also contains some supplementary bibliographical information.

438 Duggan, Joseph J., 'Formulas in the *Couronnement de Louis*', *Rom*, 87 (1966), 315–44.
A computer-assisted analysis of repeated expressions in *CL*, based on the Parry-Lord view of the formula, with inevitable circularity of argument where proper names and speech formulae are involved. The study is also unreliable because based on the Langlois CFMA composite ed. of *CL* (420).

439 Frappier, Jean, 'Remarques sur le prologue du *Couronnement de Louis* (v. 1–11)', in *Studies in Medieval Literature in Honor of Professor Albert Croll Baugh*, ed. MacEdward Leach (Philadelphia: University of Pennsylvania Press, 1961), pp. 159–67.

This study of the textual problems of the prologue to *CL* was reproduced *in extenso* in *Les Chansons de geste du cycle de Guillaume d'Orange* (79), II, pp. 59–64. The conclusion given here is that the poet was a professional writer composing in the oral style for recitation.

440   ——, 'Notes sur la composition du *Couronnement de Louis*', *MA*, 69 (1963), 281–87.
A discursively literary essay evoking the thematic unity, both moral and political, of *CL*, from which is deduced its poetic unity. *CL* is none the less described as a *chanson à tiroirs* whose narrative syntax is determinedly paratactic.

441   ——, 'Les thèmes politiques dans *Le Couronnement de Louis*', in *Mélanges Delbouille II* (1964), pp. 195–206.
Despite correctly situating the theoretical concerns of *CL* in the political context of the twelfth century, and stressing the importance of the conflicts between France and the Empire, the article is over-inclined to read notions of a unified, and unitary, centralized French State back into the poem, and into twelfth-century consciousness, from the post-Revolution Republic.

442   Györy, Jean, 'Les prières de *Guillaume d'Orange* dans le *Couronnement de Louis*', in *Mélanges Lejeune* (1969), pp. 769–77.
An excellent account of the structuring and poetic role of the prayers, interpreted by reference to Georges Poulet, *L'Espace proustien* (Paris: Gallimard, 1963), with its concept of temporal succession translated into visual panorama, although the analysis of the psychological state of the hero pronouncing the prayers is highly subjective and based on a selective choice of lines from the prayers.

443   Heinemann, Edward A., 'Sur l'art de la laisse dans le *Couronnement de Louis*', in *Rencesvals 7* (1978), pp. 383–91.
Studies the mechanisms by which the *laisse* embodies narrative transitions between episodes, arguing for the importance of the boundaries between *laisses* for understanding their construction.

444   ——, 'Silence in the Interstices: Epic Cliché and the Editorial Poetics of the *Chanson de geste* (*Couronnement de Louis*, 736–739)', *L'Esprit Créateur*, 27 (1987), 24–33.
The article is ostensibly a criticism of Langlois's editorial interventions in his ed. of *CL* (419 / 420). The criticism is based on the author's view, to be developed in much of his subsequent work, of the importance of echoes and 'semantic thrust' (also termed 'semantic weight') structured by the pauses at caesura and line-end in epic poetry. However, so many of the concepts and analyses deployed are subjective and vague that they have little practical value.

445   Hoggan, David G., 'L'unité artistique du *Couronnement de Louis*', *Rom*, 89 (1968), 313–39.
Questions the authenticity of ll. 163 & 2683 of Langlois's ed. of *CL* (419 / 420) as part of an argument framed to resolve problems of internal chronology in the poem.

446   ——, 'La version abrégée du *Couronnement de Louis* a-t-elle connu une grande diffusion?', in *McMillan Essays* (1984), pp. 55–66.
Argues from comparisons with the death of Charlemagne episode in other poems of CycG that the version of *CL* found in MS *D* is not an abridgement specially prepared for that MS, but depends on a lost version of similar length and content which also inspired the other versions.

*447   Holtschneider, Friedrich, 'Die dritte Branche des *Couronnement de Louis*' (doctoral dissertation, University of Rostock, 1913).

*448   Hoyer, Richard, 'Über die angeblichen Interpolationen im *Coronement Looïs*', in *Festschrift für Begrüssung der 47. Versammlung deutscher Philologen* (Halle, 1903), pp. 23–48.

449   Jeanroy, Alfred, 'Études sur le cycle de Guillaume au court nez: le *Couronnement de Louis*', *Rom*, 25 (1896), 353–80.
The analysis is based on the now discredited premise that each branch of *CL* derives directly from historical events of the Carolingian period.

450   Kent, Carol A., 'Fidelity and Treachery: Thematic and Dramatic Structuring of the *Laisses* in an Episode of the *Couronnement de Louis* (*laisses* 43–54)', *Olifant*, 19 (1994–95), 223–38.
A close reading of an episode of *CL*, heavily reliant on Heinemann's work on metrical artistry. The analysis is interesting, but the conclusion, that the view of Jean Rychner, *La Chanson de geste: essai sur l'art épique des jongleurs* (Geneva: Droz, 1955), on the precellence of the *laisse* structure of the *Chanson de Roland* requires revision, was far from new.

451   Langlois, Ernest, 'À propos du *Coronement Looïs*', *Rom*, 46 (1920), 330–75.
Reviews theories of the composition of *CL*, studying the nature of textual transmission in the Middle Ages, and expressing scepticism about the value of variants in late witnesses for reconstructing early poems. His conclusion stresses the importance of *mouvance* in medieval texts, suggesting that attempts to establish authentic versions are vain.

452   Larmat, Jean, 'L'orphelin, la veuve et le pauvre dans le *Couronnement de Louis*', in *Rencesvals 7* (1978), pp. 191–204.

A study of the precepts of Charlemagne in *CL* which begs questions about the social status of the widows and poor referred to by reading interpretations in from other sources, while not looking closely enough at the semantic or syntactic context of the terms in the poem. The case, that the author of *CL* is concerned only with members of the chivalric and feudal classes, is not proven.

453   Lefèvre, Yves, 'L'*Arche* de Saint-Pierre de Rome dans le *Couronnement de Louis*', *Rom*, 90 (1969), 111–21.
Sees in the double use of *arche* to mean the shrine of St Peter and the papal treasury a further proof of the clerical education of the author of *CL*.

454   Legros, Huguette, 'La réalité sociale dans le *Couronnement de Louis*', in *McMillan Essays* (1984), pp. 67–73.
A brief appeal, using Suger's *Vita Ludovici Grossi Regis* as a control text, for a sociological approach to *CL*, rather than a study of the politico-social themes of the poem.

*455   Levy, Raphael, *Glossaire du 'Couronnement de Louis'* (Turin: Erasmo, 1932).

*456   Linnenkohl, P., 'Branche I und II des *Couronnement de Louis*: gegenwartiger Stand der Forschung' (doctoral dissertation, University of Rostock, 1912).

457   Maddox, Donald L., and Sara Sturm-Maddox, 'Le chevalier à l'oraison: Guillaume dans le *Couronnement de Louis*', in *Rencesvals 12* (1993), pp. 609–15.
The thematic unity of *CL* is seen as being incorporated in the two *prières du plus grand péril* offered up by Guillaume, in which the Augustinian, teleological view of history is justified by the hero's victory. In this way the second, Corsolt, episode offers a demonstration of the truth propounded in the prologue, that Charlemagne's empire is divinely ordained. The eschatological implications of this victory justify the hero's activities in the other episodes of *CL*.

458   Micha, Alexandre, 'Le *Couronnement de Louis*, état présent des questions', *InfLitt*, 17 (1965), 185–92.
A very sound and perspicacious account of the problems posed by *CL* and of the critical responses to them. Overtaken by the publication of vol. 2 of Frappier, *Les Chansons de geste* (79).

459   Nichols, Stephen G. Jr, 'Sign as (Hi)story in the *Couronnement de Louis*', *RR*, 71 (1980), 1–9.
Guillaume's self-naming as 'Guillaume al Cort Nes' is seen as the key to reading *CL* through a systematic application of biblical exegesis to the text of the poem.

460 Niemeyer, Karina H., '*Le Couronnement de Louis* et le mythe de Guillaume', in *Rencesvals 6* (1973), pp. 639–50.
A general defence of the artistic integrity of *CL*, with reference to oral-traditional approaches and to the mixture of comic and serious to be found in many medieval epics.

461 Paris, Gaston, 'Sur un vers du *Coronement Loois*', *Rom*, 1 (1872), 177–89.
Paris starts from l. 2638 of the Jonckbloet ed. (28) to elaborate his ideas on the development of the heroic personality of Guillaume from a multiplicity of local heroes, and of CycG from two separate legends, one northern one southern. He considers the closing lines of *CL* to be a résumé of a poem, or even of a cycle of poems, dealing with the dynastic wars of the tenth century.

462 Pickens, Rupert T., 'Art épique et verticalisation. Problèmes narratifs dans le *Couronnement de Louis*', *VoxRom*, 45 (1986), 116–49.
The first part of the article offers a theoretical analysis of the distinctions between epics and other OF genres in the way they differentiate diegesis (historically oriented narrative and authorial commentary) from mimesis (presentation of direct discourse) and the implications of this for the 'horizontality' (historico-narrative progression) and 'verticality' (lyrical and ahistorical commentary) of the *chansons de geste*. The second part considers how manipulations of chronological narration bring past, present, and future together in *CL*, 'verticalizing' the narrative of Branches 1 and 2 of the poem. Finding the narrative of Branches 3–5 much less subject to verticalization, the author concludes that *CL* is a compilation, the first two parts of which are much more archaic than the remainder, although the alternative explanation proposed, that the first two branches offer a myth of which the remainder of the poem is an historical exposition, is more convincing.

463 ——, 'Comedy, History and Jongleur Art in the *Couronnement de Louis*', *Olifant*, 11 (1986), 205–18.
The separation of *CL* into two autonomous parts is not convincing, but the analysis of the poem's mechanisms, including *reprise bifurquée* and parallelism, allowing ironic readings is very sound and illuminating. As in 462 Pickens regards Branches 1 and 2 as being based on a mythographic paradigm, while the rest of the poem relies on a politico-historical one.

464 Roques, Mario, 'L'élément historique dans *Fierabras* et dans la branche II du *Coronement Looïs*', *Rom*, 30 (1901), 161–83.
The bulk of the article deals with *Fierabras*; the source of the Corsolt episode in the siege of Rome in AD 846 is dealt with on pp. 175–79. A supplement by

Gaston Paris (pp. 181–83) suggests reminiscences of a series of Muslim raids on Italy in the ninth and tenth centuries.

465   Roussel, Henri, "'L'os de la gole": réflexions sur le coup de poing meurtrier de Guillaume (*Couronnement de Louis*, vers 129–133)', in *Mélanges Louis* (1982), pp. 591–606.
A long and complex article tending to prove that the 'os de la gole' was not the cervical vertebræ but the trachea. Unfortunately a poor reading of a key text (*ChG*, l.1839), which specifically refers to the flow of marrow from the broken bone, undermines the whole argument.

466   Rychner, Jean, 'Observations sur la versification du *Couronnement de Louis*', *La Technique littéraire* (1959), pp. 161–82.
The article argues for the construction of the whole text of *CL* from formulaic elements which operate at the levels of the hemistich and the line of verse.

467   ——, 'Observations sur le *Couronnement de Louis* du MS BN fr. 1448', in *Mélanges Delbouille II* (1964), pp. 635–52.
A detailed study of the *D* version of *CL* with the 'vulgate' represented by the Langlois ed. (419) leads to the conclusion that the former is highly corrupt as a result of oral transmission. The real point of the article is to repeat the author's thesis that MS versions of medieval poems (whether epics or *fabliaux*) are accidental records of a cultural phenomenon which remains essentially oral in creation and transmission.

*468   Salzmann, H., *Die innere Einheit in 'Li Coronemenz Looïs'*, Progr. des Realprogymnasium Pillau (Königsberg in Preussen, 1897).

Rev.:   .1   Anon., *Rom*, 27 (1897), 626.

469   Scheludko, D., 'Neues über das *Couronnement de Louis*', *ZfSL*, 55 (1932), 425–74.
A wide-reaching article, which considers much of the material of *CL* to be of learned origin, but which also takes into account the contribution of folktale and oral epic. The article closes with an important statement of principle on approaching OF epic in all its complexity as the product of a twelfth-century culture at home with secular Classical and medieval Latin, as well as with biblical, hagiographic, and popular sources, all of which it exploited in free combination.

470   Schenck, David P., *'Li Coronement Looïs*: A Mythic Approach to Unity', *RR*, 69 (1978), 159–71.
The interesting attempt to demonstrate the role of the mythic, in terms of structural social-anthropological analysis, in the composition of *CL* is thwarted

by the question of the elements subtending the analysis being begged, and by a lack of rigour in analysing the semantic content of lexical items indicated as representing motifs.

471   Singerman, Jerome E., '"Si com c'est veir": The Polemical Approach to Prayer in *Le Couronnement de Louis*', *Rom*, 106 (1985), 289–302.
Shows convincingly that the *credo épique* as represented in *CL* has evolved considerably from the homeopathic charm on which it is based, but the conclusion that the prayer represents a kind of blackmail against the deity is exaggerated.

472   Suchier, Hermann, 'Die gekurzte Fassung von Ludwigskrönung (B.N.fr. 1488)', in *Bekanntmachung der Ergebnisse der Akademischen Preisbewerbung vom Jahre 1900 und der neuen für das Jahr 1901 gestellten Preisaufgeben* (Halle: Buchdruckerei des Waizenhauses, 1901), pp. 1–5.
Offers corrections to Langlois's reading of *D* from his SATF ed. (419), opines that *D* is a reconstruction from memory by a *jongleur*, and collates *D* with Langlois's published version.

473   Trotin, Jean, 'La transition dans le *Couronnement de Louis*', *Perspectives Médiévales*, 2 (1976), 39–45.
Studies the role of references to hunting and marriage in *CL* as motifs for articulating the structure of the poem and its five episodes.

474   van Waard, R., 'Le *Couronnement de Louis* et le principe de l'hérédité de la couronne', *Neophil*, 30 (1946), 52–58.
The article argues that the history of the Capetians and their need to restore to the crown of France the hereditary principle lost in AD 987 provides the only necessary explanation of the composition of *CL* in the mid-1130s. The author judiciously rejects all suggestions that *CL* and *CN*, which offers its own embroidered synopsis of *CL*, derive from a long tradition of now lost versions.

475   Vàrvaro, Alberto, 'Il *Couronnement de Louis* e la prospettiva epica', *Boletín*, 31 (1965–66), 33–44.
Uses *CL* as a model to argue that the politico-cultural nexus of the epic reflecting the cultural moment of its creation is a more important area of study than those of origins or modes of composition, whether viewed from a neo-traditionalist, historicist or individualist perspective.

476   Warren, F. M., 'The Giant Corsolt', *MPh*, 28 (1930–31), 467–68.
Suggests that the name of Corsolt in *CL* was suggested by Corseul, Côtes-du-Nord (now Côtes d'Armor), and its Iron-Age ruins.

477   Willems, Léonard, *L'Élément historique dans le 'Coronement Looïs',
       contribution à l'histoire poétique de Louis le Débonnaire*, Université de
       Gand. Recueil de Travaux de la Faculté de Philosophie et Lettres, 19
       (Ghent: Librairie Engelcke, 1896) viii + 89 pp.
       The study is in two parts: Part I attempts, inappropriately, to link the plot of *CL*
       with events in Carolingian history (although historians now put more emphasis
       than has been the case through most of the twentieth century on the difficulties of
       Louis I in establishing himself on the throne); Part II considers the evolution of
       the legend, placing too much store by the version in *CN* as a witness to an earlier
       lost version of *CL*.

       Rev.: .1   Alfred Jeanroy, *Rom*, 25 (1896), 465–72.
              .2   Ernest Langlois, *Rom*, 28 (1899), 465.

478   Zenker, R., 'Die historischen Grundlagen der zweiten Branche des
       Couronnement de Louis', in *Festgabe Gröber* (Halle: Max Niemeyer,
       1899), pp. 171–232.
       The article argues that the second, 'Corsolt', branch of *CL* blends reminiscences
       of Norman conquests in southern Italy in the eleventh century with those of
       Emperor Louis II's battles against Muslims in the ninth century. The conclusion
       that this makes the branch the most recent of the poem has no force.

       Rev.: .1   Alfred Jeanroy, *Revue Critique* (juin, 1900), 492.
              .2   Gaston Paris, *Rom*, 29 (1900), 119–21.

LES ENFANCES GUILLAUME

(i) *Editions and Translations*

479   *Die Chanson 'Enfances Guillaume'*, I, ed. Hermann Hingst (Greifswald:
       Adler, 1918); II, ed. August Becker (Greifswald: Adler, 1913).
       The ed., produced from a pair of doctoral theses, is defective in many respects,
       not least because of the uneven quality of the candidates and the varying
       conditions in which their work was produced. It is totally superseded by the
       SATF ed. of Patrice Henry (481).

480   *Les Enfances Guillaume, chanson de geste du XIIIe siècle*, ed. J.-L.
       Perrier, Publications of the Institute of French Studies (New York:
       Columbia University, 1933) ix + 151 pp.
       A superficial introduction followed by an ed. of *D* (called C^l by Perrier), variants,
       index of proper names, and brief glossary. Superseded by the SATF ed. (481).

       Rev.: .1   Ernest Hoepffner, *RLR*, 67 (1933–36), 504–08.
              .2   Grace Frank, *MLN*, 49 (1934), 555.

.3   Patrice Henry, *Rom*, 60 (1934), 117–19.

.4   K. Sneyders de Vogel, *Neophil*, 21 (1935), 47.

481   *Les Enfances Guillaume, chanson de geste du XIIIe siècle*, ed. Patrice Henry, SATF (Paris: SATF, 1935) xliii + 167 pp.

An ed. of *D* with brief introduction giving a summary of the text, establishing the stemma of MSS, and considering the language and date of the poem; there are also an index of proper names and a glossary. This is still the standard edition of the poem.

Rev.: .1   J. Straka, *Časopis pro Moderní Filologii*, 22 (1936), 384.

*482   Akainyah, Clara, 'Edition critique des *Enfances Guillaume* dans la rédaction AB' (thesis for the Doctorat de l'Université de Paris, 1969).

483   McMillan, Duncan, 'A Contribution to the Study of the *Enfances Guillaume* from the Versions Contained in the Manuscripts Royal 20 D XI (London, British Museum) and fr. 24 369 (Paris, Bibliothèque Nationale)' (PhD thesis, University of London, 1938) 281 + 119 pp.

2 vols bound as one. The first part contains a description of the MSS and a study of the MS families, studies of versification and language of *B¹* and *B²*, an establishment of the text, tables of assonances and concordance of assonances with the other redactions, and a bibliography. The second part contains an ed. of *EnfG* based on *B¹*, with rejected readings and variants of *B²* at the foot of each page, an index of proper names, and a glossary. A detailed and informative study, still the only ed. of the B family of *EnfG*.

(ii) *Studies*

484   Grisward, Joël H., 'Les jeux d'Orange et d'Orable: magie sarrasine et / ou folklore roman?', *Rom*, 111 (1990), 57–74.

A detailed study of the enchantments to which Orable subjects Tiebaut in *EnfG*, and of possible sources in a variety of areas, leads to the conclusion that what is represented is the charivari aimed at marriages provoking disapprobation.

485   Guidot, Bernard, 'Le thème du voyage dans les *Enfances Guillaume*', in *Voyage, quête, pèlerinage dans la littérature et la civilisation médiévales*, Senefiance, 2 (Aix-en-Provence: Publications du CUER MA, Université de Provence, 1976), pp. 363–80.

The article demonstrates the way in which journeys structure the narrative of *EnfG*, despite the very bald and formulaic way they are presented by the poet.

486   ——, 'Fantaisie et romanesque dans les *Enfances Guillaume*', in *Rencesvals 8* (1981), pp. 201–09.

A study of the ways in which romance modes affect the writing of *EnfG*, concluding that the poet uses comedy and humour to undermine romance rather than epic features of his poem.

487   Heinemann, Edward A., 'Rythmes sémantiques de la chanson de geste, 2: rythmes internes de l'hémistiche dans les vers où figure un nom de ville dans les *Enfances Guillaume'*, *Rom*, 110 (1989), 40–71.
        One of a long series of studies of the relationship between the semantic content and metrical structures of epic verse, this one comes to no firm conclusions but suggests some new ways of approaching the formula, literal repetition, and the privileging of the hero's name in *chansons de geste*.

488   Labbé, Alain, 'Les "jeux d'Orange": matériau onirique et illusion magique dans les *Enfances Guillaume'*, in *Magie et illusion* (1999), pp. 269–91.
        A highly perspicacious reading of *EnfG*, demonstrating that the *jeux d'Orange* episode is structurally integral to the whole message of the poem, which, in its sinister use of subconscious and mythographic imagery, is a much darker and more disturbing poem than traditional scholarship has allowed.

LES ENFANCES RENIER

(i) *Editions and Translations*

489   *Enfances Renier, canzone di gesta inedita del sec. XIII*, ed. Carla Cremonesi (Milan: Istituto Editoriale Cisalpino, 1957) 703 pp.
        The introduction offers an extensive palaeographic description of the MS, an inadequate account of the language of the text, and a section on date and author which is largely unfounded speculation. The ed. has a number of unfortunate errors. Critical notes are very few, the glossary into Italian is selective, but the table of proper names seeks to include every line reference to an occurrence of a name.

        Rev.: .1   M. Boni, *SF*, 5 (1958), 263–65.
               .2   Félix Lecoy, *Rom*, 80 (1959), 533–40.
               .3   Kurt Baldinger, *ZrPh*, 81 (1965), 190–94.

489a   Matsamura, T., 'Sur le texte des *Enfances Renier'*, *The Proceedings of the Department of Foreign Languages and Literatures*, College of Arts and Sciences, University of Tokyo, 38 (1990), 37-52.
        Offers corrections to Cremonesi's ed. See also the brief summary of the article by Gilles Roques, *RLiR*, 55 (1991), 604-05.

(ii) *Studies*

490 Colliot, Régine, 'Le personnage de Renier dans les *Enfances Renier*: romanesque et conformisme', in *Enfances 'romanesques' II, PRIS-MA,* 12 (1996), pp. 117–32,
A narrative account of the poem bringing out the motifs exploited by the author.

*491 Cremonesi, Carla, 'Le *Enfances Renier* e la Sicilia', *Bolletino del Centro di Studi Filologici e Linguistici Siciliani,* 9 (1965), 9–17.
See *BBSR,* 19 p. 128.

492 Donaire Fernández, María Luisa, '*Enfances Renier*: l'entrelacement, une technique de roman', in *Rencesvals 9* (1984), pp. 489–508.
The first half of the article is devoted to a résumé of scholarship on interlace as a compositional technique and its application to various late epics and romances. The second half looks at how the technique is applied to *EnfR* and at the linguistic markers used to articulate it.

LES ENFANCES VIVIEN

(i) *Editions and Translations*

493 '*Les Enfances Vivien*', *chanson de geste*, ed. Carl Wahlund and Hugo von Feilitzen (Upsala; Paris: s. n., 1895), viii + lii + 304 pp. Repr. Geneva: Slatkine, 1970.
A synoptic, diplomatic edition of four MSS representing different redactions and the prose text, with variants from related MSS at the foot of each page. The editorial work and the introduction by Alfred Nordfelt are of sufficient quality to make this still the standard ed. of *EnfV.*

494 *Die Enfances Vivien,* ed. H. Zorn (Leipzig: R. Noske, 1908).
A doctoral dissertation for Jena offering a critical edition, but still less useful than Wahlund and von Feilitzen (493).

Rev.:   .1   Willy Schulz, *ZfSL,* 34 (1908), 168–78.

495 *A Fragment of 'Les Enfances Vivien', National Library of Wales MS 5043E,* ed. Joseph J. Duggan, University of California Publications in Modern Philology, 116 (Berkeley: University of California Press, 1985) ix + 44 pp.
A basically sound ed. of the fragment, though not without minor errors. The exact place attributed to the fragment in the MS tradition can be questioned.

Rev.:   .1   Philip E. Bennett, *Olifant,* 11 (1986), 241–43.

.2   Gilles Roques, *RLiR*, 50 (1986), 283.
.3   Kurt Baldinger, *ZrPh*, 103 (1987), 623.
.4   Jan Nelson, *Speculum*, 62 (1987), 499–500.
.5   Wolfgang G. van Emden, *MAe*, 56 (1987), 331–32.
.6   Costanzo di Girolamo, *MedRom*, 13 (1988), 298–300.
.7   Jean Subrenat, *MA*, 94 (1988), 130–31.
.8   Madeleine Tyssens, *CCM*, 32 (1989), 364–67.
.9   Brigitte Cazelles, *RPh*, 44 (1990-91), 479-81.

496   *Les Enfances Vivien*, ed. Magali Rouquier, TLF, 478 (Geneva: Droz, 1997) xliii + 226 pp.
An ed. of A^2, with variants of other AB redaction MSS. The introduction deals mostly with the description of the MSS and provides a résumé of the narrative. The text contains a number of errors of transcription and / or interpretation.

Rev.: .1   Gilles Roques, *RLiR*, 61 (1997), 581–82.
.2   F. Duval, *Scriptorium*, 52 (1998), 39*.
.3   Alice Colby-Hall, *Speculum*, 74 (1999), 486.
.4   Philip E. Bennett, *FS*, 54 (2000), 71–72.

(ii) *Studies*

497   Cloetta, Wilhelm, *Die 'Enfances Vivien': ihre Überlieferung, ihre cyklische Stellung*, Romanische Studien, 4 (Berlin: E. Ebering, 1898) viii + 96 pp.
A sound assessment of the MS tradition and relationships of *EnfV*; only the ascription of an early date (1165–70) for an original version behind the extant redactions is dubious.

Rev.: .1   Raymond Weeks, *Rom*, 28 (1899), 450–54.

498   Guidot, Bernard, 'Les *enfances* de Vivien ont-elles un caractère romanesque?', in *Enfances 'romanesques' II*, *PRIS-MA*, 12 (1996), pp. 167–86.
The author explores the contribution of romance mode to the atmosphere and narrative structure of *EnfV*, but arbitrarily chooses B^1 from the Wahlund-von Feilitzen ed. (493) as the reference version for the study. Guidot consequently concludes a bit hastily that Vivien acquires a human dimension in this poem.

499   Nordfelt, Alfred, 'Classification des manuscrits des *Enfances Vivien*', in *Recueil de mémoires philologiques présenté à M. Gaston Paris par ses élèves suédois le 9 août 1889 à l'occasion de son cinquantième anniversaire* (Stockholm: L'Imprimerie Centrale, 1889), pp. 63–101.
A careful and still generally valid assessment of the MS tradition of *EnfV*, although some conclusions drawn about the stemma from considerations of the use of the *vers orphelin* are no longer acceptable, nor is the recommendation to

base a critical ed. on *D* (= *A* in Nordfelt's classification). Nordfelt's view that the *vers orphelin* is a late intrusion in this poem is still valid.

500   Riese, Otto, 'Untersuchungen über die Ueberlieferung der *Enfances Vivien*' (doctoral thesis, University of Halle-Wittemberg, 1900) 67 pp.
Studies the classification and filiation of the manuscripts. Wrongly sees MSS *C* and *D* as forming a family against AB. Includes résumés in German of significant episodes.

Rev.:   .1   Gaston Paris, *Rom*, 29 (1900), 639–40.

FOUCON DE CANDIE

(i) *Editions and Translations*

501   Herbert le duc de Dammartin, *Le Roman de Foulque de Candie*, ed. Prosper Tarbé, Collection des Poètes de Champagne Antérieurs au XVIe Siècle, 17 (Reims: Dubois, 1860) lxix + 227 pp.
The introduction attempts to identify the author with one of several known by the same name, analyses the poem's narrative content, and includes some stylistic and historical comment; for the purposes of the analysis the editor divides the song into 'cantos'. The ed. is an abridgement with no line numbers, but does add some notes, an index of proper names with extensive historical and biographical discussions of entries, and a brief glossary.

502   Herbert le Duc de Dammartin, *Folque de Candie nach den festländischen Handschriften*, ed. Oskar Schultz-Gora, 4 vols. 1–2, Gesellschaft für romanische Literatur, 21, 38 (Dresden: Gesellschaft für romanische Literatur, 1908 [1909]; 1915); 3, Gesellschaft für romanische Literatur, 49 (Jena: Gesellschaft für romanische Literatur, 1936); 4, Beihefte zur *ZrPh*, 111 (Tübingen: Niemeyer, 1966) xxviii + 466; xxi + 450; vi + 450; viii + 120 pp.
Vol. 1 contains a brief foreword, giving basic details of the MSS and making a concise statement of editorial practice, a synopsis of the contents of ll. 1–9882, those lines edited from BNF f. fr. 25518, with palaeographic and textual notes plus rejected readings and variants at the foot of each page. Vol. 2 contains the edited text of ll. 9883–14195 with a synopsis and variants, and five appendices giving extensive passages from other MSS. Vol. 3 contains critical and explanatory notes, a useful index to the notes, a glossary to the main text and to the appendices and table of proper names. Vol. 4 contains an introduction to the whole ed. prepared for publication by Ulrich Mölk. The introduction considers the identity of the author, the language and style of *FC*, its literary influence, and

its place within CycG. It also contains a facsimile of Vatican MS Pal. lat. 1972, f. 135^v.

Rev.: .1   Raymond Weeks, *RR*, 8 (1917), 107 (Vols 1 & 2).
     .2   Anon, *Rom*, 46 (1920), 624 (Vol. 2).
     .3   W. Schulz, *ZfSL*, 47 (1925), 212 (Vol. 2).
     .4   Ernst Gamillscheg, *ZfSL*, 62 (1939), 119 (Vol. 3).
     .5   H. Gelzer, *ZrPh*, 63 (1943), 539 (Vol. 3).
     .6   W. Ziltener, *ZrPh*, 85 (1969), 540–43 (Vol. 4).

(ii) *Studies*

503   Foerster, Wendelin, 'Zu v. 5518 des *Foulque de Candie*', *ZfSL*, 36, 2 (1910), 114–16.
Corrects *d'estre* in the Schultz-Gora ed. (502) to *destre* by comparison to Chrétien de Troyes, *Cligés*, l. 4770.

504   François, Charles, '*Foucon de Candie*: le nom *povre porveü*', *RBPH*, 49 (1971), 799–84.
Suggests that the name means 'poorly endowed'. Its use suggests the influence of *Florimont* by Aimon de Varennes, and implies a date of composition post 1188.

505   ——, 'Retouches au texte de *Foucon de Candie*', in *Hommage Delbouille* (1973), pp. 33–51.
Criticizes the Schultz-Gora ed. (502) and proposes corrections to a number of lines.

506   Grossel, Marie-Geneviève, '"Ains por Forcon tant ne fist Anfelixe con ie per vos, amis, se vos ravoie..." Composition et romanesque dans la chanson de *Fouque de Candie*', in *Mélanges Suard* (1999), pp. 351–60.
The article analyses the structure of *FC* in terms of blocks of text allotted to the various narrative sequences and of complementary pairings of characters. The romance elements identified are shown to depend greatly on lyric rather than romance models, especially the *jeu-parti*.

507   Moreno, Paola, 'Lasse inedite della chanson de geste de *Foucon de Candie*', *MedRom*, 15 (1990), 371–405.
A complete miniature critical ed. with notes and an index of proper names, but no glossary, of sixteen *laisses* of *FC* from MS Brussels, Bibliothèque Royale Albert Ier, II 7451, and the single laisse from Venice, San Marco Codex francesi XIX, not included or mentioned in the Schultz-Gora ed. (502).

508 ——, 'Sui manoscritti veneziani del *Foucon de Candie*', *MedRom*, 17 (1992), 197–99.
A close study reveals that the two MSS cannot be identical copies of a common model, as was the opinion of Schultz-Gora (502) but that Venice, San Marco, Codex francese XIX is probably a copy of Venice, San Marco, Codex francese XX, making some alterations to the text of its model.

509 ——, *La tradizione manoscritta del 'Foucon de Candie'. Contributo per una nuova edizione*, Romanica Neapolitana, 30 (Naples: Liguori Editore, 1997) 370 pp.
A detailed study of the MSS of *FC* including fragments, especially those which have been discovered since the publication of the Schultz-Gora ed. (502), and a study of the ways in which the poem was affected by *mouvance*.

Rev.: .1   Martine Thiry-Stassin, *Scriptorium*, 52 (1998), 235*–236*.

510 Schultz-Gora, Oskar, 'Der altfranzösische Name "Anfelise"', *ZrPh*, 24 (1900), 122–25.
Traces the origin of the name of the heroine of *FC* to an Arabic original, comparing it with the masculine name 'Anfelis' in *AN* and *MAN*.

511 ——, 'Der Kurzvers im *Folcon de Candie* der Boulogner Handschrift no 192', *ZrPh*, 24 (1900), 370–87.
A close analysis of representative passages in BNF f.fr. 25518 and *C* leads to the sound conclusion that the *vers orphelin* is the intrusive result of a late revision.

512 —— 'Zur Datierung des *Folque de Candie*', *ZrPh*, 53 (1933), 311–17.
A careful review of evidence leads to the conclusion that *FC* dates from 1180–87.

513 ——, 'Fragmente einer neuen Handschrift des *Folque de Candie*', *ZrPh*, 53 (1933), 566–69.
The description and discussion of two brief fragments of *FC* from an Anglo-Norman MS of 1250–1300 from a pastedown.

514 ——, 'Die Kenntnis des Verfassers des *Folque de Candie* von anderen epischen Dichtungen sowie die Anspielungen auf Herberts Epos', *ZrPh*, 65 (1949), 472–83.
The article is in two parts. In the first the author traces allusions to other poems in *FC*, often relying on minute verbal echoes as an indication. In the second part more explicit and concrete references to *FC* by other works are studied.

*515 Tischendorf, F., 'Die Behandlung des bestimmten Artikels in *Foulque de Candie*' (doctoral thesis, University of Jena, 1924).

516   Wathelet-Willem, Jeanne, '*Foucon de Candie*: une tentative de ré-
       novation du cycle des Narbonnais', in *Farai chansoneta novele* (1989),
       pp. 437–44.
       A brief general study of *FC* designed to bring out its literary merits as well as its
       relationships with other poems of CycG, especially with the Gui episode of *G1*,
       of which Herbert le Duc is shown to have extensive knowledge.

517   Weeks, Raymond, 'A Mention of the Return of King Arthur in *Foucon de
       Candie*', *RR*, 1 (1910), 436.
       Presents the lines from A^I (= P^2 in Schultz-Gora's classification, see 502, vol. 4,
       pp. 1–7) with a similar reference from *Garin le Lorrain* for comparison.

LA GESTE DE MONGLANE

*(INCLUDING VERSE TEXTS OF: LES ENFANCES GARIN DE MONGLANE; GARIN DE
MONGLANE; HERNAUT DE BEAULANDE; RENIER DE GENNES)*

(i) *Editions and Translations*

518   *Die Enfances Garin de Monglane, Einleitung, Schlussteil des Textes,
       Namenverzeichnis*, ed. Viktor Jeran (Greifswald: H. Adler, 1913) 86 pp.
       This doctoral dissertation edits BNF f. fr. 1460, ff. 57a, 9–95a, 6. The
       introduction offers a brief account of the unique MS, and an assessment of
       sources. Line numbers of the ed. and in the index of Proper Names refer to MS
       folios. Cf. Otto Bisinger (527)

519   *Die Chanson Garin de Monglane, nach den Hss. P, L, A, Teil I*, ed. E.
       Schuppe (Greifswald: H. Adler, 1914); *Teil II*, ed. Max Müller; *Teil III*,
       ed. Hermann Menn (Greifswald: H. Adler, 1913).
       These doctoral theses offer a plain text with brief philological introductions.

520   *La Geste de Monglane, Edited from the Cheltenham Manuscript*, ed.
       David M. Dougherty, E. B. Barnes, and Catherine B. Cohen (Eugene:
       University of Oregon Books, 1966) 247 pp.
       An unreliable ed. of *GM* from Cheltenham, MS Phillips 26092, now in the library
       of the University of Oregon, giving a large number of incorrect readings and
       misjudged corrections.

       Rev.: .1   Larry S. Crist, *FrRev*, 40 (1967), 883–84.
             .2   Félix Lecoy, *Rom*, 88 (1967), 561–62.
             .3   W. M. Hackett, *RPh*, 22 (1968), 121–22.

.4 Wolfgang G. van Emden, *CCM*, 11 (1968), 63–67.
.5 Giuseppe di Stefano, *SF*, 37 (1969), 116.
.6 Kurt Baldinger, *ZrPh*, 86 (1970), 252–53.

*521 Brown, Jack D., '*Les Enfances Garin*: A Critical Edition' (PhD thesis, University of North Carolina, Chapel Hill, 1971). *DAI*, 32 (1971–72), 2676.

*522 Hendrickson, William L., 'A Critical Edition of the Fragment of *Garin de Monglane* in the Garrett 125 Manuscript' (PhD thesis, Princeton University, 1969) 242 pp. *DAI*, 30 (1969-70), 2024–25.
The text with abridged introduction and apparatus was published in 523.

523 ——, 'Un nouveau fragment de *Garin de Monglane*', *Rom*, 96 (1975), 163–93.
A critical ed. of the fragment in Princeton, MS Garrett 125 collated with the Müller-Menn ed. (519).

*524 Paquette, J. M., 'Les Enfances Garin de Monglane' (thesis for the Doctorat de 3ᵉ Cycle, University of Poitiers, 1968).

*525 Williams, John L. '*Enfances Garin de Monglane*, an annotated edition' (PhD thesis, University of Arizona, 1973) 478 pp. *DAI*, 34 (1973–74), 1261.

(ii) *Studies*

526 Andrieux-Reix, Nelly, 'De quelques vers en prose. Une enquête sur la *Geste de Monglane* et des présomptions de parenté entre écritures tardives', *Rom*, 110 (1989), 493–510.
Questions the judgements made in nineteenth-century theses (518 & 519) on the antiquity of the source of the prose *Garin* of Ars. 3351 on the basis of verse inserts in the prose text. In an appendix the verses of Ars. 3351 are printed alongside the corresponding passages of the University of Oregon MS (formerly Cheltenham, Phillips 26092).

527 Bisinger, Otto, *Die Enfances Garin de Monglane, Sprache und Heimat, Eingang und Hauptteil des Textes* (Greifswald: H. Adler, 1915).
The introduction is mostly linguistic, leading to the conclusion that the poem dates from the end of the thirteenth or beginning of the fourteenth century, and is in Picard dialect. The ed. of MS BNF f. fr. 1460 ff. 1ʳ–57ʳ (*laisses* 1–101) has critical notes at the foot of each page and an index of proper names. Cf. Viktor Jeran (518).

528 di Stefano, Giuseppe, 'Flexion et versification', in *Essais sur le Moyen Français* (Padova: Liviana Editrice, 1977), pp. 97–131.

The chapter studies the mixing of OF and MF forms in the *Geste de Monglane*, using the Dougherty, Barnes, and Cohen ed. (520) as reference.

Rev.: .1   J. Bourguignon, *RLiR*, 41 (1977), 446–47.

529   Dougherty, David M., 'Characterization in the *Geste de Monglane*', in *Mélanges Frappier* (1970), pp. 253–58.
A rather superficial account of characters in the fifteenth-century revision of CycG material, concluding that characters have been edulcorated to suit a later taste.

530   Hendrickson, William L., 'Toward an Edition of *Garin de Monglane*', in *Jean Misrahi Memorial Volume: Studies in Medieval Literature*, ed. Hans R. Runte, Henri Niedzielski, and William L. Hendrickson (Columbia, SC: French Literature Publications, 1977), pp. 46–70.
Analyses MS readings, especially of the three fragments, of *GM* and proposes a revised *stemma codicon*.

531   ——, 'Quelques aspects du vers orphelin dans *Garin de Monglane*', in *Rencesvals 5* (1977), pp. 202–10.
An analysis of a sample of 288 *vers orphelins* in *GM* concluding that the device has a positive, lyric function in the poem.

532   ——, 'Les sources littéraires de *Garin de Monglane*', in *Rencesvals 6* (1974), pp. 607–17.
A rather thin paper which does little more than repeat analyses and arguments from *Durmart le Galois, roman arthurien du treizième siècle*, ed. J. Gildea (Villanova, PA: Villanova Press, 1965–66) with the added assertion that the author of the poem intended to compose a *chanson de geste* not a romance.

533   ——, '*Garin de Monglane* and *La Chanson de la croisade albigeoise*', in *Continuations: Essays on Medieval French Literature and Language in Honor of John L. Grigsby*, ed. Norris J. Lacy and Gloria Torrini-Roblin (Birmingham, AL: Summa Publications, 1989), pp. 203–15.
Argues unconvincingly on the basis of a few place names in *GM* that the poem was conceived as propaganda for the expansionist North in the thirteenth century.

534   ——, 'Quelle foi religieuse est représentée dans *Garin de Monglane*?', in *Rencesvals 12* (1993), pp. 169–76.
An attempt to show that the Saracen religion portrayed in *GM* is a disguised version of Catharism, and that Garin is a literary reflexion of Simon de Montfort.

535   Horrent, Jacques, 'Hernaut de Beaulande et le *Poema de Fernán González*', *Bulletin Hispanique*, 79 (1977), 23–52.

A detailed comparison of *Fernán González* with the version of *Hernaut de Beaulande* contained in *La Geste de Monglane* leads to the conclusion, contrary to that put forward by Ramón Menéndez Pidal, that the French poem derives from the Spanish.

536 Keller, Hans-Erich, '*Renier de Gennes*', in *Rencesvals 11* (1990), I, pp. 369–83.
Traces the evidence for a lost twelfth-century poem *Renier de Gennes* which would pre-date the *GV* of Bertrand de Bar-sur-Aube.

537 Louis, René, 'De Livier à Olivier', in *Mélanges Delbouille II* (1964), pp. 447–76.
Traces the evolution of the name of Olivier in a number of sources, and shows that the symbolic, biblically derived association of Olivier with the olive tree, and hence with peace, owes more to *GV* than to the *Chanson de Roland*.

538 Paris, Gaston, 'Le roman de la geste de Monglane', *Rom*, 12 (1883), 1–13.
An attack on Léon Gautier's view of the relationship of Ars. 3351 to the prints of *Garin de Monglave* (*sic*), expressed in *Les Epopées françaises*, vol. III, 2nd ed. (Paris: Société Générale de Librairie Catholique, 1878–82). Paris's critique is supported by a study of MS Cheltenham, Phillips 26092 (now in Eugene) which is compared to the printed versions.

*539 Rudolph, K., 'Das Verhältnis der beiden Fassungen, in welchen die Chanson *Garin de Monglane* überliefert ist, nebst eine Untersuchung der *Enfances Garin de Monglane*' (doctoral thesis, University of Marburg, 1890).

*540 Stoeriko, A., *Über das Verhältnis der beiden Romane 'Durmart' und 'Garin de Monglane'*, Ausgaben und Abhandlungen, 78 (Marburg, 1888).
Rev.: .1   Gaston Paris, *Rom*, 18 (1889), 345.

LA GESTE DE MONGLANE EN PROSE

(i) Editions and Translations

541 *La Geste de Garin de Monglane en prose*, ed. Hans-Erich Keller, Senefiance, 35 (Aix-en-Provence: Publications du CUER MA, Université de Provence, 1994) 267 pp.
The introduction is mostly concerned with situating the prose *GM* in the late-medieval traditions of the *Geste de Monglane* and with its overtly sententious and didactic tone. The study of the language is limited to listing Picardisms in the

scripta. The ed. is accompanied by textual notes at the foot of the page, a brief glossary, and appendices giving a selection of proverbs and sententious distichs. There is no index of proper names or bibliography.

Rev.: .1   Gilles Roques, *RLiR*, 58 (1994), 594–95.

(ii) *Studies*

542   Hartmann, Karl, 'Über die Eingangsepisoden der Cheltenhamer Version des *Girart de Vienne*' (doctoral thesis, University of Marburg, 1889).
Studies the parts of Prose *GM* incorporating verse quotations corresponding to *RomG* in MS Cheltenham, Phillips 26092 to show that the prose text derives from a source earlier than Cheltenham. Cf. Andrieux-Reix (526).

543   Keller, Hans-Erich, 'La chanson de geste en prose et l'amour courtois', in *Rencesvals 13* (1995), pp. 375–82.
A study of the vocabulary used to express relationships between knights and their ladies in the prose *GM* and its epic sources shows the extent to which courtly love was intrinsic to plot development in versions elaborated for the court of Burgundy.

544   Pindevic, Marie-Jane, 'Les noms propres dans la *Geste de Garin de Monglane en prose*, in *'Ce nous dist li escris…che est la verité'. Etudes de littérature médiévale offerts à André Moisan*, Senefiance, 45 (Aix-en-Provence: Publications du CUER MA, Université de Provence, 2000), pp. 217–41.
Provides the table of proper names not included in the ed. by Keller (541), and gives cross-references to early prints of other fifteenth- and sixteenth-century prose versions of *chansons de geste*.

GIRART DE VIENNE

(i) *Editions and Translations*

545   Bertrand de Bar-sur-Aube, *Le Roman de Girard de Viane*, ed. Prosper Tarbé, Collection des Poëtes de Champagne (Reims: P. Régnier, 1850) xxix + 208 pp. Repr. Geneva: Slatkine, 1974.
The literary aspects of the introduction are no longer of much academic interest, although some aspects of the historical and biographical work are still valid; the text is plain, presented continuously with no line numbers or laisse divisions; a brief glossary incorporates a list of proper names, often offering extensive explanations. The Table of Contents analyses the poem into episodes.

546   Bertrand de Bar-sur-Aube, *L'Epopée carlovingienne. Girard de Vienne, chanson de geste, d'après le trouvère Bertrand de Bar*, trans. by Gaston Armelin (Paris: Ernest Flammarion, 1911) 267 pp.
The preface, although showing some signs of erudition, is most remarkable for its disdain of the poetic qualities of OF epic. The translation, into rhyming alexandrine couplets, which carefully avoids formulaic repetition, re-orders some parts of the text, and invents whole passages for the sake of the translator's notion of clarity, is generally bombastic. The few notes are mostly concerned with relating the poem to Victor Hugo's adaptations in *La Légende des Siècles*.

547   Bertrand de Bar-sur-Aube, *Girart de Vienne, chanson de geste, ed. according to MS B XIX (Royal) of the British Museum*, ed. Frederic G. Yeandle (New York: Columbia UP, 1930) vii + 250 pp.
The brief introduction is heavily indebted to nineteenth-century scholarship. The ed. is sound, has rejected readings at the foot of each page, a glossary, and comprehensive index of proper names, but is superseded by van Emden's SATF ed. (548).

Rev.:   .1   Mario Roques, *Rom*, 58 (1932), 621.

548   Bertrand de Bar-sur-Aube, *Girart de Vienne*, ed. Wolfgang G. van Emden, SATF (Paris: Picard, 1977) cx + 407 pp.
The standard reference ed. of *GV*. The introduction considers composition and structure as well as manuscript tradition, language, and date. The ed. is conservative, based on *R*, with rejected readings and variants at the foot of each page. There are also extensive notes, a glossary, and an index of proper names.

Rev.:   .1   Anon., *Rom*, 99 (1978), 278.
        .2   L. Bartolucci Chiecchi, *Francia*, 35 (1980), 76–81.
        .3   Alessandro Vitale-Brovarone, *SF*, 24 (1980), 530–31.
        .4   John Grigsby, *Olifant*, 8 (1980–81), 181–85.
        .5   Anne Iker-Gittleman, *RPh*, 36 (1982–1983), 633–35.

549   Bertrand de Bar-sur-Aube, *The Song of Girart de Vienne by Bertrand de Bar-sur-Aube*, trans. Michael A. Newth, Medieval & Renaissance Texts & Studies, 196 (Tempe: Arizona Center for Medieval & Renaissance Studies, 1999) xxiv + 200 pp.
A poor translation into English assonanced decasyllabic verse, preceded by a brief and unreliable introduction abounding in historical and literary confusions. The accompanying table of proper names likewise has several errors in its entries.

Rev.:   .1   Wolfgang G. van Emden, *FS*, 54 (2000), 494–95.

550   van Emden, Wolfgang Georg, 'A Critical Edition of the Epic *Girard de Vienne*' (PhD thesis, University of London, 1963) 2 vols, vi + 387 & iv + 412 pp.

The edited text, critical and editorial apparatus, as well as the essence of the introduction, appear in van Emden's SATF ed. (548).

(ii) *Studies*

551 Aebischer, Paul, 'Une allusion des *Quinze signes du Jugement* à l'épisode du Jeu de la Quintaine du *Girart de Viane* primitif', in *Mélanges Delbouille II* (1964), pp. 7–19.
Having identified the source of the allusion in the *Quinze signes* as the primitive *GV*, the author uses it, rather arbitrarily in the light of the relative datings of the extant documents he is quoting, to support his thesis that originally Oliver was a more important character than Roland in epic traditions.

552 ——, 'Bavardages érudits sur Olivier, Aude et leur père Rainier, d'après les chansons de geste ayant Girard de Vienne comme protagoniste', in *Mélanges Lejeune* (1969), pp. 709–37.
A bravura performance tracing characters across *GV*, *Girart de Roussillon*, *Aspremont*, and the *Karlamagnús saga*, to demonstrate the antiquity, and temporal precedence over the Oxford *Roland*, of a primitive *GV*. The demonstration unfortunately depends on a series of begged questions, logical ellipses, and unsupported assertions, as does the ultimate conclusion that all this epic elaboration is due to a small number of clerks working on archival documents in scriptoria.

553 ——, 'Oliveriana et Rolandiana. Sur le résumé du *Girard de Viane* conservé par la première branche de la *Karlamagnus saga*: une ultime mise au point', *RBPH*, 51 (1973), 517–33.
A reply to van Emden (582) in defence of the author's original hypothesis about the 'primitive' *GV* (552).

554 Barthélemy, André (Docteur), *La Vie du fondateur de Vézelay. Histoire et légende. Influences gnostiques sur la genèse d'une épopée occitane* (Paris: Editions du Borrego, 1983) 160 pp.
A wrong-headed and failed attempt to refute René Louis's thesis on Girard de Vienne (719), as well as those of most of the major specialists of the century. The author isolates *Girard de Roussillon* from the rest of its epic context and sees a poem composed under the influence of surviving paganism and gnosticism.

555 Beretta, Carlo, 'I *Narbonnais* e il *Charroi de Nîmes* (e altre filigrane guglielmine) nella prima parte del *Girart de Vienne* di Bertrand de Bar-sur-Aube', *MedRom*, 15 (1990), 235–57.
The first part of the article reaffirms with approval the various conclusions of van Emden (579–82) about Bertrand's revision of older *GV* material; in the second,

longer, part he traces a number of intertextual references to other poems of CycG to demonstrate how Bertrand sought in ll. 1–1245 of *GV* to make his new interpretation of Girart's character acceptable by subliminal association with the heroes of that cycle.

556   Cirlot, Victoria, 'El orden de la palabra y la idea de linaje en *Girart de Vienne*', in *Rencesvals 10* (1987), pp. 351–65.
Based on R. Howard Bloch's ideas enunciated in *Etymologies and Genealogies: A Literary Anthropology of the French Middle Ages* (Chicago: University of Chicago Press, 1983), the article is less concerned with word-order in the strictly linguistic sense than with the order imposed by formulæ reflecting the increasing importance in the twelfth century of patrilineal descent. Some pertinent remarks are made, about the ways epic structures are used as guarantors of truth, but the study is too closely focused on one text, and does not take account of wider epic traditions in coming to generalizing conclusions which are consequently flawed although convincingly demonstrated in the particular case.

557   Curtius, Ernst Robert, 'Über die altfranzösische Epik V', *ZrPh*, 68 (1952), 177–208.
A set of essays, including as item three a study of *GV*, which through a commented reading of the poem and a discussion of the views of Philipp-August Becker (51& 54) and René Louis (719) seeks to anchor *GV* firmly into a humanist tradition of literary creativity in the late twelfth century.

558   Dougherty, David M., 'The *Girard de Vienne* of Bertrand de Bar-sur-Aube and that of the Cheltenham MS: A Comparison', *RoNo*, 6 (1964–65), 200–08.
A brief and superficial comparison of the two versions of *GV*, claiming for the Cheltenham version the status of autonomous work of art. The character of Robastre in the Cheltenham version is stated, without discussion, to be borrowed from Rainouart as he appears in *G2* rather than as in *Al*.

559   Elliott, Alison Goddard, 'The Double Genesis of *Girard de Vienne*', *Olifant*, 8 (1980–81), 130–60.
A detailed and subtle study of the lexical and syntactic constituents of formulæ in the different parts of *GV*, as identified by Louis (719, I, pp. 21–23) and van Emden (548, pp. xx–xxix) to confirm that the extant poem is a careful reworking by Bertrand de Bar-sur-Aube of an earlier song. The author is careful not to confuse formulaic modes of composition with oral origins.

*560   Fichera, Flavia, 'Il *Girart de Vienne* di Bertrand de Bar-sur-Aube tra vassallaggio e feudalesimo: commistione e oscillazione tra "personale" e

"istituzionale"', *Le Forme e la Storia: Rivista di Filologia Moderna*, ns 8 (1996).
See the résumé in *BBSR*, 30, pp. 94–95.

561 Guidot, Bernard, 'L'empereur Charles dans *Girard de Vienne*', in *Mélanges Foulon II* (1980), pp. 127–41.
A conventional character study leading to the conclusion that in *GV* Charles is a greatly diminished personality, but that the prestige of the royal and imperial title is undiminished despite the shortcomings of the holder of them. In this way *GV* remains aloof from the ideologies of the cycle of the *barons révoltés*.

562 Hardy, Madeleine, and Alain Labbé, 'En marge du conflit entre Charles le Chauve et Girart de Vienne: Loup de Ferrières, Rémi d'Auxerre et le peintre Fredilo', in *Mélanges Louis* (1982), pp. 119–69.
The article demonstrates the essential unity of the clerical and secular branches of aristocratic families in the late Carolingian period, a unity which accounts for a number of literary and artistic productions, among which should be numbered the promotion and diffusion (if not the origins) of *chansons de geste*.

563 Heintze, Michael, 'La présentation des caractères dans *Girart de Vienne*', in *Rencesvals 12* (1993), pp. 485–507.
The aim of the article is to demonstrate one of the mechanisms by which Bertrand de Bar-sur-Aube inserts *GV* into CycG. The character studies (of Girart, Olivier, Aymeri, and Guibourc) are not wholly original, but lead to the suggestion, proof for which is not always positive or concrete, that Bertrand imposed on characters inherited from CycG or from the primitive *GV* personality traits borrowed from characters in *Girard de Roussillon*.

564 Jordan, Leo, 'Girartsstudien', *RF*, 14,1 (1903), 321–38.
Mostly concerned with *Girart de Roussillon*; two short sections deal with questions arising from the relationship between that poem and *GV*. Subsequent work renders this redundant.

565 Keller, Hans-Erich, '*Renier de Gennes*', in *Rencesvals 11* (1990), I, pp. 369–83. See 536.

*566 Kunze, A., *Das Formelhafte in 'Girart de Viane' verglichen mit dem Formelhaften im 'Rolandsliede'* (Halle, 1885).

567 Larghi, Gerardo, 'Citations épiques et politiques en Monferrato', in *Rencesvals 13* (1995), pp. 383–89.
Studies a number of literary allusions identifying the court of Boniface of Monferrato as an active centre of cultural diffusion, and speculates on a possible direct link of Bertrand de Bar-sur-Aube with that court.

568 Lichtenstein, Gustav, *Vergleichende Untersuchung über die jüngeren Bearbeitungen der Chanson de 'Girart de Viane'*, Ausgaben und Abhandlungen, 97 (Marburg: N. G. Elwert, 1899) 72 pp.
A comparison of the narrative content of the fifteenth-century *GM* from the Cheltenham MS with the prose romance to determine the relationship between them. A long appendix gives chapter headings from the Dresden MS of the prose romance.

569 Mauron, Claude, 'Le mariage de Roland de *Girart de Vienne* à la *Légende des Siècles*', in *Les Relations de parenté dans le monde médiéval. Actes du quatorzième colloque du CUER MA (février 1989)*, Senefiance, 26 (Aix-en-Provence: Publications du CUER MA, Université de Provence, 1989), pp. 69–82.
The article is essentially concerned with the reception of *GV* in the nineteenth century, especially with Achille Jubinal's interpretations of the text, which provide the immediate source for Victor Hugo's poem 'Le Mariage de Roland'.

570 Meyer, Elard Hugo, 'Über *Gerhard von Vienne*, ein Beitrag zur Rolandsage', *Zeitschrift für deutsche Philologie*, 3 (1871), 422–58.
The first part of the study analyses the content of *GV*, dividing it into historical and mythical or legendary material. After considering the historical roots of the conflict between Girard and Charlemagne in events of the reign of Charles the Bald — cf. René Louis (719) — he treats the Roland-Oliver episode as a survival of the cyclic sun-god myth. This part of the work was roundly condemned by Gaston Paris (572).

571 Misrahi, Jean, 'Girart de Vienne et la geste de Guillaume', *MAe*, 4 (1935), 1–15.
Despite a tendentious interpretation of *ChG* ll. 1270–71 the conclusion that Bertrand de Bar-sur-Aube is the first to incorporate Girart de Vienne into the Narbonnais clan is undoubtedly correct.

572 Paris, Gaston, 'La mythologie allemande dans *Girart de Vienne*', *Rom*, 1 (1872), 101–04.
A satirical review of the article by Elard Hugo Meyer (570) protesting against the indiscriminate application of mythographic criticism to French epics. Gaston Paris refuses to see a mythological substrate in a work by a late *trouvère* like Bertrand de Bar-sur-Aube. This refusal to accept a Germanic background to French epic can be seen as part of the reaction to the Franco-Prussian War.

573 Rubaud, Roger, '*Girart de Vienne*, par Bertrand de Bar-sur-Aube. Le poète, sa vie, son milieu, ses héros', *Bulletin de la Société Historique de Langres*, 16 (1975–76), 361–90, 393–433 & 468–69.

A book-length article in three parts exploiting a wealth of local archive material to set *GV* firmly in a Champenois context, with a date of composition between 1180 and 1182. Unfortunately, in what is otherwise very solid work, some of the more picturesque conclusions about the exact circumstances of the composition and first recital of the poem are pure supposition.

574   Spijker, Irene, 'Een poging tot lokalizering van de Middelnederlandse *Gheraert van Viane* in de internationale *Girart de Vienne*-traditie', *De nieuwe taalgids*, 76 (1983), 97–108. ['An Effort to Situate the Middle Dutch *Gheraert van Viane* in the International Tradition of *Girart de Vienne*']
The author suggests that the episode of Girart's kissing the empress's foot may derive from an earlier version of *GV* than that of Bertrand de Bar-sur-Aube, since the account given in the Middle Dutch version differs notably from Bertrand's and his French derivatives, and that *GV* and the Middle Dutch version may belong to parallel branches of the tradition rather than the latter being derived from the former. Dutch text. Wolfgang van Emden (585) used this article in his rebuttal of Kurt Wais's interpretation of the relationships between the OF and Middle Dutch poems (586).

575   Subrenat, Jean, 'Dénominations de l'empereur dans *Girart de Vienne*', in *Mélanges Louis* (1982), pp. 691–702.
A detailed study of terms and expressions used by characters in *GV* to designate Charlemagne and to address him shows that Bertrand de Bar-sur-Aube rises above the constraints of metrics and rhetoric to reveal nuances in his characters' personalities and attitudes.

576   ——, 'Vienne: fief ou alleu? (A propos de *Girart de Vienne*)', in *Mélanges Jean Larmat: regards sur le Moyen Âge et la Renaissance (histoire, langue et littérature)*, Annales de la Faculté des Lettres et Sciences Humaines de Nice, 39 (Paris: Les Belles Lettres, 1982), pp. 309–18.
A closely argued article showing that the ambiguous status of Vienne is resolved by Girard's gratuitous surrender of his allod and the transformation of it into a fief at the end of the poem.

577   ——, 'De la Paix de Vienne au drame de Roncevaux', in *Reading around the Epic* (1998), pp. 1–9.
An intertextual study showing the influence of *GV* on the later redactions of the *Chanson de Roland*.

578   van Emden, Wolfgang, 'Hypothèse sur une explication historique du remaniement de *Girart de Vienne* par Bertrand de Bar-sur-Aube', in *Rencesvals 4* (1969), pp. 63–70.

The contribution tentatively proposes that *GV* would have been composed between 1181 and 1183 to coincide with the marriage of Scholastica, daughter of Marie de Champagne and Henri le Libéral, to Girart, comte de Mâcon. The dating also requires the equally tentative suggestion that Scholastica was the younger daughter of Marie and Henri, not the elder as is usually supposed.

579   ——, '*Girard de Vienne*:   problèmes de composition et de datation', *CCM*, 13 (1970), 281–90.

The article demonstrates that it was Bertrand de Bar-sur-Aube who integrated Girard into CycG, and proposes a date of 1180 for the new compilation.

580   ——, '*Rolandiana et Oliveriana*: faits et hypothèses', *Rom*, 92 (1971), 507–31.

A refutation of Aebischer's hypothesis, advanced in his study *Rolandiana et Oliveriana: recueil d'études sur les chansons de geste* (Geneva: Droz, 1967), that evidence from the *Karlamagnús saga* indicates that Oliver had the prime role in the primitive *GV*.

581   ——, '*Girart de Vienne* devant les ordinateurs', in *Mélanges Louis* (1982), pp. 663–90.

A lengthy presentation of statistical data compiled for the author by Alison Goddard Elliott confirms the tripartite division of *GV* identified by the author in his ed. of the poem (548). It also allows the conclusion that Bertrand de Bar-sur-Aube was working from a written, not an oral, source.

582   ——, 'Encore une fois *Oliveriana et Rolandiana* ou l'inverse', *RBPH*, 54 (1976), 837–58.

A further contribution to the exchanges of the author with Paul Aebischer over the nature and form of the 'primitive' *GV*, and of the importance of the Norse *Karlamagnús saga* in establishing those features distinguishing the 'primitive' version (551–553). The tone of the article is distinctly polemical, although the arguments are based on a close and precise study of the texts. Particularly at stake are the perception, based on onomastic researches, that Oliver was a more prominent hero than Roland before the appearance of the Oxford *Roland*, and above all the changing attitudes of *chanteurs de geste* and *trouvères* to the question of revolt.

583   ——, 'The Cocktail-Shaker Technique in Two *Chansons de Geste*', in *The Medieval Alexander Legend* (1982), pp. 43–56.

Analyses how the poets of *GV* and *Girart de Roussillon* exploit contamination of marital and feudal themes to influence the audience's attitude to the emperor.

584 ——, '*Girart de Vienne*: Epic or Romance?', *Olifant*, 10 (autumn, 1982–winter, 1985), 147–60.
The author provides a succinct analysis of aspects of the poem considered significant for distinguishing between epic and romance genres: the prologue, descriptions, representations of feelings, and use of *tu* vs *vous*. In addition he considers its general thematics. The overall study allows him to conclude that *GV* is essentially epic with decoratively applied romance and (in the case of the affair of the Duchess of Burgundy) *fabliau* features.

585 ——, 'Les Girart et leur(s) femme(s), et problèmes annexes. A propos de *Gheraert van Viane*', in *The Troubadours and the Epic*, pp. 238–69.
Reacting to the article by Irene Spijker on the Middle Dutch *Gheraert* (574), the author presents a line-by-line translation into French of the Dutch fragments, convincingly rebuts the opinion of Kurt Wais (586) that the foot-kissing episode was part of the primitive, pre-Bertrand de Bar, *GV* material, and concludes that the Dutch fragments derive from Bertrand's revised *GV*.

586 Wais, Kurt, 'Zum Verhältnis von Geschichte und Dichtung in den drei Girart-Epen (Vienne, Fraite, Roussillon)', in *Festgabe Ernst Gamillscheg zu seinem fünfundsechzigsten Geburtstag am 28. Oktober 1952 von Freunden und Schülern überreicht* (Tübingen: Max Niemeyer Verlag, 1952), pp. 194–213.
The article is really an attack on Bédier's views of the origins of French epic and an appeal for French and German epic to be treated again as branches of the same traditional material. The handling of the relationship between historical and poetic-legendary elements in the elaboration of *GV* and its cognate poems (*Girart de Roussillon* and 'Girart de Fraite') leaves much to be desired. See the criticisms of Wolfgang van Emden (585).

GUIBERT D'ANDRENAS

(i) *Editions and Translations*

587 *Guibert d'Andrenas, chanson de geste*, ed. J. Mélander (Paris: Edouard Champion, 1922) lxvii + 149 pp.
The ed. is a composite one based on *R* but freely incorporating readings from other MSS, plus some reconstructions of the editor's invention. It has a sound philological introduction, a glossary, and index of proper names.

588   *Guibert d'Andrenas, chanson de geste*, ed. Jessie Crosland, Modern
       Language Texts, French Series: Medieval Section (Manchester:
       Manchester UP, 1923) xv + 95 pp.
       The very brief introduction, designed for students, gives a synopsis of the story,
       situates *GA* within CycG, and makes some very sketchy remarks on language and
       MS filiations. The ed. is conservatively based on *R* and is accompanied by a list
       of corrected readings, a very brief glossary and an index of proper names. The
       readings of the MS are inadequately discussed, and some of the editorial work is
       poor.

*589   Ott, Muriel, '*Guibert d'Andrenas* édition (d'après tous les manuscrits) et
       étude littéraire' (Doctorat 3ᵉ Cycle, University of Nancy II, 1999) 588 pp.
       Abstract in *Perspectives Médiévales*, 25 (1999), 69–72.

(ii) *Studies*

590   Guidot, Bernard, 'Figures féminines et chanson de geste: l'exemple de
       Guibert d'Andrenas', in *Mélanges Wathelet-Willem* (1978), pp. 189–206.
       The article is effectively a traditional character study of two female characters in
       GA: the Christian, Hermenjart, and the Saracen, Augaiete. The lively and
       attractive personality of the latter is seen as a sign of renewal rather than of
       decadence in thirteenth-century epic.

591   ——, 'Stylistique et versification médiévales: le "vers orphelin" dans
       Guibert d'Andrenas', in *Le Génie de la forme, mélanges de langue et
       littérature offerts à Jean Mourot* (Nancy: Presses Universitaires de
       Nancy, 1982), pp. 13–25.
       A detailed and convincing analysis of the striking effects achieved by the careful
       exploitation of the *vers orphelin* even by an average poet.

*592   Siele, Carl, 'Über die Chanson de *Guibert d'Andrenas*. Classification der
       Handschriften. Analyse und Quellenuntersuchung' (doctoral thesis,
       University of Marburg, 1891).

LE MONIAGE GUILLAUME

(i) *Editions and Translations*

593   *Les Deux rédactions en vers du Moniage Guillaume, chanson de geste du
       XIIᵉ siècle*, ed. Wilhelm Cloetta, SATF, 2 vols (Paris: Firmin-Didot,
       1906–11) 391 + 384 pp.
       Vol. 1 contains the critical texts of the two redactions, with rejected readings and
       variants at the foot of each page; vol. 2 presents a detailed introduction, covering

the biography of Count Guillaume of Toulouse, the hagiographic tradition associated with St Guillaume of Gellone, and literary relationships of *MonG*. Much of the material presented and many of the opinions expressed are still of scholarly interest, although some are superseded, especially the editor's view of the relationship between the two redactions, which is now considered the inverse of that proposed by Cloetta.

Rev.: .1   Anon, *Rom*, 41 (1912), 626.

594   Hofmann, Conrad, 'Über ein Fragment des *Guillaume d'Orange*', in *Abhandlungen der kaizerlichen bayerischen Akademie*, I. Klasse, IV. Band, III. Abteil, 63 (1852), 1–42.
A simple presentation and plain text ed. of *MonG1* from *Ars*.

ii) *Studies*

595   Andrieux-Reix, Nelly, 'Le jardin saccagé: une leçon du *Moniage Guillaume*', in *Il Ciclo di Guglielmo d'Orange* (1997), pp. 362–81.
The analysis of the motif in different cyclic versions allows the author to conclude that the symbolic identification of Guillaume with the garden of his hermitage is a function of cyclic composition, finding its fullest expression in the B redaction. These MSS also add to the standard interpretation of Guillaume's destruction of his garden — the state of France from which good counsellors have been driven by Louis — the supplementary interpretation that the hero is obliged to abandon the spiritual life for the less worthy one of a secular knight in renewed service to the emperor.

596   ——, 'De l'honneur du monde à la gloire du ciel: Guillaume ermite au désert', in *Mélanges Ménard* (1998), I, pp. 37–49.
Considers the final part of *MonG* in which the hero retreats to a hermitage as the closure reconciling two contrary forces in the CycG as a whole: those of royal service as a source of warrior pride and service to God without reference to any mediating institutions. The key to this view of *MonG* is the interpretation of the destruction of the hermit's garden and cell also studied in 595.

597   Bennett, Philip E., 'Carnaval et troisième fonction: guerriers, moines et larrons dans le *Moniage Guillaume*', in *Mélanges Subrenat* (2000), pp. 61–72.
The study aims to show that the intrusion of the carnivalesque into various poems of CycG, and particularly into *MonG*, disrupts the Indo-European system of functions inherited with the epic material as discussed by Grisward (635), and tends to overlay features of the third function, associated with abundance and fertility, onto the more purely warrior (second function) features of characters such as Guillaume and Rainouart.

598   Cloetta, Wilhelm, 'Die beiden altfranzösichen epen vom *Moniage Guillaume*', *Archiv*, 93 (1894), 399–447; 94 (1895), 21–38.
The first part of this prologomenic article to Cloetta's ed. (593), still has some useful judgements, despite inverting the relationship of *MonG1* and *MonG2*. The second part studies the Boulogne version of *MonG*, reaffirming that the Synagon episode must originally have been an independent poem adapted separately into *MonG1* and *MonG2*.

599   ——, 'Die Synagon-Episode des *Moniage Guillaume II* zur Grunde liegenden historischen Ereignisse', in *Abhandlungen an Herrn Dr Prof. Adolf Tobler zur Feier seiner 25 jährigen Thätigkeit als ordentlicher Professor an der Universität Berlin von dankbaren Schülern dargebracht* (Halle: Max Niemeyer, 1895), 239–68.
Identifies the hero with Guillaume de Hauteville and associates the episode with the Norman conquest of southern Italy. The thesis has gained no currency.

       Rev.:   .1   Adolf Tobler, *Archiv*, 95 (1895), 203.

600   ——, 'Die Entstehung des *Moniage Guillaume*', in *Festgabe Foerster* (1902), pp. 99–119.
Repr. (in French) as Ch. V of the introduction to Cloetta's ed. of *MonG* (593).

601   ——, 'Ysoré im Moniage Guillaume und im Ogier', *RF*, 23 (1907: *Mélanges Chabaneau, volume offert à Camille Chabaneau à l'occasion du 75ᵉ anniversaire de sa naissance (4 mars 1906) par ses élèves, ses amis et ses admirateurs*), 541–46.
The author demonstrates that Ysoré in *MonG* derives from the same character in *La Chevalerie Ogier de Danemark*; the presence of this character in *MonG* links it to the Ogier tradition. Later MSS of *La Chevalerie Ogier de Danemark* adapt their material relating to Ysoré to the data of *MonG*, thereby completing a circle of influence among epic poems.

602   Colby-Hall, Alice, 'Le voyage d'un Orangeois, Jacques de la Pise, à l'abbaye de Saint-Guilhem-le-Désert en 1573', *Etudes sur l'Hérault*, 1989–90, 92–98.
Among other documents exploited by the historian of the house of Orange was a version of *MonG* not corresponding to the extant cyclic MSS.

603   Combarieu du Grès, Micheline de, '"Ermitages" épiques (de Guillaume et de quelques autres)', in *Guillaume d'Orange III* (1983), pp. 143–80.
A comparison of *MonG* with other epics portraying hermits and monks leads to the   suggestion that the depiction of the hero as hermit reinforces a sense of individual worth and of heroic adventure in the presentation of the warrior-saint.

604 Delbouille, Maurice, and Madeleine Tyssens, 'Du "Moniage Gautier" au *Moniage Guillaume*', in *Guillaume d'Orange III* (1983), pp. 85–142.
Studies the relationship between *MonG*, the Latin accounts of the monastic retreat of the epic hero Walter of Aquitaine, and a hypothetical 'Moniage Ogier', concluding that they all exploit a pre-existing story of a warrior-monk, without assigning the role of source to any of the three.

605 Frappier, Jean, 'Le *Moniage Guillaume*', in *Guillaume d'Orange III* (1983), pp. 19–84.
An extensive summary of the plots of *MonG1* and *MonG2*, with brief introductory remarks and a now superseded bibliography.

606 Guidot, Bernard, 'Vieillesse, fontaine de Jouvance: l'âge d'or du héros épique d'après le *Moniage Guillaume*', in *Vieillesse et vieillissement au Moyen Age*, Senefiance, 19 (Aix-en-Provence: Publications du CUER MA, Université de Provence, 1987), pp. 111–32.
Studies the character of Guillaume in *MonG2* to show that, while conserving all the attributes of youth, the hero has developed sagacity: spirituality and divine favour are represented as a Fountain of Youth.

607 Infurna, Marco, 'Gli interventi del narratore nel *Moniage Guillaume*', *MedRom*, 12 (1987) 289–306.
Authorial/narratorial interventions in *MonG2* mark it as belonging to a *jongleresque* tradition of oral presentation, while those of *MonG1* associate it with a purely literary stage of cyclic elaboration. The author is clear that such observations do not serve to attribute oral or literary composition to the redactions.

608 Lot, Ferdinand, 'Notes sur le *Moniage Guillaume*. I: Tombe Issoire ou Tombe Isoré? II: L'épisode des ronces', *Rom*, 26 (1897), 481–94.
Argues persuasively that the author of the original *MonG* consciously constructed his account of Guillaume's last years by adapting anecdotes and local legends, largely ignoring the official *Vita*.

609 Payen, Jean-Charles, 'L'érémitisme dans le *Moniage Guillaume*: une solution aristocratique à la conversion chevaleresque', in *Guillaume d'Orange III* (1983), pp. 181–208.
A general meditation on *MonG* (including a plot summary), concluding that the poem has serious hagiographic intent, creating a myth of heroic eremitism around the person of Guillaume.

610   Rajna, Pio, 'Contributi alla storia dell'epopea e del romanzo medievale, VIII: La *Cronaca della Novalesa* e l'epopea carolingia', *Rom*, 23 (1894), 36–61.
Traces the influence of the legend of Walter of Aquitaine as preserved in the *Chronicon Novaliciense* on *MonG* and the legend of Ogier le Danois. Rajna correctly saw *MonG1* as an abridgement of *MonG2*.

611   Schenck, David P., 'Couches culturelles du *Moniage Guillaume*: *bellatores, oratores*', in *Rencesvals 9* (1984), pp. 169–77.
Relates *MonG* to the rise of individualistic spirituality in the twelfth century, suggesting that Guillaume's sufferings in Synagon's prison and his incognito defeat of Ysoré are intentional depictions of a confessor's *imitatio Christi*.

612   Subrenat, Jean, 'Moines mesquins et saint chevalier: à propos du *Moniage* de Guillaume', in *Mélanges Wathelet-Willem* (1978), pp. 643–65.
Confronts the Rule of St Benedict with *MonG2* to illustrate the satire on monks, especially their propensity to avarice and envy, and the steady growth in spirituality of Guillaume, who ultimately reconciles *chevalerie* and *clergie* in his life as a hermit. The author suggests that *MonG* transcends the comic to offer a model of the spiritual life to knights, and so bears witness to changes in the Church in the late twelfth century.

613   Woledge, Brian, 'Remarques sur la valeur littéraire du *Moniage Guillaume*', in *La Technique littéraire* (1959), pp. 21–35.
An individualist argument for the adaptation of traditional techniques by specific authors to produce original literary effects.

614   ——, 'Assonance and Vocabulary in the *Moniage Guillaume*', in *The Medieval Alexander Legend* (1982), pp. 259–67.
A study of rare vocabulary found at the line end in *MonG2*. The author considers the relationship between metrical necessity and verbal invention. He acknowledges the problems raised by treating Cloetta's ed. of *MonG2* as an author's text.

615   Zenker, Rudolf, 'Die Synagon-Episode des *Moniage Guillaume II*', in *Festgabe Foerster* (1902), pp. 129–74.
Considers the episode to be an independent poem incorporated in *MonG2*, held to be later than *MonG1*, and based firmly on historical events of the ninth century. The author concludes that historical sources are more important than poetic invention in the elaboration of OF epic.

616   ——, 'Nochmals die Synagon-Episode des *Moniage Guillaume*', *ZrPh*, 28 (1903), 437–58.

Defends his and Cloetta's views (599 & 615) against the objections raised by a number of other scholars.

LE MONIAGE RAINOUART

(i) Editions and Translations

617   *Le Moniage Rainouart I*, ed. Gerald A. Bertin, SATF (Paris: Picard, 1973) lxxxi + 325 pp.

An ed. of the *C* redaction of *MonR* with rejected readings and variants at the foot of each page. The introduction deals with the formation of the Rainouart sub-cycle, the date and provenance of *MonR*, and the principles of the ed. The vol. also contains notes, an index of proper names, and an extensive glossary.

Rev.:   .1   Giuseppe di Stefano, *SF*, 56 (1975), 323.

*618   *Il 'Moniage Rainouart' secondo il ms. di Berna*, ed. Paola Bianchi de Vecchi, Collana di Filologia Romanza, 2 (Perugia: Università degli Studi di Perugia, 1980) viii + 286 pp.

619   *Le Moniage Rainouart II et III*, ed. Gerald A. Bertin, SATF (Paris: Picard, 1988) cxxii + 339.

An ed. of the *D* redaction of *MonR*, called by the ed. *MonRII*, with line numbering adapted to *MonRI* to make a synoptic ed. Rejected readings and variants are placed at the foot of each page. A complex system of line-numbering allows for lines interpolated from other MSS.   The introduction deals predominantly with the structure and elaboration of *MonR*, disputing Madeleine Tyssens's view that the poem had dual authorship.   The vol. has no critical or explanatory notes, no glossary or index of proper names.   The title page carries the indication "Tome I";   the second vol. presenting the text of the A redaction has not so far appeared.

Rev.:   .1   Jean Subrenat, *CCM*, 35 (1992), 367–68.

ii) Studies

*620   Lipke, Max, 'Über das Moniage Rainoart (auf Grund der Berner Handschrift)' (Inaugural Dissertation, Universität Halle-Wittemberg, 1904) 84pp.

Rev.:   .1   Wilhelm Cloetta, *ZfSL*, 27, 2 (1904), 22–39.

The review gives a detailed account of Lipke's dissertation (a discussion of the identity of the author-redactor of *MonR*, language and versification, and an index of proper names), concentrating on errors in Lipke's work. It also includes two long passages in which Cloetta discusses the respective roles of Graindor de Brie and Guillaume de Bapaume in the elaboration of *Al*, *BL*, and *MonR*, the relationship between the *vers orphelin* version and the 'vulgate' and modifications designed to introduce *FC*. Cloetta's views are still generally valid. The material on Graindor and Guillaume is a highly condensed version of arguments also published in *Festgabe Adolfo Mussafia*, pp. 255–75 (69).

621   Rossi, Marguerite, 'Rainouart assiégé: un exemple de transposition de motifs épiques traditionnels', in *Guillaume d'Orange III* (1983), pp. 261–90.
A detailed and interesting study of the exploitation of motifs traditionally associated with the siege for new, comic purposes.

622   Suard, François, 'L'originalité littéraire du *Moniage Rainouart*', in *Guillaume d'Orange III* (1983), pp. 291–312.
Considers *MonR* as a worthy conclusion to CycG as a whole, offering comic aspects, but with an underlying seriousness of purpose in the presentation of its main characters.

623   Subrenat, Jean, 'Aspects juridiques et religieux du duel entre Rainouart et Gadifer dans le *Moniage Rainouart I*', in *Guillaume d'Orange III* (1983), pp. 313–34.
A perspicacious analysis of the balance of burlesque fantasy and theological and juridical seriousness in the climactic duel between Rainouart and Gadifer in *MonR*.

624   Tyssens, Madeleine, 'La composition du *Moniage Rainouart*', in *Rencesvals 6* (1974), pp. 585–605 (See 152).

LA MORT AYMERI DE NARBONNE

(i) *Editions and Translations*

625   *La Mort Aymeri de Narbonne*, ed. J. Couraye du Parc, SATF (Paris: Firmin Didot, 1884) 1 + 239 pp.
A brief and no longer adequate introduction is followed by a critical ed. based on *R*; readings are incorporated from other MSS, in which cases spellings are regularized to conform with those of the base MS. Rejected readings and variants are at the foot of each page, but there are no critical or explanatory notes. The glossary and table of proper names both require updating.

626   *La Mort Aymeri de Narbonne*, ed. Paolo Rinoldi (Milan: Edizioni Unicopli, 2000) 546 pp.

The introduction is essentially philological, palaeographic, and codicological. The text is edited from B^I. There are extensive variants, a glossary translating into Italian, and an index of proper names. In many respects this ed. is preferable to the SATF ed., although it cannot fully replace it.

(ii) *Studies*

627   Dubost, Francis, 'L'autre guerrier: l'archer-cheval — du sagittaire du *Roman de Troie* aux sagittaires de la *Mort Aymeri de Narbonne*', in *De l'étranger à l'étrange* (1988), pp. 171–88.
Considers the anthropological and mythological origins of the Centaur, its humanization in *MAN*, and the way its use disrupts the normal binary oppositions of OF epic.

628   Ott, Muriel, 'Les songes d'Aymeri dans la *Mort Aymeri de Narbonne*', in *Mélanges de langue et de littérature françaises du Moyen Âge offerts à Pierre Demarolle*, ed. Charles Brucker (Paris: Champion, 1998), pp. 241–62.
A detailed study of the dreams which open *MAN*, of their interpretation and realization within the fiction, indicates that the diegetic programme they establish for the poem concerns the sub-cycle of Aimeri as a whole, and also delineates a calendrical cycle from solstice to solstice implying a cosmic cycle of death and rebirth, by which the continuity of the civilization founded by Aimeri in Narbonne is assured.

629   Suchier, Hermann, 'Die Grotten von Rochebrune', *ZrPh*, 31 (1907), 607–08.
Identifies the Rochebrune of *MAN* with the grotto of that name in the Dordogne.

LES NARBONNAIS

(i) *Editions and Translations*

630   *Les Narbonnais, chanson de geste*, ed. Hermann Suchier, SATF, 2 vols (Paris: Firmin Didot, 1898) 320 + lxxxvi + 250 pp.
Vol. 1 contains the critical ed. based on *Harley* with rejected readings and variants at the foot of each page. Vol. 2 contains a philological introduction which also deals with various aspects of the legend of Narbonne, a series of appendices giving variant passages of the poem, the texts of chapters 16 and 17 of *RomG* and of the 'Hague Fragment', a glossary, and a table of proper names. Some aspects of the introduction are obsolete, but in general this remains a reliable and informative edition.

Rev.:   .1   Wilhelm Cloetta, *ZrPh*, 27 (1903), 477.

631   Favati, Guido, 'Un ignoto frammento del poema *Les Narbonnais*', in *Omaggio a Camillo Guerrieri Crocetti*, ed. Silvana Medini Damonte (Genova: Fratelli Bozzi, 1971), pp. 493–508.
Describes and presents a fragment found in the guard papers of MS m.r.cf. 2.23 of the Berio Library in Genoa. Previously published in *La Berio: Bolletino Bibliografico Quadrimestrale*, 8 (1968), 12–13 & 18–19, with facsimiles.

632   Hutchings, Gweneth, '*Les Narbonnais* (Fragments of an Assonanced Version)', in *Studies in French Language and Medieval Literature Presented to Professor Mildred K. Pope by Pupils, Colleagues and Friends*, Publications of the University of Manchester, 218 (Manchester: Manchester University Press, 1939), 145–59.
An ed. of two fragments from paste-downs of an assonanced version of *Narb* apparently older than the rhymed version published by Suchier (630). The ed. is naturally conservative, although some rejected readings are given at the foot of each page; the corresponding lines from Suchier's ed. are given for comparison. The article contains a facsimile of one side of one of the fragments. The editor identifies the copy as Anglo-Norman on the basis of orthographic and palaeographic evidence.

(ii) *Studies*

633   Batany, Jean, 'Mythes indo-européens ou mythes des indo-européens? le témoignage médiéval', *Annales ESC*, 40 (1985), 415–22 (See 811).

634   Boutet, Dominique, 'Du mythe à la chanson de geste: le problème de l'ajustement dans les *Narbonnais*', in *Six études sur la chanson de geste*, ed. Jean Dufournet, *RLR*, 91 (1987), 25–35.
The article argues that the incompatibilities between trifunctional ideology identified in *Narb* by Joël Grisward (635) and twelfth-century Christian and feudal ideology account both for the initial illogicalities in the plot and for the way in which Charlemagne, acting as supreme power independent of and superior to the three orders, imposes peace and stability by integrating the Aymerides, representatives of an archaic system, within the new feudal-monarchic order. The argument that the literary history of *Narb* is that of the assimilation of ancestral barbaric forms to modern Christian polity, based on a supposed loss of understanding of the Indo-European ideology between the mid-thirteenth and the early fourteenth centuries, is less convincing.

635   Grisward, Joël-Henri, *Archéologie de l'épopée médiévale. Structures trifonctionnelles et mythes indo-européens dans le cycle des Narbonnais*, Bibliothèque Historique (Paris: Payot, 1981) 341 pp.

An imaginative and minutely documented study based on the anthropological and mythographic theories of Georges Dumézil, which traces the construction of characters in *Narb* back to the Indo-European ideology of the three functions. This important work, which opened a whole new field of research into the OF epic, distinguishes the mythic background of characters from the historico-legendary identities attributed to them. The dynamic structures of the epic are seen as dependent wholly on the former, the latter being more or less decorative.

Rev.:　.1　　Larry S. Crist, *Olifant*, 8 (1980–81), 317–20.
　　　　.2　　Francis Bar, *RLR*, 86 (1982), 307–14.
　　　　.3　　Victoria Cirlot, *Medievalia*, 3 (1982), 171–74.
　　　　.4　　A. Slerca, *SF*, 77 (1982), 315–16.
　　　　.5　　Jean-Claude Rivière, *ZrPh*, 100 (1984), 174–80.
　　　　.6　　M. C. Struyf, *LR*, 38 (1984), 123.

Italian translation: *Archeologia dell'epopea medievale. Strutture trifonzionali e miti indoeuropei nel Ciclo dei Narbonesi* (Genova: ECIG, 1989) 356 pp.

Rev.:　.7　　Massimo Bonafin, *MedRom*, 15 (1990), 170–74.

635a　Dufournet, Jean, '*L'Archéologie de l'épopée médiévale* de J. H. Grisward ou Dumézil au Moyen Âge', *MA*, 89 (1983), 269–80.
A review-article which uses an extended and favourable review of Grisward's book as a launch-pad for some general reflections on the ways in which Dumézil's social anthropology has been received, used, and abused by medievalists.

635b　Gallais, Pierre, 'Les Aymerides et les trois fonctions (à propos d'un ouvrage récent)', *CCM*, 27 (1984), 353–58.
A eulogistic review-article starting from a very positive critique of Grisward's *Archéologie*, which then considers the applicability of Dumézil's and Grisward's ideas to other areas of literary analysis. The article ends with a call for the approach be extended into all areas of medieval studies.

635c　Sergent, Bernard, 'Observations sur l'origine du cycle des Narbonnais', *Rom*, 105 (1984), 462–91.
This is a review-article dealing with Grisward's *Archéologie*, which it claims to admire while disputing essential parts of its argumentation. Against Grisward's scheme of an inheritance of Indo-European trifunctional structures, for which Grisward adduces Indian and Germanic parallels, Sergent proposes Celtic originals for features found in *Narb*. Like many articles of its type its weakness lies in excessive systematization, which glosses over difficult questions of cross-cultural contamination, failing to observe the common mythological and cosmographic heritage of Celts and Germans.

636   Tyssens, Madeleine, 'Le "Siège de Narbonne" assonancé', in *Mélanges Lejeune* (1969), pp. 891–917.
A close comparison of the fragments of *Narb* published by Hutchings (632) with the ed. of Suchier (630) leads to the conclusion that the extant *Narb* is the product of the combination of an older 'Siège de Narbonne' and a poem on the 'Département des Fils Aymeri' that may have been written explicitly to form a prologue to the 'Siège' in the cyclic version.

637   ——, 'Poèmes franco-italiens et *Storie Nerbonesi*. Recherches sur les sources d'Andrea da Barberino', in *Testi, cotesti e contesti del franco-italiano. Atti del 1° Simposio Franco-Italiano (Bad Homburg, 13–16 aprile 1987). In Memoriam Alberto Limentani*, ed. Günter Holtus, Henning Kraus, and Peter Wunderli (Tübingen: Niemeyer, 1989), pp. 307–24.
A consideration of passages in *StNerb* in the light of Joël Grisward's conclusions about the mythic origins of the Narbonnais (635) helps to identify two originally independent poems: 'Le Département des fils Aimeri de Narbonne' and 'Le Siège de Narbonne' (united in *Narb*) as well as guaranteeing the authenticity of the 'Testament de Charlemagne' preserved only in a Franco-Italian poem.

638   Vallecalle, Jean-Claude, 'Un emprunt d'*Anseïs de Carthage* à la chanson des *Narbonnais*', in *Rencesvals 10* (1987), pp. 1057–73.
A detailed study shows that the episode of the appeal of Anseïs for help from Charlemagne is borrowed from the corresponding siege of Narbonne episode of *Narb*. The study also highlights the weaknesses of the *remanieur* responsible for inserting the borrowed material in MS *A* of *Anseïs* (BNF f. fr. 793).

LA PRISE DE CORDRES ET DE SEBILLE

(i) *Editions and Translations*

639   *La Prise de Cordres et de Sebille, chanson de geste du XIIe siècle, publiée d'après le ms. unique de la Bibliothèque Nationale*, ed. Ovide Densusianu, SATF (Paris: Didot, 1896) cl + 194 pp.
The introduction first considers the impact of the Spanish *Reconquista* in the eleventh and twelfth centuries on the formation of CycG, then looks in detail at the MS, versification, date, and dialect of the poem. The ed. is completed by a glossary and an index of proper names.

Rev.: .1   Philipp-August Becker, *ZrPh*, 22 (1897), 417.
       .2   Gaston Paris, *Rom*, 27 (1898), 172.

ii) *Studies*

640   Guidot, Bernard, 'Ingérences romanesques dans la technique narrative de
        la *Prise de Cordres et de Sebille*', in *Études Lanly* (1980), pp. 137–53.
        A descriptive article presenting those aspects (love, increased female role,
        ornamental descriptions, magic, and *peripeteia* introduced to add suspense)
        which indicate the assimilation of epic and romance modes in the thirteenth
        century.

641   Lange, Wolf-Dieter, 'Répétition des motifs et action bipartite.
        Représentation de la réalité dans la *Prise de Cordres et de Sebille*', in
        Rencesvals 4 (1969), pp. 156–65.
        Based rather loosely on the dichotomy of 'Ideal und Wirklichkeit' formulated by
        Erich Köhler in *Ideal und Wirklichkeit in der höfischen Epik: Studien zur Form
        der frühen Artus- und Graldichtung* (Tübingen: Niemeyer, 1956), the paper
        offers a rather summary study of reality in *PCS* to suggest that the poem really
        has a romance structure.

*642   Morneau, K. A., '*La Prise de Cordres et de Sebille*, an epic poem of the
        thirteenth century' (PhD thesis, University of Pennsylvania, 1975), 278
        pp. *DAI*, 36 (1975–76), 8042.
        See *Olifant*, 4 (1976), 110–11.

643   Paris, Gaston, [No title], *Rom*, 27, (1898), 628–29.
        A response to Philipp-August Becker's review of 639, which takes issue with
        Becker, while offering separate criticisms of Densusianu. Cf. Paris's own brief
        review of *PCS* on p. 172 of the same vol. (639.2).

644   Rohde, Max, '*La Prise de Cordres*, Altfranzösisches Volksepos aus der
        Wende des 12. und 13. Jahrhunderts', *RF*, 6 (1891), 57–88.
        An introduction to the poem, giving a plot summary and a study of the phonemics
        of the text seen through its *scripta*. A second part to the article is promised, but
        appears not to have been published.

LA PRISE D'ORANGE

(i) *Editions and Translations*

645   *La Prise d'Orange, according to MS A¹, BN fr. 774, Including Excerpts
        Published for the First Time from MSS B¹, C, D, and Variants from A²,
        A³, A⁴ and B², with an Introduction, Table of Assonances, Glossary and*

Table of Proper Names, ed. Blanche Katz (Morningside Heights, NY: King's Crown Press, 1947) xxxv + 209 pp.
Includes four facsimiles (A^I, ff. 41^v–43^r). The introduction justifies the 'best manuscript' approach to presenting A^I, which is competently edited. The ed. includes excerpts from the other redactions, and variants of the A family. There is also a glossary and an index of proper names. The ed. is now superseded by that of Régnier, *Les Rédactions en vers* (646).

Rev.: .1   Charles Knudson, *RPh*, 3 (1949–50), 73–81.
       .2   M. D. Legge, *MLR*, 44 (1949), 121–22.

646   *Les Rédactions en vers de la Prise d'Orange*, ed. Claude Régnier (Paris: Klincksieck, 1966) 372 pp.
The definitive edition of *PO*, giving critical texts of the three major redactions (AB — from A^I — C and D) plus the 'Siège d'Orange' from *E*. The MS readings are maintained wherever possible; variants and rejected readings are at the foot of each page. The introduction, which deals predominantly with philological and textual matters, also considers the relationships between the different redactions. The ed. is completed by an extensive glossary, an index of proper names, and a thorough bibliography. The title page gives the publication date as 1966, but copyright and *dépôt légal* are noted as 1965. The ed. is printed from Régnier's 1964 thesis.

Rev.: .1   Raymond Arveiller, *Français Moderne*, 36 (1968), 347.
       .2   Giuseppe di Stefano, *SF*, 39 (1969), 522–23.
       .3   Jean-Charles Payen, *MA*, 76 (1970), 323–30; see 671.
       .4   Duncan McMillan, *Rom*, 94 (1973), 117–39.

647   *La Prise d'Orange, chanson de geste de la fin du XIIe siècle, éditée d'après la rédaction AB*, ed. Claude Régnier, Bibliothèque Française et Romane, Série B: Éditions Critiques de Textes, 5 (Paris: Klincksieck, 1967) 158 pp.
Excerpted from Régnier's full ed. (646), with a text based on A^I and giving variants for the other AB MSS. This is an excellent students' text of the 'vulgate' version of *PO*. The 7th ed. (Paris: Klincksieck, 1986) has minor corrections to the text and an updated bibliography.

Rev.: .1   Sam J. Borg, *FR*, 41 (1968), 723–24.
       .2   Frederick Kœnig, *RPh*, 22 (1968-69), 256–57.

648   *La Prise d'Orange: chanson de geste de la fin du XIIe siècle*, ed. Claude Régnier, trans. Claude Lachet and Jean-Pierre Tusseau (Paris: Klincksieck, 1972) 99 pp.
The first ed. of the translation is based on Régnier's 2nd ed.; the second, revised ed. (1974) is based on Régnier's 4th ed. The brief introduction concentrates on the courtly and adventure-story aspects of the poem. The translation follows the

original line by line. There are numerous informative notes and a glossary of technical terms.

ii) *Studies*

649   Andrieux, Nelly, 'Une ville devenue désir: la *Prise d'Orange* et la transformation du motif printanier', in *Mélanges de langue et de littérature médiévales offerts à Alice Planche*, ed. Maurice Accarie and Ambroise Queffelec, Annales de la Faculté des Lettres et Sciences Humaines de Nice, 48 (Paris: Les Belles Lettres, 1984), pp. 21–32.
A semiotic study showing the transfer onto the urban site 'Orange' of motifs previously associated with nature and the countryside (Spring-*raverdie*) and love (the Lady).

650   Bennett, Philip E., 'The Storming of the Other World, the Enamoured Muslim Princess and the Evolution of the Legend of Guillaume d'Orange', in *McMillan Essays* (1984), 1–14.
Postulates that the extant cyclic *PO*, dating from the 1190s, revises an older poem based on the mythological-folklore motif of the hero's conquest of a female spirit of sovereignty by exploiting the 'amorous Saracen princess' motif popularized by poems like *Fierabras* and *Floovent*.

651   Bertoni, G., 'Sur quelques vers du "Siège d'Orange"', *ZfSL*, 33 (1908), 233.
Proposes a few corrections to the readings of the 'Siège d'Orange' published by Fichtner in his study (656). Cf. also 679.

652   Brucker, Charles, 'L'adjectif qualificatif dans les chansons de geste du XIIe siècle: la *Prise d'Orange*', in *Études Lanly* (1980), pp. 37–49.
A brief statistical survey of noun phrases including epithets, illustrating the importance of studying such systems for the rhetorical analysis of epics and other genres, whether or not in the context of oral-formulaic studies.

653   Colby-Hall, Alice, 'Le substrat arlésien de la *Prise d'Orange*', in *Rencesvals 8* (1981), pp. 83–86.
Argues from a literalist reading of archaeological evidence that the extant *PO* must have replaced a lost 'Prise d'Arles'. The case is not compelling in the light of the *Vita Willelmi*.

654   ——, 'Orange et Arles: un royaume pour deux Guillaumes', *Bulletin des Amis d'Orange*, 22 (1981), 13–19.
Designed for a generalist audience, the article looks at the historical background to *PO*, but extrapolates too freely from *StNerb* and other late sources in re-creating the lost original of the poem.

655   Dufournet, Jean, 'La métamorphose d'un héros épique ou Guillaume Fierebrace dans les rédactions A et B de la *Prise d'Orange*', *RLR*, 78 (1968), 17–51.
Studies the presentation of the character of Guillaume, considering him to be largely supplanted as hero by Guielin and subject to a humour deriving from the tension between tradition and innovation. The article is not without factual errors, including a confusion in the chronological relationship between *PO* and *CN*, which is highly oversimplified.

656   Fichtner, Adolf, 'Studien über die *Prise d'Orange* und Prüfung von Weeks' Origin of the *Covenant Vivien*' (doctoral dissertation, Universität Halle-Wittemberg, 1905) 58 pp.
This brief study rejects Weeks's theories on the origins of *ChV* (679) and includes the first ed. of the 'Siège d'Orange' from MS *E*, treated as a lost poem and as source of the episode in *StNerb*.

Rev.: .1   Raymond Weeks, *Rom*, 36 (1907), 309–11.

657   Grunmann-Gaudet, Minette, 'From Epic to Romance: The Paralysis of the Hero in the *Prise d'Orange*', *Olifant*, 7 (1979), 22–38.
A semiological analysis of *PO*, presenting its structures as romance rather than epic.

658   Heinemann, Edward A., 'Some Reflections on the Laisse and on Echo in the Three Versions of the *Prise d'Orange*', *Olifant*, 3 (1975–76), 36–56.

Makes a close factual study of repetitions, predominantly in *laisses* 32–35 of MS A^1 of *PO*, with reference to corresponding passages of MSS *C* and *D*, but does not come to any real conclusions about the nature of their use.

659   ——, 'Toward a History of the Metric Art of the *Chanson de Geste*: Laisse and Echo in the Opening Scene of the Three-Verse Versions of the *Prise d'Orange*', in *Echoes of the Epic*, (1998), pp. 93–114.
A comparison of the lines corresponding to *PO*, AB 39–238 in redactions AB, *C*, and *D* indicates that the move from epic to romance techniques of verse narration is not one of simple linear progression through time, but involves fundamental changes in attitudes to the structure of the epic decasyllabic line.

660   Heintze, Michael, 'L'Amour de loin dans la *Prise d'Orange*', in *Contacts de langue, de civilisations et intertextualité*, ed. Gérard Gouiran, 3 vols (Montpellier: Centre d'Études Occitanes, Université de Montpellier III, 1992), III, 943–55.
This study of the relationship between Guillaume and Orable in *PO* correctly identifies all that the epic poem owes to courtly and other traditions, but treats the

appearance of similar motifs in the poems of Jaufre Rudel as inventions of that poet, thus allowing the gratuitous assertion that *PO* depends directly on the poetry of Jaufre Rudel for its exploitation of *amor de lonh*.

661   Kibler, William W., 'Humor in the *Prise d'Orange*', *Studi di Letteratura Francese*, 3 (1974), 5–25.
A ground-breaking study showing how the revised cyclic version of *PO* exploited epic compositional technique, the portrayal of the hero, and a mixture of themes from epic and romance, all to comic effect.

662   Kindrick, Robert, 'La femme et la guerre dans la *Prise d'Orange* AB', in *Rencesvals 8* (1981), pp. 253–61.
The study links comic features in *PO* both with aristocratic satire of an outmoded genre and with aspects of a supposed class struggle between the aristocracy and the bourgeoisie. Neither argument carries real conviction.

663   Knudson, Charles A., 'Le thème de la princesse sarrasine dans la *Prise d'Orange*', *RPh*, 22 (1968–69), 449–62.
A general study of the theme, designed to show that the author of *PO* distanced Orable / Guibourc from earlier portraits of amorous Saracen princesses in stressing her modesty and by refusing to make her a sorceress.

664   Lachet, Claude, *La 'Prise d'Orange' ou la parodie courtoise d'une épopée*, Nouvelle Bibliothèque du Moyen Âge, 10 (Paris: Champion, 1986) 248 pp.
Studies the use of romance and lyric motifs and language in *PO* from the perspective of comic intent, but views literary evolution as unidirectional, with romance commenting on epic, never the reverse.

Rev.: .1   Jean Dufournet, *RLR*, 90 (1986), 256–60.
      .2   Gilles Roques, *RLiR*, 51 (1987), 280–81.
      .3   Philippe Ménard, *InfLitt*, 40, 3–4 (1988), 61–62.
      .4   Peter Noble, *MAe*, 57 (1988), 128–29.
      .5   Bernard Guidot, *Annales de l'Est*, 5e série, 41(1989), 149–50.
      .6   Alice Colby-Hall, *Olifant*, 15 (1990), 185–88.
      .7   Michael Heintze, *ZrPh*, 109 (1993), 203–07.
      .8   Duncan McMillan, *CCM*, 36 (1993), 190–96.

665   ——, 'Les procédés parodiques dans la *Prise d'Orange*', in *Burlesque et formes parodiques (Actes du colloque de l'Université du Maine, Le Mans: 4–7 décembre, 1986)*, ed. Isabelle Landy-Houillon and Maurice Ménard, Papers on French Seventeenth-Century Literature / Biblio, 17 (Seattle; Tübingen: W. Leiner, 1987), pp. 171–83.

The study offers a very general survey of comic, burlesque, and parodic elements in *PO*, but does not seek to differentiate systematically between the different types of humour.

666   ——, 'Nouvelles recherches sur la *Prise d'Orange*', *RLR*, 91 (1987: *Six études sur la chanson de geste*, ed. Jean Dufournet) 55–80.
The article comprises two short autonomous studies. The first, on *vers similaires*, considers the subtle complexities of verbal echoes in redaction A of *PO*, both in contiguous *laisses* and across wider stretches of the poem, and how they contribute to the parodic effect of the *chanson*; the second argues against Régnier (646) that the sending of the message to Tiébaut after the first capture of the Franks belongs to the archetype of *PO*, before looking briefly at the implications of the modification of this episode in *D* for the psychology of the characters.

667   Luongo, Salvatore, 'Tra periferia e centro del discorso epico: note sulla *Prise d'Orange*', *MedRom*, 15 (1990), 211–34.
The first part of the article offers a critical synopsis of *PO*, emphasizing the mythological and folklore dimensions of the plot and presentation of characters; the second part renews the synopsis, now emphasizing humour and parody and relating these to Bakhtin's ideas on carnival; the third part concludes that the interferences between epic and romance discourse are resolved in favour of the epic, so that potentially comic and disruptive intergeneric dialogism is negated and monologism restored.

668   Macinnes, John W., 'Gloriette: the function of the tower and the name in the *Prise d'Orange*', *Olifant*, 10 (autumn 1982– winter 1985), 24–40.
The article, based on the erroneous premise that because *PO* contains romance features in its plot structure it must reflect a psychological conflict within the hero, posits the name of Gloriette as a catalyst in resolving the poem's tensions. The argument is unfortunately based on a number of misreadings and misinterpretations of the text.

669   McMillan, Duncan, '*La Prise d'Orange* dans le ms. fr. 1448', in *Rencesvals 6* (1974), pp. 543–60.
A detailed study of the construction of the MS and of the text of five episodes of *PO* in MS *D* leads to the conclusion, as gratuitous as Régnier's (673), that the weaknesses of this version of *PO* are due to a scribe making good the lacunae of a badly damaged model.

670   Myers-Ivey, Sharon, 'Repetitive Patterns for Introducing Speech in the Manuscript Tradition of the *Prise d'Orange*', *Olifant*, 8 (1980–81), 51–65.

Studies formulæ describing emotional or mental states in the context of announcements of direct speech in the different redactions of *PO*. The theoretical underpinning is very firmly that of Joseph J. Duggan's interpretation of oral-formulaic theory in *The Song of Roland: Formulaic Style and Poetic Craft* (Berkeley: University of California Press, 1973), so that conclusions about the positions of AB and *E* within literary, cyclic traditions are of limited value.

671   ——, 'A Thematic and Formulaic Study of the Manuscript Tradition of *La Prise d'Orange*' (PhD thesis, University of California, Berkeley, 1982) 298 pp. *DAI*, 43 (1982–83), 2662.
Considers the themes of *PO* in relation to other poems of the cycle, with particular reference to the theme of love, then analyses the formulaic system with special regard to the problematic 'syntactic formula'.

672   Payen, Jean-Charles, 'Considérations sur *La Prise d'Orange*, à propos d'un livre récent (I)', *MA*, 76 (1970), 323–30.
This article begins as a review of Régnier's synoptic ed. (646), with particular attention paid to Redaction *D* and the problems it poses to editor and critic, before extending into general considerations of the place of *PO* in the epic tradition. Its penchant for satire, especially of *amor de lonh*, is noted. Although the article's title includes the indication '(I)', no sequel appears to have been published.

673   Régnier, Claude, '*La Prise d'Orange* dans le manuscrit BN fr. 1448', in *Mélanges Rychner* (1978), pp. 439–47.
The study of several passages in redaction *D* of *PO* leads to the conclusion that it is a 'popular' version, in contrast to the 'aristocratic' version of B, that it is more archaic than the cyclic compilations, and that it bears the hallmarks of oral performance if not of oral composition. The extrapolations of the conclusion are based on entrenched positions in a long-running polemic with McMillan, cf. 669.

*674   Riggs, Elizabeth P., '*La Prise d'Orange* or William in Love: A Study and Translation of an Old French epic of the William Cycle' (PhD thesis, Columbia University, 1971) 156 pp. *DAI*, 34 (1973–74), 7734.
See *Olifant*, 2 (1974–75), 44–45.

675   Schurfranz, Barbara D., 'Strophic Structure versus Alternative Divisions in the *Prise d'Orange*: *Laisses* versus Similar and Parallel Scenes and the *reprise bifurquée*', *RPh*, 33 (1979–80), 247–64.
The article considers the importance of summary passages, based on a re-interpretation of the *vers d'intonation*, and of episodic ring composition in establishing the narrative and poetic structure of *PO*. However, the observation that these repetitive elements are not related to *laisse*-structures is not extended to

consider the implications of the clash or combination of epic and romance modes of composition in *PO*.

676   Tuailon, Gaston, 'L'emploi de la déclinaison dans la *Prise d'Orange*', in *Mélanges Rychner* (1978), pp. 501–18.
300 faults of declension, mostly failures of agreement not affecting the sense of a line, are noticed in *PO* in Régnier's ed. of MS A^1 (647) and studied by category. Although most of these are imputable to scribal error, it is also noted that the author's usage was already tending in the direction of later developments of the language.

677   Tyssens, Madeleine, 'Le "Siège d'Orange" perdu', *Boletín*, 31 (1965–66), 321–29.
Starting from a résumé of the elaboration of the existing CycG from two kernels, as discussed in the author's thesis (22), the article finds a trace of the 'Siège d'Orange' in the survival of Bertrand's nickname 'le timonier' in *PO* MS *E*, reviews allusions to the episode in other poems, and suggests that it was eliminated from CycG because the death of Tiebaut it reported clashed with his role in later poems. The further deduction that the changed role of Vivien in cyclic poems also required the removal of the 'Siège d'Orange' from CycG makes the unsound assumption that the isolated report of Vivien's role in the 'Siège' found in *ChG* belongs to the earliest stratum of the tradition.

678   Weeks, Raymond, 'The Primitive *Prise d'Orange*', *PMLA*, 16 (1901), 361–74.
Weeks's belief in the value of *StNerb* for reconstructing lost versions of OF epics is undermined by the evident dependence of *StNerb* on *CN* and *PO* in extant versions. His reconstruction of a 'lost' *PO* cannibalizing parts of *CN* and *Al* is pure fantasy.

679   ——, 'Concerning Some Lines of the "Siège d'Orange" ', *RR*, 1 (1910), 313–14.
Disagrees with G. Bertoni (651) that Suchier's transcription of *PO* used by Adolf Fichtner in his 'Studien über die *Prise d'Orange*' (656) was careful.

LE ROMAN DE GUILLAUME D'ORANGE EN PROSE

(i) *Editions and Translations*

680   *Die Prosafassung des 'Couronnement de Louis', des 'Charroi de Nîmes', und der 'Prise d'Orange'*, ed. Carl Weber (Halle: Buchdruckerei Hohmann, 1912), 128 pp.

A doctoral dissertation (Halle-Wittenberg). A detailed study of the contents of chapters 29–38 of *RomG* and their relationship to the epic sources. The text is edited from BNF f. fr. 1497, with rejected readings and variants from BNF f. fr. 796 at the foot of each page. There is no glossary.

681 *Le Roman de Guillaume d'Orange*, vol 1, ed. Madeleine Tyssens, Nadine Henrard, and Louis Gemenne, Bibliothèque du XVe Siècle, 62 (Paris: Champion, 2000) xii + 587 pp.
The first volume of what is effectively the *editio princeps* of *RomG* establishes the principles of the ed. and the place of *RomG* in late-medieval literary culture. The text is edited from BNF f. fr 1497.

Rev.: .1   Gilles Roques, *RLiR*, 64 (2000), 607.

682 Castedello, Wilhelm, *Die Prosafassung der 'Bataille Loquifer' und des 'Moniage Renouart'* (Halle-Wittenberg: Buchdruckerei Hohmann (Halle), 1912) 193 pp.
A detailed study of the sources of *RomG* Chaps 94–110 with an attempt to relate elements of the prose version to specific MS families. The text is edited from BNF f. fr. 1497, with rejected readings and variants of BNF f. fr. 796 at the foot of each page. There is no glossary.

683 Reuter, F., *Die Bataille d'Arleschant des altfranzösischen Prosaromans 'Guillaume d'Orange': eine Quellenuntersuchung mit kritischem Text* (Halle: Niemeyer, 1911) 162 pp.
A close study of the sources of the *Al* episode of *RomG* in BNF f. fr. 1497 followed by an ed. of the episode with rejected readings and variants of BNF f. fr 796 at the foot of each page. The transcriptions are not without errors.

Rev.: .1   Raymond Weeks, *RR*, 2 (1911), 462–66.

684 Scherping, W., 'Die Prosafassung des *Aymeri de Narbonne* und der *Narbonnais* (doctoral thesis, Universität Halle-Wittemberg, 1911).
An ed. of extracts from the *RomG*, with a study of sources.

685 Theuring, H., 'Der Prosafassung der *Enfances Guillaume*', *RF*, 29 (1911), 779–925.
An ed. of the *EnfG* section of *RomG*. The introduction is mostly taken up by résumés in German of *EnfG* in MS *C* and the corresponding passage of *RomG* to provide a comparison of their narratives.

(ii) *Studies*

686 Guidot, Bernard, 'Le *Siège de Barbastre* dans le *Guillaume d'Orange en prose*: l'originalité dans l'écart', in *Conformités et Déviances au Moyen Âge: Actes du deuxième colloque international de Montpellier, Université*

Paul-Valéry (25–27 novembre 1993), Les Cahiers du Centre de Recherche Interdisciplinaire sur la Société et l'Imaginaire au Moyen Âge, 2 (Montpellier: Université de Montpellier, 1995), pp. 171–89.
Studies chapters 39–57 of *RomG* to conclude that it is the work of a genuine literary creator.

687   Luongo, Salvatore, 'Il "picolo ciclo" di Guglielmo nel *Roman* in prosa', in *Il Ciclo di Guglielmo d'Orange* (1997), pp. 382–403.
Analyses the way in which *RomG* restructures the three poems, *CL*, *CN*, and *PO*, reduces the burlesque elements in the presentation of both Louis and Guillaume, and integrates epic and romance features to celebrate an idealized chivalric heroism.

688   Schläger, Georg, and Wilhelm Cloetta, 'Die altfranzösische Prosafassung des *Moniage Guillaume*', *Archiv*, 98 (1897), 1–58.
The first part (pp. 1–45) by Schläger is a detailed account of how closely *RomG* follows the cyclic poems, despite much original work by the new author; the second part (pp. 45–58) by Cloetta studies the links of *RomG* with redaction B (Cloetta's *D*) of *MonG* and with *La Chevalerie Ogier le Danois*.

689   Suard, François, *Guillaume d'Orange: étude du roman en prose*, Bibliothèque du XVe Siècle, 44 (Paris: Champion, 1979) xxvi + 661 pp.
A study of the sources of *RomG*, showing that the prose romance derives only from known versions of all the poems exploited, is followed by an illuminating study of the literary techniques of *RomG*, and by a comparison with other fifteenth-century *mises en prose* of *chansons de geste*.

Rev.: .1   William W. Kibler, *Olifant*, 7 (1979–80), 364–70
       .2.   Larry S. Crist, *Speculum*, 55 (1980), 842–45.
       .3   Jean Dufournet, *Rom*, 101 (1980), 410–19.
       .4   Bernard Guidot, *RF*, 93 (1981), 250–55.
       .5   L. Rovero, *SF*, 25 (1981), 335–36.
       .6   Terence Scully, *RR*, 72 (1981), 243–44.
       .7   Roger Dubuis, *RBPH*, 60 (1982), 658–63.
       .8   C. E. Pickford, *CCM*, 25 (1982), 308–09.
       .9   Jean Subrenat, *MA*, 88 (1982), 155–59.
       .10   Jeanne Wathelet-Willem, *MR*, 31 (1982), 110–13.
       .11   R. Aubert, *Revue d'Histoire Ecclésiastique*, 79 (1984), 248.

690   Tyssens, Madeleine, '*Le Roman de Guillaume d'Orange*: étude d'une mise en prose', in *Rencesvals 5* (1977), pp. 45–63.
A brief but important study of the aesthetic merits of the prose version of CycG, a history of critical and editorial approaches to it, and an appreciation of its importance as a witness to the MS tradition of the verse texts.

691   ——, '*Le Roman de Guillaume d'Orange*: trois notes de lecture', in *Mélanges Suard* (1999), pp. 915–26.
Three independent studies, the first of which identifies the rare survival of a decasyllable from *EnfG* in *RomG* and analyses its new context; the second uses lexicographic evidence to reinforce the importance of MS *D* in the stemma of *PO*; the third, and longest, analyses the use made by *RomG* of the designation of Hernaut le Roux, contrary to the poetic tradition, as the eldest of Aymeri's sons.

*692   Weiske, H. [Johannes], *Über die Quellen des altfranzözischen Prosaromans von Guillaume d'Orange* (Halle: Ehrhardt-Karras, 1898).
Argues for lost sources of elements of the *RomG* not known to extant poems.

Rev.:   .1   Anon, *Rom*, 28 (1899) 159–60.

LE SIÈGE DE BARBASTRE

(i) *Editions and Translations*

693   *Le Siège de Barbastre*, ed. J.-L. Perrier, CFMA, 54 (Paris: Champion, 1926) viii + 278 pp.
A brief and inadequate introduction is followed by a critical ed. of the poem from *R*. Rejected readings and variants, misleadingly called 'notes critiques', are inconveniently mixed together. The vol. also contains an index of proper names and a very brief glossary. The ed. is marred by misreadings and typographic errors. It is now replaced by the editions of Muratori (694) and Guidot (695).

694   *Le Siège de Barbastre, canzone di gesta del XIII secolo*, ed. Emilia Muratori, Biblioteca di Filologia Romanza della Facoltà di Lettere e Filosofia dell'Università di Bologna, 9 (Bologna: Pàtron, 1996) 586 pp.
The introduction provides a brief history of editions of and critical work on *SB*, an account of the capture of Barbastro in 1064–65, a description of the MSS, the establishment of a stemma on strictly Lachmannian grounds, a brief assessment of scribal language, and a description of versification. The sigla used for MSS are those adopted by Perrier (693), not those now in common use. MS *P* (= *D*) is surprisingly assigned to the same family as *A* and *B* (= *B¹* and *B²*), with contaminations from the other group. The text is edited from *A* (= *B¹*), and, although the editor claims a conservative approach, corrections are made on the grounds of a majority reading or on the basis of subjective aesthetic judgements. There are extensive variants at the foot of each page, a glossary, an index of proper names, and a bibliography. The introduction and all critical commentary are in Italian.

Rev.:   .1   T. Matsamura, *RLiR*, 64 (2000), 591–97.

695   *Le Siège de Barbastre*, ed. Bernard Guidot, CFMA, 137 (Paris: Champion, 2000) 448 pp.
A sound ed. of the poem based on B^2. The introduction has a brief account of the MSS, an analysis of the linguistic features of the base MS, a lengthy narrative presentation of the content of the poem, and a section dealing with epic technique and inspiration. The ed. is accompanied by variants from B^1, *R*, and *Harley* at the foot of each page, copious explanatory notes, a useful index of proper names, and an extensive glossary.

Rev.: .1   T. Matsamura, *RLiR*, 64 (2000), 591–97.

696   Weeks, Raymond, 'The *Siege de Barbastre*', *RR*, 10 (1919), 287–321; 11 (1920), 349–69; 12 (1921), 57–61.
The three parts of this long article form an ed. of *SB* from MS *D*, in the form of extensive extracts. Linking passages are mostly résumés of the plot, although some involve discussion of poetic technique and especially of the intertextual allusions to *ChG* and other poems of CycG. Part 1 edits ll. 1–776, part 2 ll. 777–1186, and part 3 ll. 1187–1335. See also the *Appendice* in *PCS*, ed. Densusianu (639).

(ii) *Studies*

697   Becker, Philipp-August, 'Der *Siège de Barbastre*', in *Festgabe Gröber* (1899), pp. 252–66.
A plain résumé of the plot of *SB*.

698   Cazanave, Caroline, 'Barbastro/Barbastre ou quand la légende épique s'empare d'un territoire appartenant à l'histoire', in *Le Territoire, études sur l'espace humain: littérature, histoire, civilisation*, Cahiers CRLH-CIRAOI, 3 (Paris: Publications de l'Université de la Réunion; Didier-Érudition, 1986), pp. 31–50.
Shows the symbolic and poetic importance of the fictive geography of *SB*, and particularly the importance of the *Pseudo-Turpin Chronicle* in forming this geography.

699   Colliot, Régine, 'L'étrange et les belles étrangères dans le *Siège de Barbastre*', in *De l'étranger à l'étrange* (1988), pp. 89–107.
Studies animal imagery and other exotica in dreams relating to *belles Sarrasines*, but fails to identify the 'dragon' as the imperial standard, and does not draw the threads of any argument together.

700   Guidot, Bernard, 'L'esprit du chevalier dans le *Siège de Barbastre*', in *Rencesvals 7* (1978), pp. 629–42.

A realist and positivist character analysis of the young knights of *SB*, which treats them as autonomous beings. Although some account is taken of epic convention in relation to the presentation of their attitude to the clan, there is no reference to the play of inter-generic motifs of which their literary *personae* are really constructed.

701 ——, 'Un personnage typique du *Siège de Barbastre*, le païen qui trahit les siens', in *Mélanges de langue et littérature françaises du Moyen Âge offerts à Pierre Jonin*, Senefiance, 7 (Aix-en-Provence: Publications du CUER MA, 1979), pp. 287–304.
The depiction of Clarion de Vaudune as a traitor inspired by motivation typical of the g*este des barons révoltés* is seen as a sign of the psychological enrichment of *SB*, in which the Saracen espousing the Christian cause because his overlord has despoiled him of his fief is portrayed as the returning Prodigal Son.

702 Gundlach, Adolph, *Das Handschriften-Verhältnis des 'Siège de Barbastre'* (Marburg: R. Friedrich, 1883) 32 pp. Also published in Ausgaben und Abhandlungen aus dem Gebiet der Romanischen Philologie, 4 (Marburg: Elwert, 1882), pp. 141–73.
A still valid account of the MS tradition of *SB*.

*703 Keller, Victor, *'Le Siège de Barbastre' und die Bearbeitung von Adenet le Roi* (Marburg, 1875).

704 Micha, Alexandre, '*Le Siège de Barbastre*: structure et technique', *TraLiLi*, 6, 2 (1968), 37–52.
A brief account of the narrative structure of *SB* is followed by an assessment of its themes (clan solidarity, fidelity to the crown, and love) a note of the motifs used (and, as interestingly, of those common in epic which are not found in *SB*), and an appreciation of its handling of *laisses* and formula. There is no conclusion, but the whole tone of the article is to suggest that *SB* is a better poem than has traditionally been thought.

705 Muratori, Emilia, 'L'assedio di Barbastro, prima crociata di Spagna, e la canzone di gesta omonima: occasioni della storia e scarto retorico', *Francofonia*, 8 (1985), 23–35.
SB reflects events of the 'crusade' of 1064, but uses Carolingian heroes to exalt the French nobility, while Barbastro becomes the symbol of the opulent Muslim world to be conquered for Christendom.

706 Nichols, Stephen G., Jr, 'L'intervention de l'auteur dans le *Siège de Barbastre*', *Boletín*, 31 (1965–66), 243–50.

Notes the systematic use of authorial intervention to structure the poem, and the distance this places between audience and characters. The argument that the role of the poet-persona changes from early to late epics is unconvincing, as it does not allow for the interposition of the voice of the *jongleur* between poem and audience.

707   Sullivan, Penny, 'Le *Siège de Barbastre*: la description concrète dans un texte épique', *Olifant*, 8 (1980–81), 367–75.
The study of description in *SB*, which tends to be impressionistic rather than analytic, leads the author to conclude that description is used both to unify the poem and to increase verisimilitude.

708   Vesce, Thomas E., *Feudal and Courtly Values in the 'Siège de Barbastre' and the 'Beuvon de Commarchis'* (Millwood, NY: the author, 1969) 55 pp.
This rather slim study takes a normative view of epic, using *La Chanson de Roland* as the sole benchmark. The presence of romance and courtly features in the poems is considered to be a sign of decadence. *SB* in particular is criticized for a lack of unity, and for introducing female interest in a way that distracts from the epic action.

'LE SIÈGE D'ORANGE' SEE *LA PRISE D'ORANGE*

D. STUDIES OF CHARACTERS, TOPOGRAPHY, AND THEMES

(i) *Characters and Personal Names*

AÏMER LE CHÉTIF

709   van Waard, R., 'Aïmer le chétif', *Neophil*, 25 (1940), 82–88.
The article traces a possible poetic history of Aïmer. This will have started from a gratuitous insertion in a list of kinsmen given by Guillaume to Corsolt in *CL* (Lepage, 422, AB, ll. 820–31), based on memories of Carolingian chronicles, a process which will have been repeated independently by *Al*. The culminating point is given as the poem cited by Aubry des Trois Fontaines, which van Waard sees as a late work exploiting *PO* as well as *CL* to create the character and career of Aïmer.

710   Weeks, Raymond, 'Aïmer le chétif', *PMLA*, 17 (1902), 411–34.

This study of the legend of Aïmer still has some useful material, but the general argument concerning the antiquity of the story, and of essential details from it, is vitiated by Weeks's habitual belief that *StNerb* preserves older material than any of the OF poems, which is probably true only of *Narb* (see 635 & 637); his view that *ChV* is a poem with a long pre-history is equally mistaken. Weeks was further hampered in writing this article by lack of knowledge of the still unpublished *ChG*.

AIMERI DE NARBONNE

711 Grisward, Joël-Henri, '*Aymeri de Narbonne* ou la royauté masquée', in *Farai chansoneta novele* (1989), pp. 199–210.
The article revisits an element of the author's *Archéologie* (635), using comparisons with Irish, Indian, and Persian texts to reinforce the argument that Aimeri de Narbonne fulfils the role of supreme king in the trifunctional system elaborated by Georges Dumézil.

712 Lejeune, Rita, 'La question de l'historicité du héros épique Aimeri de Narbonne', in *Mélanges offerts à Edouard Perroy*, Études, 5 (Paris: Publications de la Sorbonne, 1973), pp. 50–62.
An anthroponymic study identifying the epic Aimeri de Narbonne with the Carolingian Count Haimric, about whom Occitan legends would have grown, producing a number of bishops, and later viscounts of Narbonne bearing the same name. The exploits of these viscounts would have rekindled interest in the epic legends among French speakers in the twelfth century. The argument is persuasive.

713 Paris, Gaston, 'Naimeri — n' Aymeric', in *Mélanges Léonce Couture* (Toulouse: Privat, 1902), pp. 349–57.
Demonstrates the widespread use of the Provençal form with the noble prefix (*e*)*n* in French and Spanish references to Aimeri de Narbonne, without concluding that lost Occitan epics must have existed; Paris is content to deduce that Aimeri's origins as an Occitan hero were recognized in other regions.

LES AIMERIDES

714 Pastré, Jean-Marc, 'Le thème des Aymerides dans le *Willehalm* de Wolfram von Eschenbach', in *Mélanges Fourquet* (1999), pp. 355–65.
Beginning from Grisward's tri-functional reading of *Narb* (635), the article shows that Wolfram's handling of the essential characteristics of the Narbonnais clan and his re-organization of the group of seven brothers to emphasize the theme of the warrior in his poem reveals a knowledge of many poems of CycG

beyond his main source, *Al*. His modifications confirm the interpretation of the brothers' roles given by Grisward.

ESTOURMI

715   Longnon, A., 'Estourmi de Bourges', *Rom*, 33 (1904), 93–94.
Identifies Estourmi from *ChG* with the Carolingian count Sturminus. The loss of final *-n* would indicate an Occitan source for the character.

716   Lot, Ferdinand, 'Estormi de Bourges', *NM*, 32 (1931), 246–47.
Considers that the Sturminus recorded as count of Bourges *ca* AD 780 is to be identified with the Sturmion who was count of Narbonne from AD 791 to 800. Lot suggests that this transfer may account for the apparent proximity of Bourges to L'Archamp in *ChG*.

GARIN D'ANSEÜNE

717   Lauer, Philippe, 'Garin d'Anseüne et l'oppidum d'Ensérune', *Rom*, 69 (1946), 112–14.
Confirms the identification of the epic Anseüne with the Celtic *oppidum* of Ensérune, called Anseduna in Latin. The site remained fortified until the Wars of Religion in the sixteenth century.

GIRART DE VIENNE

718   Gaiffier, Baudouin de, 'Hagiographie bourguignonne: à propos de la thèse de doctorat de M. René Louis', *Analecta Bollandiana*, 69 (1951), 139–47.
Offers some minor corrections to the hagiographic section of Louis's *Girart, comte de Vienne* (719).

719   Louis, René, *De l'histoire à la légende*. I. *Girart, comte de Vienne, 819–877 et ses fondations monastiques*; II–III. *Girart, comte de Vienne dans les chansons de geste: Girart de Vienne, Girart de Fraite, Girart de Roussillon*, 3 vols (Auxerre: Imprimerie Moderne, 1946–47) 244 + 416 + 355 pp.
A detailed and wide-ranging study of the historical archetype of the epic heroes Girard de Roussillon, Girard de Fraite and Girart de Vienne. It also considers the literary evolution of the three legends from one archetype. Despite much solid factual research some of the argumentation is based on speculation and conjecture. Notwithstanding these shortcomings it remains essential reading as

the standard study of the problems surrounding the multiplex development of the character of Girart.

Rev.: .1   G. Drioux, *Revue d'Histoire Ecclésiastique* (1948), 123–26.
     .2   Edmond Faral, *Journal des Savants* (1948), 5–15.
     .3   J. Laurent, *Annales de Bourgogne* (1948), 42–58.
     .4   C. Margueron, *CN*, 8 (1948), 288–90.
     .5   Georges Tessier, *Revue d'Histoire de l'Église de France* (1948), 123–26.
     .6   Anon., *Neophil*, 33 (1949), 186.
     .7   Raymonde Foreville, *Revue du Moyen Âge Latin*, 5 (1949), 159–62.
     .8   G. Le Bras, *Revue d'Histoire de Droit Français et Étranger*, 4e sér., 27 (1949), 592.
     .9   L. Levillain, *MA* (1949), 225–45.
     .10   Ferdinand Lot, *Rom* (1949), 192–233 & 355–96.
     .11   J. Perret, *Revue des Sciences Humaines*, ns 16 (1949), 129–32.
     .12. Robert Guiette, *RBPH*, 28 (1950), 555–68.
     .13   Rita Lejeune, *MA*, 4ᵉ sér. 5 (1950), 1–28.
     .14   Clovis Brunel and Jean-François Lemarignier, *BEC*, 109 (1951), 311–18.
     .15   André Burger, *Bibliothèque d'Humanisme et Renaissance*, 10 (1951), 205–14.
     .16   Georges Gougenheim, *Annales ESC*, 6 (1951), 406–08.
     .17   Paul Zumthor, *ZrPh*, 67 (1951), 384–88.

719a Calmette, J., and Henri David, 'De l'historique Girart de Vienne au légendaire Girart de Roussillon: à propos d'une thèse récente', *Annales du Midi*, 62 (1950), 259–77.

Beginning as a positive critique of both Joseph Bédier's and Ferdinand Lot's often conflicting views of epic origins and development, this review-article, almost all of which is by Henri David, gives a commented résumé of René Louis's book, with criticisms mostly drawn from the extended review of Ferdinand Lot (719.10), of which David is careful to approve. Joseph Calmette adds a brief note at the end criticizing Louis's treatment of the translation of Count Bégon, Girart's father, from Catalonia to Paris. The cause of this concerted attack is the perceived lack of deference shown to the ideas of his academic elders and betters by René Louis, whose youth and inexperience is repeatedly stressed.

GUIBOURC (SEE ALSO ORABLE)

720   Brach-Pirotton, Nicole, 'Guibourc, sœur de Rainouart', in *Mélanges Lods* (1978), pp. 88–94.
Following the study by McMillan (750) the suggestion is made that in *G2*, and thus in *Al*, Rainouart and Guibourc are half-siblings on the mother's side, only the former being the child of Desramé. The argument *ex silencio* is not totally convincing, especially since the triangular relationship Orable-Rainouart-Desramé is known in several cyclic poems, while Oriabel, Rainouart's mother, appears to be an invention of the poet of *G2*.

721   Kloocke, Kurt, 'Giburg.   Zur altfranzösischen *Wilhelmsepik* und Wolframs *Willehalm*', in *'Getempert und gemischet' für Wolfgang Mohr zum 65. Geburtstag von seinen Tübinger Schülern*, ed. Franz Hundsnurcher and Ulrich Müller, Göppinger Arbeiten zur Germanistik, 64 (Göppingen: Kümmerle-Verlag, 1972) pp. 121–46.
Suggests that the first part of *G1* presupposes an earlier poem in which Guibourc had a genuinely heroic role. There is a continuous evolution of Guibourc towards the courtly in later poems, with an increasing absorption of her into the Saracen world and, especially in the German poems, an emphasis on her sainthood. While *ChG* exploits traditional motifs to sketch a figure, Wolfram develops a full artistic portrait.

722   de Kok, Bertha Louise, *Guibourc et quelques autres figures de femmes dans les plus anciennes chansons de geste* (Paris: PUF, 1926) 189 pp.
Originally a thesis for the University of Amsterdam, the study offers a series of very brief remarks about women as wives, mothers etc. in a number of poems from CycG (Guibourc, Hermenjart, Aëlis) and elsewhere.

723   Rocher, Daniel, 'Guibourc, de la *Chanson de Guillaume* au *Willehalm* de Wolfram', in *Guillaume et Willehalm* (1985), pp. 125–44.
Postulating that *ChG* in its extant form is anterior in its entirety to *Al*, the paper traces the evolution of Guibourc across the poems from social to moral then to spiritual force. This is seen as a simple linear development.

GUILLAUME (D'ORANGE, AU CORT NEZ, AU CORB NEZ, FIEREBRACE; ST GUILLAUME DE GELLONE)

724   Becker, Philipp-August, *Die altfranzösische Wilhelmsage und ihre Beziehung zu Wilhelm der Heiligen, Studien über das Epos vom Moniage Guillaume* (Halle: Niemeyer, 1896) 175 pp.

A narrative overview of the life of William of Toulouse, followed by an account of the development of his legend from Ermoldus Nigellus to the cyclic poems. *MonG* is related to the history of Gellone and Aniane, to the other cyclic poems, and to foreign adaptations. Becker maintains the view, refuted by Tyssens (22), that *MonG1* is the original version, dating from 1150s.

Rev.: .1   Gaston Paris, *Rom*, 25 (1896) 384–89.

725   Bennett, Philip E., 'Guillaume d'Orange: Fighter of Demons and Harrower of Hell', in *Myth and Legend in French Literature: Essays in Honour of A. J. Steele*, ed. Keith Aspley, David Bellos, and Peter Sharratt, Publications of the Modern Humanities Research Association, 11 (London: Modern Humanities Research Association, 1982), pp. 24–46.
Studies the role of christological figuration in the elaboration of the legend of Guillaume d'Orange, and its survival in the fourteenth-century Franco-Italian *Huon d'Auvergne*.

726   Colby-Hall, Alice, 'L'héraldique au service de la linguistique: le cas du "cor nier" de Guillaume', in *Rencesvals 10* (1987), pp. 383–98.
Working back from the fourteenth-century *Roman d'Arles*, the author posits an early epithet for Guillaume in Occitan: *al cor nier* ("with the black huntinghorn"). Most evidence comes from late heraldry (fourteenth and fifteenth centuries). None of the author's evidence points to the use of this epithet before the mid-thirteenth century.

727   ——, 'In Search of the Lost Epics of the Lower Rhône Valley', in *Romance Epic* (1987), pp. 115–27.
Posits a lost Occitan original for *PO*, and returns to the author's insistence that the original epithet for Guillaume was *al cornet*, this places undue weight on the evidence of *StNerb* while ignoring evidence from the 'Nota Emilianense', which knows Guillaume as alcorbitunas. The illustration published with the article of two seals belonging to successive princes of Orange (one with a horn, one with a star) undermines the case for the importance of the supposed family or local tradition about Guillaume's diminutive horn.

728   ——, 'From *curb niés* to *cor nier*: The Linguistic Metamorphoses of William's Epic Nose', in *The Tenth Lacus Forum 1983*, ed. Alan Manning, Pierre Martin, and Kim McCalla (Columbia, SC: Hornbeam Press, 1984).
This study of the various linguistic forms of Guillaume's sobriquet (*al curb n(i)es, al curt nes, al cor nier*) in French, Occitan and Franco-Italian texts from the twelfth to fourteenth century, insists, unlike later studies by the same author (729 & 730), on the priority of the form *al curb nes*. Unfortunately the

concluding suggestion that the sobriquet has Occitan origins is derived through a complex series of unsupported suppositions from the spelling 'nies' of the Anglo-Norman MS of *ChG*.

729   ——, 'Saint Guillaume de Gellone et Saint Bénézet: le témoignage de Gervais de Tilbury', *Mémoires de l'Académie de Vaucluse*, 7e série, 7 (1986–87), 61–70.
A contribution to the historical background of *MonG*.

730   ——, 'Guillaume d'Orange sur un nouveau sceau médiéval de l'abbaye de Saint-Guilhem-le-Désert', *Olifant*, 15 (1990), 3–13.
Presents a mid-thirteenth-century seal from St-Guilhem-le-Désert showing a knight carrying a horn. The conclusions the author derives from this concerning primitive iconic attributes of Guillaume d'Orange fail to distinguish late witnesses and early traditions in establishing the hero's legend.

731   ——, 'Guillaume au Court Nez et les premiers historiens d'Orange', in *Keller Studies* (1993), pp. 151–64.
An account of the sources of sixteenth- and seventeenth-century historians of the city and house of Orange. The authenticity of the sobriquet 'Guillaume au Cornet' is taken for granted with no investigation of the date of its appearance.

732   Hannedouche, Simone, 'A propos de Guillaume d'Orange', *Cahiers d'Études Cathares*, 26 (1975), 39–45.
Deals, very unscientifically, with the associations that Wolfram von Eschenbach establishes between Guillaume d'Orange and the Grail legend.

733   Huby-Marly, Marie-Noël, 'Les personnages de Guillaume et de Willehalm', in *Guillaume et Willehalm* (1985), pp. 31–47.
Although Wolfram remains in many respects faithful to the portrait of Guillaume he found in *Al*, this study shows how he turns his hero into a model of courtly chivalry, which diminishes much of his immediate impact as a character.

734   Hüe, Denis, 'Brèves remarques sur l'écu de Guillaume', in *De l'aventure épique à l'aventure romanesque: hommage à André de Mandach*, ed. Jacques Chocheyras (New York: Peter Lang, 1997), pp. 115–33.
A study of the shield which Guillaume captures from Aarofle in *Al*, and which is later destroyed in an enigmatic fire in the abbey where it was deposited, leads to the suitably hesitant conclusion that the shield symbolized a step on the hero's road from secular warrior to hermit-saint. Comparisons are made to the handling of shields in similar episodes of *La Mort le roi Artu* (Lancelot's shield left at Escalot) and the *Continuation de Perceval* by Gerbert de Montrueil (the shield of

Le Chevalier au Dragon). The author rejects the view that there is a possible allusion to the arms of the Plantagenets in the presentation of Guillaume's shield.

735   Infurna, Marco, 'Guillaume d'Orange o "le chevalier au déguisement": il motivo del travestimento nel ciclo di Guillaume', *MedRom*, 10 (1985), 349–69.
      After invoking structural semiotics to establish Guillaume's essential role as defender of the realm and conquistador in pagan lands in *CL*, the article argues that *CN*, *PO*, and *MonG* are merely variations on the themes established in *CL*. An appeal is made to the thought of Bakhtin (in which there is a confusion between carnival and dialogism). The final thesis of the article is that disguise threatens to suppress the real function of the hero, a threat he has to overcome. It is odd that Guillaume is considered to be merely disguised as a monk in *MonG*.

736   Lejeune, Rita, 'La naissance du couple littéraire "Guillaume d'Orange" et "Rainouart au Tinel"', *MR*, 20 (1970: *Hommage des romanistes liégeois à la mémoire de Ramon Menéndez Pidal*), 39–60.
      Onomastic studies of entries in cartularies suggest that the name Rainouart belongs to south-eastern France, and leads the author to conclude that the 'Chanson de Rainoart' must originally have been in Occitan.

737   Mölk, Ulrich, 'Ein Buch für den lebenden und ein Gedicht auf den verstorbenen Wilhelm, Mönch in Gellone', in *Mittelalterstudien* (1984), 218–28.
      Studies two Latin texts. The first, written for St William of Gellone during his lifetime, praises his asceticism in its prologue; the second is an early-ninth-century eulogy of a nobleman, which Mölk deduces from its content to be about Count William of Toulouse. The article includes two photographs of the MS sources.

738   Press, Alan R., 'More Light on William's Lethal Punch', *FMLS*, 22 (1986), 263–72.
      Starting from a consideration of Guillaume's epic punch, as reported initially in *CL*, the article analyses the elements of the *Carmen in honorem Ludovici Pii* by Ermoldus Nigellus, which already show signs of knowing what amounts to a popular legend of Guillaume as an epic character in the 820s. The arguments advanced in favour of Ermoldus's exploiting pre-existing stories rather than inventing his own version of Guillaume's deeds are convincing.

739   Saxer, Victor, 'Le culte et la légende hagiographique de Saint Guillaume de Gellone', in *Mélanges Louis* (1982), pp. 565–89.

The article is concerned almost exclusively with liturgical and hagiographic documents referring to St Guillaume de Gellone, but includes a few comments on the exploitation of the epic legend of Guillaume by hagiographers.

740   Soutou, André, 'Le vrai emblème de saint Guilhem: le cor noir, et non le court nez ou le nez courbe', *RLR*, 100 (1996), 131–34.
Proposes that the horn predates any reference to William's nose, but wrongly has references to 'cort nez' predating those to 'corb nes' and generalizes from confusions in chronology.

741   Suard, François, 'Guillaume d'Orange dans la *Chronique de France jusqu'en 1380* (MSS BN fr, 5003 et Vatican Reg. Lat. 749)', *Rom*, 99 (1978), 363–88.
An ed. of six episodes of the *Chronique* dealing with Guillaume d'Orange and Aimeri de Narbonne. The study of the episodes both allows a close dating of the *Chronique* to 1450–76, and indicates that the author consciously melded epic and historiographic material to produce his new version of French history.

742   van Waard, R., 'La postérité de saint Guilhem et la formation de sa légende', *Neophil*, 31 (1947), 153–61.
Traces references in Ermoldus Nigellus and other Carolingian writers to demonstrate that the origins of the epic legend of Guillaume and his family do date from his own life time or soon after. The critique of Bédier's view that no legend of Guillaume existed before the end of the eleventh century, as expressed in *Les Légendes épiques*, I (56), is judicious and accurate.

743   Wathelet-Willem, Jeanne, 'La pénétration en Italie de la légende de Guillaume vue à travers l'onomastique', *CN*, 21 (1961), 155–63.
Onomastic evidence, which the author admits to being very fragile in this case, suggests that poems of CycG, in a form that it is impossible to determine, may have been known in Italy from the early twelfth century.

744   ——, 'Charlemagne et Guillaume', *Rencesvals 7* (1978), pp. 215–22.
While CycG makes Guillaume the moral heir of Charlemagne, it constantly misrepresents chronology and historical relationships to have him serve Louis. This may have been caused partly by a memory that he served Louis as King of Aquitaine, partly by the rise of Roland as the main hero of the *geste du roi*. A significant synthesis of individualism and traditionalism leads to extant poems being ascribed to a succession of poets without clerical collaboration.

HERNAUT / HERNAÏS

745   Gemenne, L., 'Comment Hernaut de Gironde devint-il Hernaïs d'Orléans?', in *Rencesvals 11* (1990), I, pp. 275–90.
A close study of allusions to the usurper from the first episode of *CL* in later literature leads to the conclusion that his original name was Hernaut d'Orléans, that he became confused with Guillaume's brother, Hernaut de Gironde, because of the identity of their names, and that the name Hernaïs was introduced through contamination with a character in the Lorraine Cycle. The influence of a lost twelfth-century poem 'Arnaïz d'Orléans' is also posited, without a proper source for the name in that poem being identified.

MAUDUIT

746   Barnett, Monica J., 'Mauduit de Rames', *MAe*, 46 (1977), 35–40.
A study of allusions to Mauduit's relationship to Anfelise indicates that the author of *BL* must have known a version of *FC* earlier than the currently extant one.

747   Kunitzsch, Paul, 'Noch einmal: Mauduit de Rames. Bemerkungen zur Echtheit Sarazenennamen in der mittelalterlichen europäischen Literatur', *GRM*, 61; ns, 30 (1980), 350–54.
Using Mauduit as an example, the article argues that Saracen names in epics are not fantastic, but forms known in the West of genuine Muslim names, and that the business of scholars is not to explore the symbolic resonances of such epic names, but to trace the texts from which the original was borrowed in order to establish a *terminus a quo* for the poem in which the name appears.

ORABLE (SEE ALSO GUIBOURC)

748   Latrouitte-Armstrong, Christine, 'D'Orable à Guibourc, ou l'évolution guidée de l'adorable supplément: une étude onomastique de l'héroïne de la *Prise d'Orange*', in *Mélanges Fourquet* (1999), pp. 301–12.
A reading of *PO*, mixing feminist and deconstructionist approaches to demonstrate that Orable-Guibourc remains a threatening and unassimilable presence in the patriarchal society of the epic. An inherent weakness of the approach is the failure to take account of chronology, either in the cyclic development of the poems or in the history of French vocabulary, an appeal being made to the connotations of the lemma |orange| which would have been unavailable to a twelfth-century audience.

749   Luongo, Salvatore, 'La femme magicienne: Orable tra epopea e folclore', in *Rencesvals 12* (1993), pp. 345–59.
Studies the figure of Orable in *ChG*, *EnfG*, and *PO*. The extrapolation from Guibourc back to Orable in *ChG* is based on the allusion to Guibourc's powers as a magician by Blanchfleur (ll. 2591–94).

750   McMillan, Duncan, 'Orable fille de Desramé', in *Mélanges Lejeune* (1969), pp. 829–54.
The study attributes the formation of the clan of Desramé in *Al* to later redactors keen to elaborate the role of Rainouart as a popular folkloric hero. The author also suggests, as an aside, that *ChV* may have existed independently of its function as a prologue to *Al*. The main weakness of the article is its failure to take account of the fact that Rainouart and Guibourc are brother and sister in both *Al* and *ChG*, a relationship which must therefore date back to the 'Chanson de Rainouart', and that in both poems it is the evocation of the name of Desramé that causes Guibourc to acknowledge Rainouart as her brother.

PICOLET

*751   Delbouille, Maurice, 'Les origines du lutin Pâcolet', *Bulletin de la Société de Langue et Littérature Wallonnes*, 69 (1953), 131–44.

RAINOUART

752   Barnett, Monica J., 'Renoart au Tinel and Ogier de Danemarche: A Case of Contamination', *MAe*, 40 (1971), 1–5.
Suggests that the episode of the hero's encounter with Morgain la Fée in Avalon originated in *BL* before being applied to Ogier.

753   Beckmann, Gustav Adolf, 'Das Beispiel Renewart: Geschichte und Folklore als Inspirationsquelle der altfranzösischen Epik', *Romanistisches Jahrbuch*, 22 (1971), 53–83.
Sees the historical elements in *G2* and *Al* as more important than folktale as a source of these poems. Folktale may influence the way the epic developed, but the author considers the story of Rainouart to have influenced 'fairy stories' such as *Starke Hans* of the Bothers Grimm, rather than to have derived from such tales.

754   Bennett, Philip E., 'Havelok and Rainoart', *Folklore*, 90 (1979), 77–99.
A comparison of the various versions of the Havelok legend in English and French with the Rainouart material of *ChG* and *Al* suggests an influence of the

latter on the French *Lai d'Haveloc* unknown either to the medieval or the modern English variants.

755   Evers, Hélène M., 'Notes on Rainouart', *RR*, 2 (1911), 144–62.
        Attempts to trace the development of the legend of Rainouart from two folktales through its various literary manifestations, including *StNerb* and the *Willehalm* of Wolfram von Eschenbach. The sociological explanation of epic evolution, presupposing a downwards displacement of epic by the adoption in aristocratic circles of the romance, is no longer widely accepted.

756   Grisward, Joël-Henri, 'La naissance du couple littéraire Vivien et Rainouart', in *Il Ciclo di Guglielmo d'Orange* (1997), pp. 441–56. See 773.

757   Guidot, Bernard, 'Un éminent protagoniste d'*Aliscans*: le tinel de Rainouart', in *Burlesque et dérision* (1995), pp. 133–50.
        The article shows that the close association between Rainouart and his *tinel*, which, like its owner, is also closely associated with fire, allows an element of the sublime to temper the comic in the portrayal of this couple of protagonists. Guidot argues that this tends to negate the normal associations of clubs with base characters, reducing the potential for burlesque and parody in the poem.

758   Herman, Gerald, 'Rainouart au Tinel and the Rustic Hero Tradition in *Baudouin de Sebourc*', *RoNo*, 16 (1974–75), 415–21.
        Although certain parallels are adduced between Rainouart, Baudouin de Sebourc and the Povre-Pourveü, another character in *Baudouin de Sebourc*, no unequivocal case is made for Rainouart as the direct source of these characters. It is clear from the author's own evidence that other gigantic characters from CycG and elsewhere share similar characteristics.

759   Lejeune, Rita, 'La naissance du couple littéraire "Guillaume d'Orange" et "Rainouart au Tinel"', *MR*, 20 (1970: *Hommage des romanistes liégeois à la mémoire de Ramon Menéndez Pidal*), 39–60. See 736.

760   Martin, Jean-Pierre, 'Le personnage de Rainouart entre épopée et carnaval', in *Comprendre et aimer* (1994), pp. 63–86.
        This study of the character of Rainouart, which extends to all poems in which he appears, considers him as a carnivalesque reflex of Guillaume who is presented as a purely heroic character.

761   Moisan, André, 'Du "tinel" à l'épée ou le lent apprentissage du métier des armes chez "Rainouart au tinel"', in *Le Geste et les gestes de table au Moyen Âge*, Senefiance, 41 (Aix-en-Provence: Publications du CUER MA, Université de Provence, 1998), pp. 626.

The article seeks to show how Rainouart and his *tinel*, originally two facets of one indissociable folklore persona, evolve so that Rainouart is humanized and ennobled by his contact with the members of the Narbonnais clan.

762   Pastré, Jean-Marc, 'Rainouart et Rennewart: un guerrier aux cuisines', in *Burlesque et dérision* (1995), pp. 123–31.
The study is firmly founded on the social anthropological and mythographic theories of Georges Dumézil, and while demonstrating that Rainouart is essentially to be attributed as a warrior to the second function, his association with the kitchen also gives him characteristics of the third function.

763   Walter, Philippe, 'Rainouart et le marteau-tonneau: essai de mythologie épique et pantagruélique', *InfLitt*, 46 (1994), 3–14.
The article casts doubts on the applicability of Rita Lejeune's historical research (736) to Rainouart as a character in *Al*. The author prefers to exploit Indo-European mythology, and defines Rainouart's *tinel* as a barrel, thus identifying the character with a Greco-Celtic psychopomp.

764   Wathelet-Willem, Jeanne, 'Quelle est l'origine du tinel de Rainouart?', *Boletín*, 31 (1965–66), 355–64.
A seminal article for identifying Rainouart's *tinel* with a yoke for carrying barrels (the meaning derived by metonymy), and noting a steady upward movement in the presentation of Rainouart in *Al* from his burlesque association with the kitchen to a sublime status as warrior, his yoke achieving full chivalric symbolism.

765   ——, 'La femme de Rainouart', in *Mélanges Frappier* (1970), pp. 1103–18.
Speculates on possible historical prototypes for the two different names of Rainouart's wife in different poems of CycG.

766   ——, 'Le personnage de Rainouart dans la *Chanson de Guillaume* et dans *Aliscans*', in *Rencesvals 4* (1969), pp. 166–78.
A comparative study of the presentation of Rainouart and his *tinel* in *ChG* and *Al*, concluding that the former is closer to the lost original, since it treats Rainouart as a character new to the audience, while *Al* presupposes audience knowledge. The author also defends the literary quality of *ChG* against *Al* and raises objections to the opinions of Rychner (316) and Becker (51).

767   ——, 'Les parents de Rainouart', *MA*, 83 (1977), 53–70.
Considers the relationships between *ChG*, *Al*, and their lost source(s) in the light of the presentation of Rainouart's kin.

768   ——, 'Rainouart et son cycle', in, *Mittelalterstudien* (1984), pp. 288–300.

Studies the evolution of Rainouart from *G2* through the cyclic poems, noting that his gigantic and comic traits become more marked with time, and that his origins may have been serious. Also suggests that *BL* and the 'Gadifer' episode of *MonR* may be pastiches of both epic and romance.

769   Williamson, Joan B., 'Le personnage de Rainouart dans la *Chanson de Guillaume*', in *Guillaume et Willehalm* (1985), 159–71.
Rainouart is seen as an ambiguous character, innocent and wild, predestined as saviour of the Christian cause.

VIVIEN

770   Adler, Adolf, 'A propos de l'article de M. K. Urwin "La mort de Vivien et la genèse des chansons de geste" (*Rom*, LXXXVIII [*sic*], 1957, p. 392–404)', *Rom*, 79 (1958), 129–30.
Uses a phrase of St Bernard, applied strictly to the Order of the Temple, to suggest that all Crusaders could be considered monks and knights at the same time, and thus to explain Guillaume's giving communion to Vivien.

771   Greenfield, John T., 'Vivien und Vivianz', in *Chansons de geste in Deutschland, Schweinfurter Kolloquium 1988*, ed. Joachim Heinzle, L. Peter Johnson, and Gizela Vollmann-Profe, Wolfram-Studien, 11 (Berlin: Erich Schmidt Verlag, 1989), pp. 47–64.
After a summary of scholarship on Vivien, *ChG*, *ChV*, and *Al* are analysed to show an increasing emphasis on both Vivien's martyrdom and his youth, but the author seems to misunderstand the technical sense of *enfant* in *ChV*. The final part of the article studies the development of the martyrdom theme in Wolfram.

772   ——, *Vivianz: An Analysis of the Martyr Figure in Wolfram von Eschenbach's 'Willehalm' and his Old French Source Material*, Erlanger Studien, 95 (Erlangen: Palm und Enke, 1991) 263 pp.
A study of the evolving biography of Vivien as martyr in *ChG*, *ChV*, and *Al*, followed by a comparative study of the presentation of Vivien in *Al* and in Wolfram's *Willehalm*.

773   Grisward, Joël-Henri, 'La naissance du couple littéraire Vivien et Rainouart', in *Il Ciclo di Guglielmo d'Orange* (1997), pp. 441–56.
An analysis, adopting the author's usual method based on the work of George Dumézil, which seeks to demonstrate that Vivien and Rainouart are the two necessary and indissociable components of the second (warrior) function: Vivien representing the 'warrior of Oðin' through his asceticism, his wisdom, and his

role as sacrificial victim, Rainouart being the more rumbustuously humorous 'warrior of Þor'.

774   Jeanroy, Alfred, 'Etudes sur le cycle de Guillaume au court nez, III: Notes sur la légende de Vivien', *Rom*, 26 (1897), 175–207.
An analysis of the legend of Vivien and a consideration of the relationships between *EnfV*, *ChV*, and *Al*, which makes some points that are still of interest. The main weakness comes from a lack of knowledge of the still undiscovered *ChG*.

775   Legros, Huguette, 'De Vivien à Aiol: de la sainteté du martyre à la sainteté commune', in *Rencesvals 9* (1984), pp. 931–48.
A comparison of the careers of Vivien and Aiol reveals the evolution of thought from St Bernard to St Francis as well as changes in crusading mentality and the increasing importance of urban culture.

776   Lejeune, Rita, 'Le nom de Vivien, héros épique: étude anthroponymique', in *Symposium Riquer* (1984), pp. 115–36.
The study, which begins by stressing the linguistic and textual difficulties posed by the name of Vivien in the different poems of CycG, emphasizes the importance of St Vivian of Saintes for the popularity of the name. Lejeune considers it probable from onomastic evidence that the epic couple Guillaume and Vivien emerged in the later eleventh century in southern Poitou and the Bordelais.

777   Lot, Ferdinand, 'Vivien et Larchamp', *Rom*, 35 (1906), 258–75.
A reply to Suchier (786) considering the history and topography of Charles le Chauve's campaign of AD 851 against the Bretons to rebut the simple identification of the Vivien of *ChG* with Vivianus, Count of Tours, and to demonstrate that the battle site could not be Larchamp (Mayenne).

778   ——, 'Encore Vivien et Larchamp', *Rom*, 38 (1909), 599–602.
A simple rebuttal of Suchier's hypothesis that L'Archamp of *ChG* should be identified with Larchamp in Brittany (786 & 787).

779   Moisan, André, 'Deux noms une légende: la légende épique de Vivien et la légende hagiographique de Saint Vidian à Martres-Tolosanes', 2 vols (Doctorat d'Etat, University of Lille III, 1973) 224 + 223 pp. Distributed by the Service de reproduction des thèses de l'Université de Lille III.
Vol. 1 contains a detailed study of the epic legend of Vivien from CycG and of the life of Vivien, Count of Tours, indicating the probable role of the Templars in forming and disseminating the epic legend. Vol. 2 studies the development of the legend of St Vidian of Martres-Tolosane under the influence of the epic legend of

Vivien, especially of *EnfV*, and its contamination with the legend of St Vivien of Saintes.

*780   ——, 'Le Vivien historique, abbé laïc de Saint-Martin de Tours, et le Vivien épique de la *Chanson de Guillaume*', in *Mémoires et exposés présentés à la semaine d'études médiévales de Saint-Benoît-sur-Loire du 3 au 10 juillet 1969*, Cahiers d'Archéologie et d'Histoire (Auxerre: Société des fouilles archéologiques et des monuments historiques de l'Yonne, 1975), pp. 267–78.

781   ——, 'Réflexions sur la genèse de la légende de Vivien', in *Rencesvals 8* (1981), pp. 345–52.
A highly speculative article, as the author admits, which considers a variety of possible exchanges between popular-oral and ecclesiastical sources in maintaining and transmitting the legend of Vivien and in attaching it to that of Guillaume d'Orange. Moisan makes the significant observation that the crusading ideology of St Bernard, evident in the founding of the Order of the Temple, is of great importance to our understanding of the portrait of Vivien in *ChG*.

782   ——, 'Face à la violence, Vivien le martyr: thèmes et variations', in *La Violence dans le monde médiéval*, Senefiance, 36 (Aix-en-Provence: Publications du CUER MA, Université de Provence, 1994), pp. 333–47.
A comparison of the ways in which the death of Vivien and his vow are presented in *G1*, *G2*, *Al*, and *ChV*, revealing the increased insistence on the precision of his vow in each subsequent reworking, and the effect this has on the representation of his death as martyrdom. This leads to the important suggestion that the portrayal of Vivien's heroic persona was influenced by St Bernard's *De laude novæ militiæ*.

783   Scinicariello, Sharon G., 'The Evolution of Vivien's Vow', *RoNo*, 18 (1977–78), 388–93.
A rather schematic account of the evolution of Vivien's vow compared with those of Moisan (782) and Subrenat (784), which fails to take into account that the consummation of the vow made in *ChV* is presented in *Al*.

784   Subrenat, Jean, 'Vivien, a-t-il respecté son voeu?', in *Il Ciclo di Guglielmo d'Orange* (1997), pp. 313–32.
Considers the evolution of Vivien's vow from *ChG* to *EnfV*, taking particular account of the changing juridical and theological context, to bring out the way Vivien's epic persona evolves between *ca* 1150 and *ca* 1220.

785   Suchier, Hermann, 'Vivien', *ZrPh*, 29 (1905), 641–82.
The article starts with an analysis of *ChG* in its two main sections, making some pertinent remarks on language and giving an assessment of the use and sense of the refrains; the longest sections deal with the identity of Count Vivien of Tours

and the battle of AD 851; a concern with history rather than poetry makes the comments on Guillaume worthless. The article closes with some reflexions on the elaboration of the epic legend of Vivien, supposing a ninth-century origin, relating it to both Guillaume and Rainouart material, before considering *EnfV*, *ChV*, and *Al*. Much of this is still of interest, although the relative chronology proposed for the poems is no longer accepted.

786   ——, 'Nochmals die Vivianschlacht', *ZrPh*, 33 (1909), 41–58.
A series of three responses on points of detail to the work of other scholars. I: Ferdinand Lot on the age of the historical and fictitious Vivien at the time of his death and the site of the battle of AD 851 (777); II: Paul Meyer (298) and Raymond Weeks (218) on the localization of L'Archamp / *Aliscans* in the poems; III: Franz Rechnitz on the meaning of the refrain *lunsdi al vespre* (310). The discussion is largely misguided as it seeks to interpret poetic features by reference to extrapoetic *realia*, often identified by intuition.

787   ——, 'Nochmals die Vivienschlacht', *ZrPh*, 34 (1910), 343–48.
Another attempt to rectify Lot's opinions (777 & 778) by reference to archival documents relating to Count Vivien of Tours, thereby confusing historical and poetic reality.

788   Toja, Gianluigi, 'Postilla arnaldiana: la fame del "nebot sain Guillem"', *CN*, 39 (1959), 239–50.
Argues that the nephew of Guillaume referred to in the poem by Arnaut Daniel must be Vivien, but see 295.

789   Urwin, Kenneth, 'La mort de Vivien et la genèse des chansons de geste', *Rom*, 78 (1957), 392–404.
Uses the episode of Guillaume administering the sacrament to Vivien to argue against Bédier's theory of the clerical origins of the French epic, given the climate of reform surrounding priestly functions in the late eleventh and twelfth centuries.

(ii) *Geography, Topography, and Place Names*

790   Payen, Jean-Charles, 'Encore le problème de la géographie épique', in *Rencesvals 4* (1969), pp. 261–65.
An abstract and general reflection, which is mostly concerned with *ChG* and *CN*. Payen considers epic geography and topography to be essentially symbolic.

ALISCANS / L'ARCHAMP

791   Lejeune, Rita, 'A propos du toponyme "L'Archamp" ou "Larchamp" dans la geste de Guillaume d'Orange', *Boletín*, 31 (1965–66), 143–51.

An interesting article suggesting that the original formula of *ChG* was 'en l'are champ sur mer', a poetic invocation of sterility rather than a toponym. Its weakness lies in the assumption that the noun not the preposition of the formula has been modified in transmission despite the invariable presence of the disyllabic form 'l'Archant' in *ChV* and *Al* which confirms the reading 'L'Archamp' of *ChG*.

792　Mandach, André de, 'Le "Fragment de La Haye" et le site des "Campi Strigilis"', in *Rencesvals 7* (1978), pp. 617–28.
Identifies the *Aliscans* of *Al* with the 'campi strigilis' of the 'Hague Fragment', and identifies both with the palæo-Christian cemetery of Arles, partly on the grounds of the number of sarcophagi found there which are marked by incised scroll-work decoration. Since Latin *strigilis* is more properly the flute of an Ionic column the derivation is unwarranted.

*793　Terracher, A., 'Notes sur "L'Archant" dans les chansons de geste de Guillaume au court-nez', *Annales du Midi*, 22 (1910), 1–16.

794　Wathelet-Willem, Jeanne, 'A propos de la géographie dans la *Chanson de Guillaume*', *CCM*, 3 (1960), 107–15.
A study of the problems posed by the form and the identification of L'Archamp in *ChG*, which concludes that the poem reveals strata of recomposition by different poets with different perspectives.

795　——, 'Le champ de bataille où périt Vivien', in *Hommage Delbouille* (1973), pp. 61–74.
Identifies L'Archamp in *Al* strictly with the battlefield on which Vivien dies, while *Aliscans* itself covers the wider field of Guillaume's combats.

FONTAINE SAINT-GUILLAUME

796　Suchier, Hermann, 'Die Fontaine de Saint Guillaume', *ZrPh*, 30 (1906), 463–64.
A number of sites bearing this or a similar name, mostly in the *départements* of Orne and Mayenne, are named after a twelfth-century St Guillaume Firmat, not after the epic hero.

LUISERNE

*797　Bédier, Joseph, 'La ville légendaire de Luiserne', in *Studi letterari e linguistici dedicati a Pio Rajna nel quarantesimo anno del suo insegnamento* (Milano: Ulrico Hoepli, 1911), pp. 29–40.

798　McMillan, Duncan, '"Mais l'am que qui.m des Luserna" — Arnaut Daniel', in *The Troubadours and the Epic* (1987), pp. 218–37.

Despite the topographic precision and pseudo-realism with which the town of Luiserne-sor-mer is treated in *EnfV*, the presentation of the town appears to derive from the deliberate exploitation of mythic material about a 'lost city'. Despite his other known references to CycG material (see 295 & 788), it is probable that in making this allusion Arnaut Daniel was referring to the mythic substratum and not to its exploitation by the poet of *EnfV*.

NARBONNE

799 Combarieu, du Grès Micheline de, 'Une ville du sud vue du nord: Narbonne dans le cycle d'Aymeri', *Perspectives Médiévales*, 22 (1996) Supplément, Actes du Colloque Languedoc et Langue d'oc (Toulouse, janvier 1996), 59–77.
A syncretic account of Narbonne compiled from all the songs of the subcycle of Aimeri, concluding that the town is presented as an idealized vision of the New Jerusalem, or of Cockaigne. There is a close identification between the town and the person of Aimeri, its count.

800 ——, 'De l'histoire à la légende: Narbonne dans le cycle d'Aymeri', in *Mélanges Fourquet* (1999), pp. 205–15.
Compares the historical city of Narbonne with its ideal representation in the poems of the Aymeri Cycle to show how poetic imagination transformed it into an independent kingdom, and its lord, Aymeri, effectively into an independent monarch, symbolic of the struggle for the reconquest of Spain from the Moors.

PORTPAILLART

801 Barnett, Monica J., 'Portpaillart in the Cycle of Guillaume d'Orange', *MLR*, 51 (1956), 507–11.
Studies topographical indications accompanying the name Portpaillart in a number of poems of CycG to conclude that the name corresponds to Lattes, the medieval port of Montpellier.

802 Worthington, Martha G., 'Odiene and Porpaillart: Epic Names in a Twelfth-Century Chronicle', *RPh*, 24 (1970–71), 101–07.
A study of the *Chronicle* of Roger of Hoveden suggests that Odiene (in *Mainet*) may not be an error for Odierne as found in CycG; it is identified with the river Guadiana. Roger's placing of a 'Purpallar' on the Catalan coast between Barcelona and Ampurias serves, according to the author, not to identify a historical site, but to confirm the fame of epic Portpaillart in the twelfth century.

TOMBE-ISSOIRE

803   Lauer, Philippe, 'Le siège de Paris dans l'épopée médiévale et la localisation de l'épisode d'Isoré à la Tombe-Issoire', *Mémoires de la Société de l'Histoire de Paris et de l'Ile-de France*, 49 (1927), 123–33.
The first part of the article, finding historical sources for the episode in tenth-century battles, mistakes the role of myth in historiography, but the second part is important for demonstrating the probable contribution of the Hospitallers to the formation of the legends surrounding the Tombe-Issoire, and its role in *MonG2*.

VENICE

804   Cremonesi, Carla, 'Venice', *Filologia e Letteratura*, 9 (1963), 214–22.
Reconsiders geographical and historical evidence, particularly that associated with the preliminaries of the Fourth Crusade, to reaffirm the identification of 'Venice' in *EnfR* with the Italian city of that name.

(iii) *Themes*

ENFANCES

805   Carney, Anna, 'A Portrait of the Hero as a Young Child: Guillaume, Roland, Girard, Gui', *Olifant*, 18 (1993–94), 238–77.
An impressionistic and unscientific article which takes for granted an equivalence between modern English 'child' and OF 'enfes-enfant', and which makes no reference to the extensive literature discussing the meaning and use of these terms in medieval literature and society.

EPIC CREDO *(PRIÈRE DU PLUS GRAND PÉRIL)*

806   Garel, J., 'La prière du plus grand péril', in *Mélanges Le Gentil* (1973), pp. 311–18.
The author is principally concerned with *CL*, *CN*, *PO*, and *MonG*, which he compares with Latin sources for prayers and with Norse texts. He suggests that the appeal to a form of prayer reflecting popular religion derived from ritual pagan incantations is the result of the Christianization of the ancient epic motif that the hero participates in the divine.

807   Legros, Huguette, 'Les prières d'Isembart et de Vivien: dissemblances et analogies: la fonction narrative de la prière', in *La Prière au Moyen Âge (littérature et civilisation)*, Senefiance, 10 (Aix-en-Provence: Publications du CUER MA, Université de Provence, 1981), pp. 361–73.

A textual comparison of the prayers pronounced *in articulo mortis* by the two heroes leads to the conclusion that the structure and content of the *prière du plus grand péril* are determined by narrative context.

808   Scheludko, D., 'Über das altfranzösische epische Gebet', *ZfSL*, 58 (1934), 67–86.

A reply to Spitzer (809) using the Longinus episode of the epic prayer to show that the presentation of material in *chansons de geste* differs substantially from that in hagiographic texts (exemplified by the *Legenda aurea*). The author concludes that all epic prayers are generically related, being derived from Guillaume's prayers in *CL*. The last part of the proposition is unsound.

809   Spitzer, Leo, 'Zu den Gebeten im *Couronnement Louis* und im *Cantar de mio Cid*', *ZfSL*, 56 (1932), 196–209.

Starting from a comparison of prayers by Ximena in the *Cid* and Guillaume in *CL* the article argues that all art in the Middle Ages was based on biblical-clerical culture, so that to distinguish learned from popular art is an anachronism.

HISTORY, MYTH, AND EPIC

810   Barbero, Alessandro, 'Les chansons de geste et la mutation féodale de l'an Mil', in *Il Ciclo di Guglielmo d'Orange* (1997), pp. 457–75.

The article attempts to demonstrate that poems of CycG reflect the socio-political situation of the late ninth and early tenth centuries. However, the analysis of historical data is inadequately nuanced, and the choice of *ChG*, *CL*, *CN*, and *PO* as representing the oldest stratum of poems is tendentious because of the ways in which these poems, even *ChG*, have been adapted to the cyclic context established at the end of the twelfth century.

811   Batany, Jean, 'Mythes indo-européens ou mythes des indo-européens? Le témoignage médiéval', *Annales ESC*, 40 (1985), 415–22.

A jocularly satirical review-article inspired by Joël Grisward's *Archéologie* (635), which questions the mutual distrust between historians and the disciples of Georges Dumézil in interpreting the background to, and fundamental meanings of, the OF epic. The author sees no contradiction between the supposed historical existence of characters called 'Guillaume d'Orange' or 'Aymeri de Narbonne' and the myth that has been created around them.

812   Dion, R., 'La leçon d'une chanson de geste: *Les Narbonnais*', *Fédération des Sociétés Historiques et Archéologiques de Paris et de l'Ile-de-France, Mémoires*, 1 (1949), 23–45.

Studies the relationship of the presentation of the Aymerides at the court of Charlemagne and events of the reign of Philip Augustus to suggest that the high-handed independence of the former constituted a satire on the policies of the latter. It concludes, rather in advance of the *Annales* school, that such literary documents are an important resource for studying the mentalities of an age.

813   Flori, Jean, 'L'idée de croisade dans quelques chansons de geste du cycle de Guillaume d'Orange', in *Il Ciclo di Guglielmo d'Orange* (1997), pp. 476–95.
Sees in the representation of conflict between Christians and Saracens less a reflection of the Crusades than an interpretation in chivalric terms of the ancient Augustinian ideology of the just war.

814   Frappier, Jean, 'Réflexions sur les rapports des chansons de geste et de l'histoire', *ZrPh*, 73 (1957), 1–19.
A contribution to the individualist-traditionalist debate which comes down circumspectly on the side of tradition. The article first considers the nature of truth in the epic and its tendency to mythography, then studies three specific cases: the syncretism of the opening scene of *CL*, the satirical value for a thirteenth-century audience of the arrival of Aymeri's sons in Paris in *Narb*, and the sense of historical perspective generated by the poet of *MonG2* in describing Guillaume's arrival in Paris for the duel with Isoré. Frappier makes extensive use of the study by R. Dion (812), a debt duly acknowledged (p. 18).

815   Grisward, Joël-Henri, 'Epopée indo-européenne et épopée médiévale: histoires ou histoire?', *Perspectives Médiévales*, 8 (1982), 125–33.
Reconsiders the formation of the epico-historical characters Guillaume, Louis, Bernard, and Aïmer to suggest an influence of epic and mythological archetypes on the structuring of historiographic narrative.

INDEX OF SCHOLARS

This index contains the names of authors of articles, chapters, book reviews, and monographs, and those of editors of critical editions of medieval texts listed in the bibliography. It also contains the names of scholars referred to in the commentary on items listed.

SUBJECT INDEX

This index includes references to manuscripts, titles of poems, names of characters, and of authors of *chansons de geste* and of other literary works. Many items include the terms 'Cycle de Guillaume' or 'Geste de Guillaume' or an equivalent in their titles, while dealing only with a limited selection of poems from the cycle. As far as possible the following index identifies and refers to the actual poems edited or studied in such works. Numbers in bold type indicate items listed under a main headword.